A
Doric
Dictionary

By the same author

Teach Yourself Doric: A Course for Beginners; 1 898218 14 5
Also available as a cassette giftpack (book & tape); 1 898218 17 X

The Minister's Cat: An A–Z of cats in verse;
1 898218 18 8

Here's Tae Us! Wha's Like Us? A Personal view of Scottish History;
1 898218 46 3

Conversations with a Cat: Mewsings on Church Life and Christian Doctrine;
0 948643 16 1

A
Doric
Dictionary

Two-way Lexicon of North-East Scots

**Doric~English
English~Doric**

Compiled and edited by
Douglas Kynoch M.A. (Aberdeen)

SCOTTISH CULTURAL PRESS

First published 1996
Scottish Cultural Press
Unit 14, Leith Walk Business Centre
130 Leith Walk
Edinburgh EH6 5DT
Tel: 0131 555 5950 • Fax: 0131 555 5018

British Library Cataloguing in Publication Data
A catalogue record for this book is available from the British Library

ISBN: 1 898218 86 2 (hardback)
ISBN: 1 898218 80 3 (paperback)

Printed and bound by
BPC-AUP Aberdeen Ltd

FOREWORD

Doric is a name given to broad and rustic dialect. Deriving from that spoken by the Dorians in ancient Greece, it has been applied in more recent times to the dialects of England and of Scotland, while in Scotland itself the term refers pre-eminently to the dialect of the Scots language which is spoken in the north-eastern corner of the country. The Doric of North-east Scots meets both the traditional qualifications. On the one hand, its broadness can present difficulty even for Scots in other parts of Scotland, while on the other, its richest manifestation has always been found in the rural hinterland, where the language has recorded and labelled all the trappings of everyday life in what was a largely farming and fishing community.

It may be useful to establish what we mean in the present context by the term 'North-east'. For the purposes of this dictionary, it has been taken to include the old counties of Moray and Nairn, Banffshire and Aberdeenshire, along with Kincardineshire, where there are language differences between North and South. Additionally, as the North-east has always claimed as its own such writers as Violet Jacob, Helen Cruickshank, Sir Alexander Gray and Marion Angus, their home county of Angus has been included, or at least that part of it, the east, which has strong linguistic ties with Kincardine. Certain forms appear in Angus which are unknown in, even alien to the rest of the North-east (for example *no* for *nae*); but the similarities are strong and argue for inclusion.

It should come as no surprise to anyone that over so extensive an area there should be a considerable number of linguistic differences. If language can change slightly from village to village, as it does, then changes from county to county may be expected to be even greater. It would be a rash man who would say that this or that expression was not Doric simply because it was not *his* Doric. The truth is that there is not one monolithic form of Doric but a multiplicity of forms, differing to a greater or lesser degree here and there. Not only is there a northern and southern Doric, a Banffshire and Mearns Doric, there is a farming and fishing Doric and a now somewhat diluted urban Doric. It is interesting to note how the word for a *scarecrow* changes from county to county and that for a *seagull*, from town to town.

A North-east born journalist recently took me to task for using the word *gae* in a Doric context, protesting that *gyang* was the only allowable rendering of the English verb, *to go*. This is, quite simply, untrue. It was certainly the form used in the area the speaker was brought up in; but, as is clear from the ensuing text, there are other widely used and acceptable forms such as *ging* (Aberdeen city) and *gang*, *gaan* (coastal) and *gae*. Individual Doric speakers appear to use more than one.

The vocabulary in this dictionary has been drawn from the works of North-east writers published between 1871 and the present day, while Helen Beaton's book, *At the Back of Benachie*, attempts to reproduce the speech of 100 years before its publication, taking us back approximately to 1815. Some may question the value of including words long obsolete; but they are part of the Doric heritage and are useful for reading older Doric texts. The list of writers is very far from exhaustive but contains as many as could be conveniently referred to by one individual over the six and a half month period in which the dictionary was compiled.

Of greatest value has been the work of writers of prose or dialogue, of which, sadly, there have been few. Into this category come not only Helen Beaton but Wm. Alexander, the creator of *Johnny Gibb*; James Alexander, the author of the dialogues, *Mains and Hilly*; several newspaper contributors from Wm. Donaldson's Victorian prose collection, *The Language of the People*; and the autobiographical work of the Rev. David Ogston. Alexander Smith's work was of invaluable service in pointing to the linguistic variants to be found in Kincardineshire, and, although he spent the latter half of his life in Buchan and his Doric could conceivably have got a little *throwder*, I was never myself aware of any confusion.

Poetry, though much more readily available than prose, can be something of a minefield for someone in search of purity of language, since purity of language need not the poet's first concern. For one thing, a poet uses language creatively and moves it on from its original sense to mean something imaginatively different. For another, he or she may borrow terms used in other parts Scotland, believing any Scots word to be fair game for the writer. Hugh MacDiarmid certainly subscribed to this view and various other writers were to follow his example in the Scottish Renaissance of the early 1920s. For this reason, I had, at an early stage, to abandon Helen Cruickshank, a devotee of MacDiarmid, as a reliable example of Angus dialect, when I found several intrusions of the kind described (although a few cullings from Miss Cruickshank survive to confirm some of the more basic differences of Angus speech). The work of other well-known poets has, for similar reasons, been avoided or used with similar circumspect. Even Charles Murray, that revered exponent of the Aberdeenshire tongue may on occasion have borrowed from outwith the Doric-speaking area. His use of *toom* rather than *teem* being one of the factors which suggests the possibility.

In using the dictionary, readers will occasionally find words marked with an initial letter. This points to the writer in whose work the word was found and is an indication either of the part of the North-east he or she comes from, or in what period the word was used. A list of authors and appropriate code signs is provided. This system of word identification is quite unscientific but may prove useful as a general guide for writers and readers alike.

It may be fairly pointed out that much of the vocabulary listed here is not, strictly speaking, Doric at all but merely a Doric form of English. *Suppersteeshun* for *superstition* for example. Yet if this is or was the way in which the word was commonly spoken in the North-east, then it is right that it should be recorded and preserved rather than that the pure English form should be used in the speaking of Doric. As for what is pure Doric and what is Doric slang, it is not within my competence to distinguish between the two.

A Doric Dictionary is offered to the people of the North-east, wherever they may be, in gratitude for having been nurtured by our shared culture.

Douglas Kynoch
Glasgow, August 1996

SPELLING

Despite signs of increasing standardisation, there is no generally recognised way of spelling Scots; and readers of the language will find considerable variation. This will become apparent in the first part of the dictionary, where, with a few exceptions, spelling is generally as I found it in the text from which the word was culled. In turning the dictionary around, however, and compiling the English to Doric section, I have thought it sensible to review the orthography to some extent and to reduce the number of spelling options. It is not uncommon, therefore, for a word to be spelt one way in Part One and another in Part Two, the latter being considered preferable for one reason or another.

There may, in fact, be more than one acceptable spelling in Part Two; and, as I have not eradicated the forms used in other parts of Scotland, a North-east Doric form may be followed by a more common all-Scotland form (e.g. *daad* and *daud*; *meen* and *mune*; *stoor* and *stour*). Both spelling forms are capable of being spoken in the Doric way, or alternatively, the latter (e.g. *daud* and *mune*) may sometimes be spoken using a vowel sound alien to the North-east but heard in other parts of Scotland. In writing, then, one has the choice of appealing to an exclusively North-east audience on the one hand or a wider Scots audience on the other. Charles Murray adopted the latter course and perhaps in consequence, won himself a national following. Few other North-east poets have followed suit.

Modern practice is to eradicate the apostrophe as far as possible and certainly in common words such as *an* meaning 'and' and *amo* meaning 'among'. This is understood by some to indicate that the word in question exists in its own right and is not a mere corruption of English. Whatever the validity of that view, I am happy to respect the convention and apostrophes have been eliminated as far as possible, surviving only occasionally in Part II, where the meaning of a word would otherwise be unclear.

PRONUNCIATION

Vowels and Dipthongs

a, aa and *aw* are pronounced as in the English *car.*

a before *bb, m, mp* and *nk,* however, is pronounced *u* in both English and Scots words (e.g. *cabbage, crabbit, stamp* and *bank).* Before *g, a* may be pronounced *u* (e.g. *bag, baggie)* or *a* as in *car* (e.g. *stag).*

ai and *ae* are pronounced as in the English *hate* (e.g. *mait, maet).*

a_e as in the English *seen* (e.g. *ane, bane, stane,* more usually rendered *een, been, steen).*

ee and *ei* (sometimes also *ie)* as in the English *feet.*

i is pronounced somewhere between the English *i* and *e.*

ie is sometimes pronounced as in *feet* and sometimes as in *fit.* Several words are spelt now *ie,* now *ei.* To attempt to clarify the situation, I have classified those in Part Two according to pronunciation, so that *speil, speir, sheilin, deil* and *neist* are spelt *ei,* the first letter indicating the pronunciation, while *fient* and *nieve* are spelt *ie,* the first letter pointing once more to pronunciation. As the *diphthong* in *bien, brier, chief, chiel, feish, neiper, reive, remeid* and *sheil* appears to be spelt only one way, I have left these as they stand, though there is obviously room for further standardisation.

oi as *i_e* or *y,* being rendered this way in Part Two, e.g. *dytit, doitit.*

oo as in *moon.*

ou may be pronounced either as in *moon* or as in *cow.* With a few words like *clout,* both pronunciations are possible, though generally with different meanings. For this reason, I have eliminated the *ou* spelling as far as possible in Part Two, replacing it either with *oo* or *ow* according to pronunciation. Where this was uncertain, I left *ou* untouched.

u is pronounced as in the English *ju.*

u_e as in *mune* is generally pronounced *ee.* Hence *meen* and *sheen.*

ui is problematic being susceptible to different pronunciations in different areas. In the words *buird* and *buirdly,* for example, *boord(ly)* would appear to apply to Angus and South Kincardineshire, with *beerd(ly)* or *byoord(ly)* applying in the rest of the North-east. The *ui* division line is said to run from Mount Battock to Skateraw on the Kincardineshire coast.

Consonants

ch is pronounced as in the Scots *loch.*

g and *k* should be pronounced before *n* (e.g. *knowe* and *gnap).*

ng in the middle of a word is followed by no *g* sound, so that the *ng* in the Doric *hunger* is spoken like the *ng* in the English *singer.*

s or the *s* sound is sometimes replaced by *sh* in such words as *vessel, officer* and *sew (shoo).*

wh at the start of a word is, with the exception of Angus, pronounced *f,* the words *whaar, whan* and *what* being rendered *faar, faan* and *fat.*

Diminutives

North-east Scots is much given to the use of diminutives. 'Bairn' can become *bairnikie;* 'babbie', *babbitie;* 'lass', *lassock* or *lassockie.* The most popular of the diminutive forms, however, is the simple *ie* ending which appears most commonly in one-syllable words such as *loonie*, though it can also be found in words of two-syllables *(boorrachie)* and, exceptionally, in longer words. Diminutives appear rarely in this dictionary; but, by the use of the *ie* ending, can be created from appropriate nouns.

BIBLIOGRAPHY
and
KEY TO CODE SYMBOLS

The code symbols shown here indicate the writer in whose work the word was found and may point either to the part of the North-east where the word came from or to the period in which use of the word was current, the home area and dates of the writer being given where known. The symbol usually indicates an unusual word or an unusual variant of a word. A commonplace word is coded, where it is one of several having the same meaning. The system offers no more than a rough guide to the provenance of the word.

A   **George Abel of Aberdeenshire** (1856–1916); brought up on farms in the parish of Kintore; minister of Udny Free Church for 35 years; author of the verse collection *Wylins fae My Wallet*, published 1916.

A1   **James Alexander of Ythan Wells, Aberdeenshire;** author of *Mains and Hilly*, a collection of dialogues in the Aberdeenshire dialect, originally published in the *Aberdeen Weekly Free Press* and brought out in book form in 1929.

A2   **William Alexander of Aberdeenshire** (1826–94); author of *Johnny Gibb of Gushetneuk*, first published 1871; ploughman, journalist and editor of the *Aberdeen Free Press*, in which *Johnny Gibb* was serialised.

B   **Peter Buchan of Peterhead** (1917–1991); a fisherman like his father; author of a collection of poems, *Mount Pleasant* and a collection of North-east tales, *Fisher Blue*. What has been drawn on here is his contribution to **Buchan Claik**, a compendium of North-east words and phrases which he compiled in collaboration with David Toulmin.

B1   **Helen Beaton of Aberdeenshire.** Mrs Beaton's account of life in the Garioch in the nineteenth century is based in particular on the parish of Rayne and relies on the stories and language of her grandmother. Entitled *At the Back o' Benachie*, it was published in 1915.

C   **J. M. Caie of Banffshire** (1879–1949). John Morrison Caie was born in Banchory-Devenick, the son of a Banffshire minister, he was brought up on a farm in the parish of Enzie. Trained both in law and agriculture, he spent much of his working life with the Board of Agriculture for Scotland. Of his two volumes of verse, it is *'Twixt Hills and Sea* which helps give the dictionary its Banffshire flavour.

C1   **Helen B. Cruickshank of Angus** (1886–1975). Helen Burness Cruickshank was reared at Hillside between Montrose and the North Esk. The greater part of her working life with the civil service was spent in the Department of Health in Edinburgh. A devotee of Hugh MacDiarmid, her Scots vocabulary, tends to be eclectic, so only the most basic terms are quoted as examples of Angus speech.

F   **Alexander Fenton of Aberdeenshire** (1929–   ). Director of the European Ethnological Research Centre in Edinburgh, Prof. Fenton, himself a native of Auchterless, has used a farm in that parish as the basis of a study of the words and expressions describing farm equipment and techniques in the second quarter of the twentieth century. This invaluable record of North-east farm practice, is described in his book, *Wirds an Wark 'e Seasons Roon*, published in 1987.

G   **Flora Garry of Aberdeenshire** (1900–   ). Of farming stock, Mrs Garry was brought up at Mains of Auchmunziel, New Deer. Trained as a teacher, she taught at Dumfries and Strichen, married R. Campbell Garry, Regius Professor of Physiology at Glasgow University and ultimately retired to Comrie. Her verse collection, *Bennygoak* was first published in 1974.

G1   **Sir Alexander Gray of Angus** (1882–1968). Gray was first Jeffrey Professor of Political Economy at Aberdeen University from 1921–34, to which period much of his Scots verse belongs. The linguistic variants of Angus become apparent in his verse collection, *Any Man's Life* which appeared in 1924.

J   **Violet Jacob of Angus** (1863–1946). Mrs Jacob (née Kennedy-Erskine) was sister of the 19th laird of Dun, the family having owned for centuries the Dun estate between Brechin and Montrose. Author of four books of verse, her *Scottish Poems* were published in 1944.

M   **Charles Murray of Aberdeenshire** (1864–1941). Born in Alford, Dr Murray was a civil engineer who spend most of his professional life in South Africa, where he was ultimately appointed the Union's Secretary for Public Works. He retired to the North-east, where several books of verse were published his lifetime, *Hamewith: the Complete Poems* appearing in 1979.

M1 **J. C. Milne of Aberdeenshire** (1897–1962). Another writer of farming stock, John Milne was born at Memsie near Fraserburgh. After a brilliant academic career at Aberdeen University, he turned to teaching, later becoming Master of Method at Aberdeen College of Education. His verse collection, *The Orra Loon*, was published in 1946; his collected *Poems* in 1963.

O **David D. Ogston of Aberdeenshire** (1945–   ). In two volumes of autobiography, *White Stone Country* and *Dry-stone Days*, David Ogston, minister at St John's, Perth described in Doric his upbringing on farms in Buchan and the Garioch. *Dry-stone Days* was on the reading list for the dictionary.

R **Elsie S. Rae of Banffshire**. Elsie Ray was the wife of the Rev. Robert Wilson. Her verse collections include *Private John McPherson* (1917) and *Hansel Fae Hame and other Scots Poems* (1927), the latter forming part of this bibliography.

S **Alexander Smith of Kincardineshire** (1911–1993). Alex Smith is remarkable for having, in the years before his death, written three substantial books in Doric. Two of them, *Forty Years in Kincardineshire* and *Forty Years in Buchan and Banff*, are autobiographical; the third, *Fairmin the Wey It Wis* records farm life over the period of a year. As well as having what appears to be total recall, Smith had a keen ear, which discerned the differences between the Doric of Kincardineshire and that of Buchan and Banff.

T **David Toulmin of Aberdeenshire**. This is the pen-name of John Reid (1913–   ) born at Rathen in Buchan, the son of a farm-worker. He himself spent his working life in farm labour but turned, in due course, to the writing of novels. He contributed the farming data to *Buchan Claik*, while his collaborator, Peter Buchan provided the fishing material.

Additional Bibliography

Sheena Blackhall of Aberdeen and Deeside: *The Cyard's Kist* (1984);
George Bruce of Fraserburgh and Edinburgh: *Perspectives* (1984);

A. M. Davidson of Midmar: *Tinkler's Whussel* (1981);
Joyce Everill of Torry, Aberdeen and Fife: *Granny's Button Box* (1989);
William Imray of Tarland: *Langstene Nou and Syne* (1991);
M. S. Lumsden of Rothiemurchus and Aberdeen: *Affirmations* (1990);
Liliane Grant Rich of Glenlivet: *White Rose of Druminnor* (1969);
Alexander Scott of Aberdeen (1920–1989): *Collected Poems* (1994);
Margaret Smith of Gardenstown and Banff: *Hard Graft* (unpub. dialogue);
Wm. Thom of Inverurie: *Rhymes and Recollections of a Hand-Loom Weaver* (1845);
Rev. James Wood of Portnockie and Aberdeen: *The Wind on the Hill* (1988);
The Living Doric verse anthology (1985);
The Language of the People: Scots Prose from the Victorian Revival edited by William Donaldson (1989).

Acknowledgements

Further vocabulary was provided by the late Mrs Bella Sandison of Adendale, Strachan. To Mrs Sandison, to the writers of all published work listed, to the compilers of the *Scottish National Dictionary*, the *Concise Scots Dictionary* and *Chamber's Dictionary*, the author is greatly indebted. For kindnesses rendered, thanks are due too to the Aberdeenshire Library and Information Service, to James Slater of Portsoy, Bill Middleton of Ardlair, Strachan, Anne MacWilliam of Stonehaven and Olivia Scott of Glasgow.

ABBREVIATIONS

Abdn.	Aberdeen	phr.	phrase
adj.	adjective, -ival	pl.	plural
adv.	adverb	ppl.	participle (present
aux.	auxiliary		or past)
cf.	compare with	pred. adj.	predicative
chf.	chiefly		adjective
conj.	conjunction	pr. n.	proper noun
contempt.	contemptous	prep. phr.	prepositional
corr.	corruption		phrase
def. art.	definite article	pro.	pronounced
deriv.	derivative of,	pron.	pronoun
	deriving from	obs.	obsolete
dim.	diminutive	ref.	reference
e.g.	for example	rel. pron.	relative pronoun
Eng.	English	v.	verb
esp.	especially	var.	variant
excl.	exclamation	vb. n.	verbal noun
f.	female	v. pr.	verb present tense
fig.	figuratively	v. pt.	verb past tense
gen.	generally	v. tr.	verb transitive
imp.	imperative	v. intr.	verb intransitive
incl.	including		
indef.	indefinite article		
int.	interjection		
interrog.	interrogative		
lit.	literary		
liter.	literally		
m.	male		
n.	noun		
naut.	nautical		
neg.	negative		
n. pl.	noun plural		
orig.	originally		
perf.	perfect		
perh.	perhaps		

PART ONE

Doric~English

— A —

A *pron.* I. *cf.* **Aw, I**

a *indef. art.* a

'a' *v.* (in perf. tense with *aux. v.*) have; *e.g.* **mith 'a' been** might have been

aa, a' *adj.* all, every; **aa come** in one's right mind; **aa gate** everywhere; **aa his lane** all on his own; **aa itherbody** everyone else; **aa the airts** in all directions; **an aa** also, too

aabody *n., pron.* everybody

aacre *n.* acre. *cf.* **awcre**

aafa, aafu *adj., adv.* awful

aagent *n.* agent

Aagist *n.* August

aal *adj.* old. *cf.* **aul; aaler** older; **aalest** oldest

aam *v.* thrash. *cf.* **aum**

aat, 'at *adj., pron., conj.* that

aathing *n.* everything

aawye *adv.* everywhere

abeech, abeich *adv.* at a distance, aloof

abeen *adv., prep.* above. *cf.* **abune**

ablach *n.* dwarf; insignificant person

ablins *adv.* perhaps (B1). *cf.* **aiblins**

ablo(w) *prep.* below (S)

abody *pron., n.* everybody

aboot *prep.* about

abreist *adv.* abreast

abune *prep., adv.* above. *cf.* **abeen**

accep *v.* accept; *ppl.* **acceppit**

accommodat *v.* accommodate

accoont *n., v.* account

accoontable *adj.* accountable

acht *adj.* eight. *cf.* **aicht, echt** *n.* ownership; *v.* own; owe. *cf.* **aucht, yacht**

achteen *adj.* eighteen. *cf.* **auchteen**

ack *n.* action; *v.* act

ackir *n.* actor

acquant *ppl.* acquainted (G)

acquantance *n.* acquaintance

acquaint *ppl.* acquainted (B)

acquint *ppl.* acquainted (S)

adappit *v. pt.* adapted

adaya *n.* idea

adee *n.* a to-do; *v.* to do; **muckle adee** much to do

ae *adj.* one, single

aefaul(d) *adj.* sincere (B1, O)

aenoo *adv.* now. *cf.* **ivnoo, eyvnoo**

aet *n.* a feed; **a gweed aet** a good feed; *v.* eat; **aeten** *ppl.* eaten

afen *adv.* often. *cf.* **aft, aften**

aff *adv., prep.* off; **aff his stotter** losing the thread of his thought

affa *adj., adv.* awful. *cf.* **aafa, yafa**

aff-cast *n.* anything cast off

affeckit *adj.* moved, touched

aff-go *n.* start

aff-han *adj.* blunt, plain; without warning or preparation

affint *prep. phr.* off it; from it (S)

affint *adj.* upset (S)

afflat, an *n.* time off, leave of absence

afflickit *adj.* afflicted

affoord *v.* afford

aff-pittin *ppl., adj.* procrastinating

1

affrontit *adj., ppl.* ashamed; embarrassed; **black affrontit** deeply embarrassed

afore *adv.* in front; *prep., conj.* before, in front of

afore-han *adv.* beforehand; **to be afore-han wi** to forestall

aft, aften *adv.* often. *cf.* **afen**

agee *adj.* awry; in a disordered state, out of order

agin *prep.* against

agley *adv.* off the straight, obliquely

aggravation *n.* irritation

a-gyaun *ppl.* going about; going on

aheid *prep., adv.* ahead

ahin *prep.* behind; *adv.* late

ahint *adv.* behind

Aiberdeen *pr. n.* Aberdeen

Aiberdour *pr. n.* Aberdour

aiblins *adv.* perhaps (M1). *cf.* **ablins**

aicht *adj.* eight (S)

aidder *n.* udder

aifter *prep., conj.* after. *cf.* **efter** *adv.* afterwards

aifterhin *adv.* afterwards

aifterneen *n.* afternoon

aifternin *n.* afternoon (S)

aig *n.* egg

aik *n.* oak

ail *v.* to be unwell, to be amiss; (with *at* to be dissatisfied with)

ain *adj.* own

aince *adv.* once (S). *cf.* **eence**

aipple *n.* apple

air *adv.* early (A)

airch *n.* arch; *adj.* (**ch** gutteral) anxious (A2); timorous. *cf.* **arch**

airels *n. pl.* musical tones

airish *adj.* chilly

airly *adv.* early. *cf.* **air**

airm *n.* arm

airm-cheer *n.* armchair

airmy *n.* army

airn *v.* earn

airt *n.* direction; art

airth *n.* earth. *cf.* **yird**

aise *n.* ease. *cf.* **aiss**

aishan *n.* generation; family connection (A2). *cf.* **ation**

aisp *n.* asp, serpent

aiss *n.* ash, ashes

aiss-backet *n.* ash-can

aiss-midden *n.* ash-heap

aisy *adj., adv.* easy (S)

ait, aits *n.* oats; **ait kyaaks** oat cakes (A1); **aitmeal** oatmeal

aiten *adj.* oaten

aith *n.* oath

aits *n.* oats

aiven *adv.* even

aiv(e)rin *n.* cloudberry

aivis *n.* trick; fad (B1)

aixle *n.* axle

ajee *adv.* to one side, off the straight; (of a door) ajar. *cf.* **agee**

Ake, Akie *pr. n.* Alexander

alairm *n.* alarm

alane *adj., adv.* alone. *cf.* **aleen**

alang *prep.* along

ale *n.* ale; lemonade etc.

aleberry *n.* oatmeal boiled in ale, sweetened with sugar (A2)

aleen *adj., adv.* alone. *cf.* **alane**

aleyven *adj.* eleven

alis(s) *excl.* sudden cry of pain, alas!

alist *in phr.* **come alist** recover consciousness

alloo, allou *n.* approval; *v.* allow, *pt.* **alloot**

Almichty *adj.* Almighty

alow, in alow *prep.* below (S)

alow(e) *adv.* on fire, ablaze

alunt *adv.* ablaze. *cf.* **alow(e)**

amang *prep.* among. *cf.* **amin, amo**

ameesement *n.* amusement

amin *prep.* among (S). *cf.* **amo**

amint, oot *prep. phr.* out of things (S)

ammuneetion *n.* ammunition

amnin *v.* am not; **amnin aw** am I not? (A2)

amo, amon *prep.* among. *cf.* **amin**

amous *n.* alms

amshach *n.* accident, mishap (B1)

amunt *n.* amount

amus *See* **amous**

an *conj.* and

ance *adv.* once (G1). *cf.* **aince, eence**

Andra *pr. n.* deriv. of Andrew

ane *n., numeral* one. *cf.* **een**

anent *prep.* opposite; in front of; over against

Anersmas *pr. n.* Andrewmas

aneth *prep., adv.* beneath (A, M, M1). *cf.* **ablow, alow**

aneu, aneuch *adj.* enough

angersome *adj.* annoying, provoking

anidder *adj., pron.* another. *cf.* **anither, anodder**

anint *prep.* opposite. *cf.* **anent**

anither *adj., pron.* another; **anither kind** much improved (B)

annwal *adj.* annual

anodder *adj., pron.* another (A2). *cf.* **anidder, anither**

anse *adv.* else (C)

antrin *adj.* occasional

apairt *adv.* apart

apen *v.* open

appale *n., v.* appeal

appearandly *adv.* apparently

appint *v.* appoint

appruv *v.* approve

arch (ch guttural) *adj.* timorous; anxious (A2). *cf.* **airch**

aready *adv.* already

argie *v.* argue

argie-bargie; argle-bargle (A2) *n.* argument; *v.* to argue, contend

argiement *n.* argument

arles *n.* earnest given on striking a bargain

arn-tree *n.* alder (J)

aroon *adv., prep.* around

arreenge *v.* arrange

as *in phr.* **as much** so much

ashet *n.* large serving dish

aside *adv.* close by; present; *prep.* beside

asklent *adv.* askance

(asser), asseer *v.* assure (B1)

asteer *adv.* astir

astonisher *n.* a big surprise (A1)

astonishment, an *n.* shock (A1)

atheen *prep.* above (B1). *cf.* **abeen**

athin(g) *n.* everything

Athole brose *n.* honey or meal mixed with whisky

athoot *prep., conj.* without

athort *adv.* all over; *prep.* across

ation *n.* generation; family connection (A2). *cf.* **aishan**

attrack *v.* attract

atween *adv., prep.* between; **atween hans** *adv.* between times (B)

atweesh *prep. See* **atween**

Auchmacoy bummer *n.* the Buchan bumble bee

aucht *adj.* eight; *n., pron.* anything; *n.* possession; *v.* owe; own; **auchtin** due; **aucht nor ocht** nothing at all; neither one thing nor another

auchteen *adj.* eighteen

audiscence *n.* audience; hearing

aul, auld *adj.* old; **auler, aulest**; **aulder, auldest**

aul-farran(t) *adj.* old-fashioned

Aul Nick *pr. n.* the Devil

Auld Kirk, the *n.* established Church of Scotland; whisky

aum *v.* thrash. *cf.* **aam**

aumrie *n.* cupboard (A); pantry; press above a press (B1)

auncient *adj.* ancient

Australya *pr. n.* Australia

ava *adv.* at all

aven *adv.* even

Aw, aw *pron.* I

awa *adv.* away; **awa forrin** away abroad; **hine awa** far away; **keep her awa** change course to leeward (B). *cf.* **tee**

awaar *adj.* aware

awat *adv.* I wot, indeed, truly. *cf.* **awyte**

awcre *n.* acre

awe *v.* owe; **awin** owing

aweel *adv.* well

aweers o *adv.* on the point of, just about to

awfu *adj.* awful. *cf.* **afa, aafa**

awmous *n.* alms

Awprile *n.* month of April. *See* **Prile eeran**

awpron *n.* apron; leather covering for use in open carriage

Aw'se *pron. with v.* I'll

awyte *pron. with v.* I wot, know; *adv.* assuredly

ay *adv.* yes

ay, ay *int.* hello

aye *adv.* always; still

ayoke *adv.* at work

ayon, ayont *prep., adv.* beyond

ayven *adv.* even

— **B** —

ba *n.* ball

baabee *n.* halfpenny; *in pl.* money. *cf.* **bawbee**

Baabie *pr. n.* deriv. of Barbara

baal *n.* ball, dance

baathe *v.* bathe

babbity *n.* baby

babbity bowster *n.* (bab-at-the-bowster) an old country dance to end a ball etc.

bacca bree *n.* the spittle of a tobacco-chewer

back *n.* wooden vessel for carrying peat; outermost board of a sawn tree; **back o** *prep.* just after (of time); **at the back o beyond** *phr.* far off the beaten track

back-been *n.* back-bone

backbin *n.* back band in harness

back-birn *n.* back burden

back-cheyn *n.* chain over saddle supporting cart shafts
back-door *n.* tail board of cart
backet *n.* bucket; three-sided wooden box with hand-holes, used for carrying peats, sliced turnips or potatoes and pre-dating sculls; wooden scuttle for carrying ashes
backie *n.* back-green; back-garden
backin *n.* address on a letter
backlins *adv.* backwards
backs *n.* refuse of sawmill
backset *n.* setback; *v.* disgust (B1)
back-spier *v.* question a speaker
bad *v. pt.* bade
badder *v.* bother. *cf.* **bather**
bade *v. pt.* lived. *cf.* **bed**
baet *v.* beat; *ppl., adj.* beaten, defeated
baggerel *n.* worthless woman
bag-raip *n.* rope around eaves of stack
baignet *n.* bayonet
baikie *n.* short iron stake to hold tether for cattle and goats
bailie, baillie, bylie *n.* cattleman; alderman; water bailiff (M); **little bailie** under-cattleman
baird *n.* beard
bairn *n.* baby, child; **bairnikie** little child; *v.* make pregnant
bairnheid *n.* childhood
baith *adj., pron.* both
bajan *n.* first year student at Aberdeen University
baket *n.* bucket. *cf.* **backet**
bale-fire *n.* bonfire
ballant *n.* ballad
ballie *n.* ball

ban *v.* to scold; curse, swear
bandie *n.* minnow, stickleback
bandster *n.* one who binds sheaves. *cf.* **banster**
bane *n.* bone; **near the bane** tight-fisted. *cf.* **been**
banie *adj.* boney
bang *v.* hasten (M)
bangstrie *n.* violence to person or property
bannock *n.* round, flat cake (usually of oatmeal) baked on a girdle; oatcake (S)
banster *n.* one who binds the sheaves. *cf.* **bandster**
banter *v. tr.* scold; tease
bantin *n.* a bantam
bap *n.* floury breakfast roll; *v.* walk in a plodding, flat-footed way
bapteese *v.* baptise
bapteesement *n.* baptism
bar *n.* a joke, funny story; *v.* fix door with a bar (B1)
barbet *n.* arrow; **bow an barbet** bow and arrow
barbit-weer *n.* barbed wire
barfit *adj.* barefooted
bark *n.* the skin; preservative for fishing nets; *v.* skin
bark-an-bowff *n.* scolding
barkit *adj., ppl.* skinned; encrusted with dirt, dirty
barleys-on *See* **parley**
barm *n.* yeast; ferment
barra *n.* barrow
barrie *n.* a baby's flannel coat (B1)
barritchfu *adj.* harsh (G)
bass *n.* doormat
batchie *n.* bachelor
bather *v.* bother (S). *cf.* **badder**

Baubie *pr. n.* deriv. from Barbara.
 cf. **Baabie**
bauch *adj.* shy, bashful; timid
bauchle *n.* old shoe; *v.* shamble;
 trouble (B1); defeat (B1)
bauchle-ban *n.* shoe-tie (B1)
bauk *n.* uncultivated strip of land
 between fields; cross-beam
 between rafters
baukie *n.* bat
baul *adj.* bold (A2); strong (B1)
bauld *adj.* bold (J)
bauldie-heidit *adj.* bald-headed. *cf.*
 beld
bau(l)drins, bawdrons *n.* ref. to a
 cat, puss
bawbee *n.* halfpenny; *in pl.* money
bawd *n.* hare (M). *cf.* **maukin**
baxter *n.* baker
bear *n.* four- or six-rowed barley
beardie *n.* good-natured rubbing of
 a man's beard on a child's face
beas' *n. pl.* animals in general,
 cattle in particular (C)
beat *v.* lash a hook to a fishing line
beck *v.* curtsey; do obeisance
bed *v.* spread straw for animals for
 the night
bed-claes *n. pl.* bed clothes
bed(d) *v. pt.* lived. *cf.* **bade**
beddal *n.* a bedridden person
beddie *n.* (small) bed
beddies *n.* hopscotch
beddit *ppl.* in bed, put to bed
bed-lids *n. pl.* doors of box-bed
bedraigle *v.* to bedraggle
beed *v. pt.* must, had to. *cf.* **beet**
beef *n.* beef; the term used on board
 fishing boats for all butcher meat
 (B)

beek *v.* warm before the fire
beelin *n.* whitlow. *See* **futlie**
been *n.* bone. *cf.* **bane**
beerial *n.* interment, funeral
bee-ruskie *n.* simple form of beehive, covered in ropes of twisted
 straw (T)
beery *v.* bury, *ppl.* **beeriet**
beesom *n.* a broom; untidy woman
 (A1); disparaging term used of a
 woman. *cf.* **besom**
beesom-ticht *adj.* swept-clean (B1)
beet *n.* boot. *cf.* **buit**; *v.* bet; replace
 lost hooks on a fishing line. *cf.*
 beat
beet tae *v. pt.* (**be tae** by wrong
 division) had to; **that beet tae be
 gran** that must have been grand;
 sometimes used as *v. pr.*
beezer *n.* something of huge size
befa *v.* befall
begeck *n.* disappointment; trick;
 shock
begood *v.* begin; *v. pt.* began
begowk *v.* trick, fool
begrutten *adj.* tear-stained
behauden *adj.* beholden
beheef *n.* behoof
beheeld *v. pt.* beheld
beheeve *v.* behove
beil, beilin *n.* boil, sore
bek (B1) *See* **beek**
belaabour *v.* belabour
belang *v.* belong; belong to a place;
 he belangs Aiberdeen
beld *adj.* bald
Beldie *pr. n.* deriv. of Isabella
belike *adv.* perhaps, likely
bellas, bellaws *n.* bellows
belly-ban *n.* harness belly-band

belly-rive *n.* indigestion
belly-thraw *n.* colic, stomach-ache
belt *n.* narrow plantation
beltie *n.* water-hen (G1)
belyve *adv.* by-and-by, before long
ben *adv., prep.* inside, through; **far ben wi** intimate with, esp. with God; *n.* hill, mountain
bencape *adj.* first rate
benmaist, benmost *adj.* innermost
Ben(n)achie *n.* well-known hill near Monymusk, Aberdeenshire
bennin *n.* bend (T)
bent *n.* coarse grass growing near sea; hillock covered in such grass; sand dune
bere *See* **bear**
besom *n.* broom; term of reproach for woman. *cf.* **beesom**
besom-shaft *n.* broom-handle
bess *n.* bass; *v.* sing bass
bestial *n.* cattle (A2)
beuk *n.* book. *cf.* **buik**
bevie *n.* large fire (B1)
bewotifie *adj.* beautiful (B1)
bibblie-nibbit *adj.* snotty-nosed
bick *n.* bitch
bicker *n.* scrimmage; wooden brose basin; *v.* move quickly and noisily; ripple; laugh heartily
bid *v.* invite; **bidden** *ppl.* asked; invited; told; stayed; **bidden gang** asked to go
bide *v.* wait; remain; live; tolerate; **bide ye** *excl.* wait
bidie-in *n.* a live-in lover
biel, bield *n.* shelter; **bieldy** sheltered
bien *adj.* well-to-do; comfortable; **bienless** *adj.* comfortless

big, bigg *v.* build; **biggit** *pt., ppl.* built
bigger *n.* builder
biggin *n.* building, house
biggit oot *ppl.* having abundance of (B)
bigsie *adj.* conceited
bike *n.* nest of wild bees
bikk *See* **bick**
bile *v.* boil; **bilt egg** boiled egg. *cf.* **bylt**
biler *n.* kettle
bilin *n.* a boiling (e.g. of rhubarb)
billet *n.* lot; situation (A)
billie, billy *n.* fellow; comrade
billie *n.* notice posted in seaports with news of herring fleet catches (B)
bin *v.* to bind (rhymes with tin)
bin *n.* humour, mood
bin' *v.* to bind. *cf.* **bin**
binch *n.* bench
binder *n.* tall story; an outstanding thing of its kind (B)
bing *n.* crowd; heap; bin for corn, turnips etc.
bink *n.* hob (B)
binna *v. neg. imp.* (of 'be') don't be
binner *n.* a quick movement; sounding blow; *v.* move rapidly and noisily
binnin *n.* binding for cattle
bird-alane *adj.* quite alone (B)
birdies' eenies *n. pl.* sago pudding (T)
birk *n.* birch tree
birken *n.* birch tree (C)
birkie *n.* lively, smart fellow
birl *n.* twirl; brisk dance; *v.* twirl
birn *n.* burden; large collection

birr *n.* force, energy, passion; whirr. *cf.* **virr**

birse *n.* bristle; bristle on cobbler's thread; beard; bruise; pressure, *esp.* of crowd

birse, birss *n.* fit of bad temper; **get yir birse up** to get angry; **set up your birss** make you angry; **birse** *v.* press, squeeze, push; bruise; **birse ben a bit** move along a bit; **birse tee** push to. *cf.* **birze**

birsel, birstle *v.* toast, roast; **birslet, birslin** *adj.* scorched, scorching

birsin *ppl., adj.* out of breath

birst *n.* over-exertion causing injury; *v.* burst, split

birze *v.* squeeze, press. *cf.* **birse**

bishop *v.* beat down earth or stones; *n.* device for doing this

bit *conj.* but; *n.* crisis; **at the bit** in a crisis

bittock *n.* small bit

bizz *v.* buzz; hiss

bizzar *n.* jade (J) probably from **bizzard** buzzard

bizzin *n.* buzzing

blackguaird *v.* to blackguard, abuse

blackie *n.* blackbird

black yarn *phr.* empty herring nets (B)

blad *v.* spoil. *cf.* **blaud**

bladderskite *n.* foolish, noisy talker

blae *adj.* blue; bluish; black and blue (B1)

blaeberry *n.* bilberry

blaewort *n.* blue cornflower

blaffert *n.* blast of wind (C). *cf.*

bluffert

blaik *v.* blacken

blaiken *v.* blacken

blain *n.* bare patch in field where grain has not sprung

blainy *adj.* covered with bare patches

blake *n.* black polish

blate *adj.* bashful

blatter *n.* sharp shower (C); *v.* dash noisily

blaud *v.* spoil. *cf.* **blad**

blauve *See* **blyaav**

blaw *v.* blow; brag; *n.* braggart

bleart *ppl.* bleary-eyed

bleat *adj.* dull, stupid. *cf.* **blate**

bleb *v.* sip; tipple (A)

bleck *adj.* black

bleck, bleckin *n.* blacking

bleck *n. joc.* blackguard, scoundrel (M2). *cf.* **blake**

bleck *v.* puzzle; defeat; beat, prove too much for

blecken *v.* blacken. *cf.* **blaik**

bledder *n.* bladder; *v.* talk idly

bleed *n.* blood. *cf.* **bluid; bleedy cooter** bleeding nose, nosebleed

bleed-jeelin *adj.* blood-chilling, blood-curdling (G)

bleed-reid *adj.* blood-red

bleery *adj.* bleary

bleeter *n.* blethering person, gasbag

bleeze *n., v.* blaze

bleezin *adj.* very drunk

blether *n.* a talk, chat; *v.* chat; talk nonsense

blewart *n.* bluebell (B1)

blibber *v.* sip a small amount of liquid (T)

blicht *n.* blight

blickers *n. pl.* nonsense
blin *adj.* blind
blin-bridle *n.* bridle with blinkers
blin lump *n.* boil
blin sieve *adj., n.* sieve with solid base
blin tit *adj., n.* blind teat
blink *n.* beam, ray; *v.* wink
blinter *v.* blink weakly or sorely
blithe(some) *adj.* cheerful, merry
blobbie-like *adj.* humid
blocher *v.* cough with phlegm in the throat
bloiter *n.* blast of wind. *cf.* **blouter**
blon *n.* blonde; girlfriend
blood *v.* bleed (S)
blouter *n.* blast of wind. *cf.* **bloiter**
blue *adj.* downcast (A1)
Bluemoggener *pr. n.* native of Peterhead
bluffert *n.* blast of wind
blyaav *v.* blow, pant; boast
blythe *adj.* glad, cheerful. *cf.* **blithe**
boakie *See* **bokie**
bob *v.* curtsey
bobbie, bobby *n.* policeman
bobbinjohn *n.* tin cylinder perforated at one end for sowing turnip seed by hand where it has failed in the drills
bocht *v.* bought
bockie *n.* hobgoblin
Boddam Coo *pr. n.* fog horn at Boddam Head (B)
boddom *n.* bottom
bode *n.* bid at a sale
bodie *n.* person
bodle *n.* small coin (J)
bodsie *n.* short, dapper person
body bulk *quasi-adv.* physically

bog *v.* stick in the mire or bog; confuse, dumbfound; **boggit** bamboozled
bogie *n.* two-wheeled open wagon
bogie-rowe *n.* bogie-roll tobacco
bogjavelt (B1), **bogshaivelt** *adj.* knocked out of shape, distorted
boiler *n.* kettle. *cf.* **biler**
bokie *n.* bogie, scarecrow; fisher term for small boy (B)
bondy *n.* bonfire (O). *cf.* **bale-fire**
bone *in phr.* **in richt bone** in fine fettle (M2)
bone davie (davy) *n.* horse-drawn manure distributor, spreading fertiliser including bone-meal (S, T)
bonnet *n.* a man's cap
bonnet-laird *n.* yeoman farmer; proprietor of the land he farms
bonnie, bonny *adj.* lovely, pretty; handsome; attractive
bonspeil, bonspiel *n.* contest, especially curling
boo *v.* bow; **boot, boo't** *ppl., adj.* bent; **boot twa faal** bent over
boodie *n.* ghost (B1); scarecrow (M1). *cf.* **tattie-boodie** etc.
booet, booit *n.* hand-lantern (without glass)
bool, bowl *n.* a marble
bools *n. pl.* marbles; bowls
boons *n. pl.* bounds; **oot o kent boons** in unknown territory; off the beaten track
boorach(ie) *n.* group, crowd
boortree *See* **bourtree**
boo't *See* **boo**
bore *n.* crevice, chink, hole
borra *v.* borrow; **borrat licht**

indirect light

bosie *n.* bosom

bosky *adj.* wild, unfrequented

boss *adj.* hollow

bossie *n.* large wooden bowl used for oatmeal in baking (B1)

bothy *n.* cottage where farm servants were lodged and cooked their own food

bouch *v.* bark; cough

bouk *n.* size, build; **boukit** large, bulky; **sma boukit** of small build, bulk; **muckle-boukit** pregnant (B1); **nairra-boukit** of lean build

boun *n.* boundary

bourach(ie) *See* **boorach**

bourtree, boortree *n.* elder tree

bout *n.* swathe cut by scythesman, corn or hay cut by a scythe and lying in rows

bow *n.* boll, an old Scottish dry measure of not more than six bushels; the part of the harness bent under the neck of an ox to fasten the yoke; **ower the bows** in a disorderly way (A2); **go through the bows** misbehave (A2)

bow-cheer *n.* armchair

bowden *v.* to fill; **bowdent** replete (after eating)

bowe *n.* fishing float

bowel-crappit *adj.* (hair) cut with a bowl

bowff *n., v.* bark (of dog)

bow-hoched *adj.* bow-legged

bowie *n.* barrel

bows *See* **bow**

bowsell *n.* iron cattle-binding (F)

bowster *n.* bolster

bowsterous *adj.* boistrous

box *phr.* **i the same box** in the same boat, or position

bracken *n.* fern. *cf.* **breckan**

braddie *n.* meat pie. *cf.* **bridie**

brae *n.* hill, slope, steep road

braeset *adj.* situated on a slope

braid *adj.* broad

braig *v.* brag

braird *n.* first sprouting of young grain

braith *n.* breath (G). *cf.* **breith**

braivity *n.* show, splendour; finery

brak *v.* break

brakfast *n.* breakfast

brak-fur *v.* plough shallow furrows (F)

bramble *n.* blackberry

brammle *See* **bramble**

brander *n.* gridiron; drain-cover

branert *adj.* baked on **brander**

branks *n.* halter of wood or metal

braw *adj.* fine, handsome, excellent; *in pl.* fine clothes

brawlies *adv.* well, finely. *cf.* **brulies**

brawly *adv.* well, splendidly

braxy *n.* internal inflammation in sheep; sheep that has died a natural death (M)

break *n.* hollow in a hill

brecham *n.* collar for a draught horse

breckan *n.* fern. *cf.* **bracken**

bree *n.* liquid, juice; liquor. *(See* **snaw-bree**); *v.* to drain boiled solids *e.g.* **tae bree the tatties; throwe the bree** (of potatoes) overboiled

breed *See* **breid**
breeder *n.* brother. *cf.* **bridder**
breeks *n.* trousers. *cf.* **briks**
breem *n.* broom; a thatch of broom
breem-buss *n.* broom bush
breenge *v.* rush forward impetuously; batter, bang
breer *n.* briar; first sprouting of a crop (A1); *v.* sprout. *cf.* **braird**
breest *n.* breast. *cf.* **breist**
breet *n.* brute (not always unsympathetic)
breid *n.* oatcakes taken as dessert in bowl of milk (F, T); bread; breadth
breist *n.* breast. *cf.* **breest**
breith *n.* breath (J)
brench *n.* branch
brent *ppl.* burned (G1). *cf.* **brunt**
bress *n.* brass
brevity *n.* fine show or display
brichen *v.* brighten
bricht *adj.* bright
bridder *n.* brother. *See* **breeder, brither, broder**
bridegreem *n.* bridegroom
bridie *n.* beef or mutton pie (S)
brier *n.* eyelash; **by the briers o the een** by the skin of his teeth (T)
brig *n.* bridge
briks *See* **breeks**
brinch *n.* branch
britchin *n.* breeching, the piece of harness that passes round the hind-part of a horse in shafts, to let it push backwards; **intae the britchin** into reverse
brither *n.* brother. *See* **bridder**
broadcast *n.* broadcast sowing machine (F)
brob *v.* to prick; **brobbit** *pt., ppl.* pricked
Broch, the *pr. n.* nickname for Fraserburgh
broch *n.* burgh; halo round sun or moon (round moon, predicting storm); Pictish tower
brochan *n.* oatmeal boiled thicker than gruel, with butter and honey
Brocher *pr. n.* nickname for native of Fraserbugh
brocht *v. pt.* brought
brod *n.* board; collecting box in church
broder *n.* brother (A2). *cf.* **breeder, bridder, brither**
brodmell *n.* brood (B1, A2)
broke *v. pt.* became bankrupt
broncaidis *n.* bronchitis
Broo *n.* Employment Office
broo *n.* brow
broobin *n.* harness brow band
brook *n.* soot on pots; *v. pt.* broke. *cf.* **bruik**
brookie *n.* blacksmith (A); *adj.* sooty, grimy
brookit *adj.* (of cattle, sheep) speckled
broon *adj.* brown
brose *n.* oatmeal or peasemeal mixed with boiling water, milk etc; a meal
brose-caup *n.* wooden bowl for oatmeal dish
brosy *adj.* stout, well-fed
brow *adj.* handsome (M, R). *cf.* **braw**
browst *n.* a brew
bruckle *adj.* brittle, crumbly (C1)

bruik *v. pt.* broke. *cf.* **brook**
bruise-box *n.* corn-chest (F)
bruised corn *n.* pounded oats
bruk *v. pt.* broke (R). *cf.* **brak,**
bruik
brulies (B1) *See* **brawlies**
brulzie *n.* brawl
brunt *v., ppl.* burned. *cf.* **brent**
bubble *v.* blubber, snivel
bubbly *n.* paraffin torch used at sea
bubbly-bairn *n.* cry-baby
bubbly(jock) *n.* turkey-cock
Buchan *pr. n.* Buchan's *Domestic*
Medicine
Buchaner *n.* native of
Buchanhaven, now part of
Peterhead
Buchanie, the *pr. n.* the *Buchan*
Observer
bucht *n.* a sheep-, cattle-fold
Bucker *pr. n.* native of Buckie
bucker *n.* annoyance; nuisance (A);
v. botch, bungle (B1)
buckie *n.* refractory, mischievous
person; periwinkle; spiral shell of
winkle; **as fou's a buckie** drunk
buckle *v.* dress (for a journey) (R)
bucklins *n. pl.* paraphernalia of
marriage (A2)
buddick *n.* small useless fish found
in harbours (B)
buff *n.* nonsense
buffet steel *n.* square stool (B1)
buik *n.* bulk; book; *v.* book,
register; record names of
betrothed couple in church
register before marriage. *cf.* **beuk,**
byeuck
buikin-nicht *n.* the night on which
the names of persons about to be

married are given to the church
Session Clerk to have the banns
proclaimed
buird *n.* board; table. *cf.* **brod**
buirdin-squeel *n.* boarding-school
buirdly *adj.* burly; fine-looking
buit *n.* boot. *cf.* **beet**
bul(l) *n.* bull; bill; *v.* serve a cow
bullaments *n. pl.* outer garments
usually ragged or untidy (B1)
bullyrag *v.* scold, hector, treat in a
bullying manner
bum *v.* hum, drone
bumbee *n.* bumble-bee
bummer *n.* anything outstandingly
large
bun, bunt *v. pt., ppl.* bound. *See*
bin; bun-bed wooden bed shut
in with folding or sliding doors
buncher *n.* machine attached to
mill for making straw bunches
bung *n.* ill-humour; huff (A); **on**
the bung in the huff
bunkert *n.* obstacle
burn *n.* stream
burn the witchie *v.* to burn effigy
on a boat deck to change bad luck
(B)
buroo *n.* bureau
burr *n.* the uvular 'r'; *v.* pronounce
the letter 'r' in the throat
burssen *ppl.* bursting
burssen-ile *n.* discarded lubricating
oil used to soothe the skin of pigs
(B) and prevent rust on farm
machinery (T)
bushle, bussle *n.* bushel measure
busk *v.* dress; adorn
buss *n.* bush
but-an-ben *n.* two-roomed cottage;

from end to end; **but-bed** the bed in the semi-parlour end of the cottage

but-the-hoose *n.* kitchen

butt *n.* tail of a sheaf

butterflee *n.* butterfly (R). *cf.* **buttery**

buttery (-rowie) *n.* flat morning roll

buttery *n.* butterfly (M1)

buttock mail *n.* a spanking

buzness *n* . business

buzzle *n., v.* (of grain, indicating ripeness) rustle

by, by wi't *adv.* over, past; **by the warst** past the worst

byaakin *n., ppl.* baking

byes *prep.* compared with; besides

byeuck *n.* book. *cf.* **beuk, buik**

bygaein, bygaun, bygyaun, i the *phr.* as you go by; incidentally

bygane *adj.* (of time) past

byle *n., v.* boil. *cf.* **bile**

bylie *See* **bailie**

bylin *n.* a boiling

byock *v.* vomit (B1)

byordnar *adj.* extraordinary

byous *adj.* extraordinary; *adv.* exceedingly

byowty *n.* beauty

byowtifu *adj.* beautiful

byre *n.* cowshed

bywye *n.* byway

— C —

ca, caa *v.* call; drive; knock; **ca for** head for; **ca** (a person) **for aathing** defame; **on the ca** on the move; **ca canny** take care; **ca the crack** chat; **ca the door tee** shut the door. *cf.* **caw**

caal *adj.* cold; **caal roch shooers** cold blustery showers. *cf.* **caul**

caav *v.* give birth to a calf

cack *v.* defecate. *cf.* **kich**

cackie-stammackit *adj.* having imperfect digestion; squeamish (T)

caddis *n.* cotton-wool; flock; padding; (cotton- or wool-) fluff; any kind of fluff

cadge *n.* shake, jog; *v.* carry loads; peddle wares; shake roughly, knock about; sponge

cadger *n.* carrier; itinerant dealer, hawker; sponger

caff *n.* chaff; **caff-bed, caff-seck** mattress filled with chaff. *cf.* **cauff**

caip *n.* cap

caird *n.* tinker; *v.* card (wool)

cairn *n.* loose heap of stones; *v.* form a cairn or heap

cairry *v.* carry

cairry-on *n.* carry-on

cairt *n.* cart; *v.* carry

cairter *n.* carter

cairtin *ppl.* playing cards

cairts *n. pl.* playing-cards

caithick *n.* monkfish

calfie's mooie *n.* small cowrie shell (B). *cf.* **Johnny Groatie, kysie**

callant *n.* stripling, lad

caller *adj.* fresh; cool, refreshing

cam *v. pt.* came; **cam in aboot** approached

camsteerie *adj.* perverse, quarrelsome

can *n.* ability

cankert *adj.* ill-humoured, fretful; (of weather) stormy, threatening; gusty

canle *n.* candle

Canlemas *n.* Candlemas

canna *v. neg.* cannot

cannas *n.* canvas, esp. that used in winnowing grain

canny *adj.* prudent, cautious; gentle; frugal; safe; moderate in price

cantle *v. intr.* brighten up; recover one's health or spirits

cantle (up) *v.* brighten (up), recover health

cantrip *n.* mischievous trick

canty *adj.* cheery, good-humoured

capawcity *n.* ability

capawshus *adj.* capacious

caper *v.* dance

capernicious *adj.* short-tempered; fretful

capital *adj.* excellent

capshon, caption *n.* lucky acquisition, windfall, prize

captire, in *phr.* in suspense (B1)

car *n.* calves. *cf.* **caur;** *v.* care

carefu *adj.* careful

carena *v. neg.* do not care; **carena doit** do not care in the least

cargie *n.* cargo

cark *n.* care, anxiety; **nae cark nor care** not a care in the world

carl *n.* churl; man; old man

carl-doddie *n.* stalk of rib-grass

carlers *n.* heavy seaweed. *cf.* **tangles**

carlie *n.* a little old man

carlin(e) *n.* old woman; witch

carn *n.* cairn (also in placenames)

carritch(es) *n.* catechism; *in pl.* the Shorter Catechism (M)

cartil *n.* cartload (B1)

carvel-biggit *adj.* (boat) built with planks edge to edge. *cf.* **clinker-biggit**

carvy, carvey, carvie *n.* caraway

case be *conj.* in case

cassen *See* **cast**

cassie *See* **causey**

cast *v.* cut with a spade (e.g. peat); dig; to throw off (e.g. coat); **casen, cassen** *ppl.* cast; (of colour) faded

castell *n.* castle

castock *n.* stalk of kail or cabbage

cast-oot *n.* quarrel; fall-out

catcher *n.* truant officer (S); townkeeper at weekends (F)

catch her (*phr.* used by fishermen) fall asleep; **he's catched her**

catecheese *v.* catechise, instruct by question and answer by use of the Church Catechism

catechis *n.* catechism (A)

cat's dicht *n.* quick wipe or wash

cattie's tailie *n.* plaything made from scraps of knitting wool on makeshift loom, using a cotton reel and pins (B)

cattlie *n.* cattleman (S)

cauf(ie) *n.* calf

cauk *v.* to chalk; challenge for repayment of a debt; calk, fix guard on horse's hoof to prevent slipping

caul(d) *adj., n.* cold; **caul steer** sour milk or cold water and meal stirred together

cauldrife *adj.* cold, chilly

caulker *n.* iron rim fixed on shoe to minimise wear

caum *n.* mould for ball, spoon etc.

caunle *n.* candle. *cf.* **canle**

caup *n.* wooden bowl; **cauper** maker of caups, wood-turner

caur *n.* calves. *cf.* **car**

cause *conj.* because

causey *n.* causeway, paved area; the granite sett or cobblestone it is paved with. *cf.* **cassie**

caw *v.* to drive. *cf.* **ca**

cawpable *adj.* capable

ceety *n.* city

ceevil *adj.* civil

'cep, 'cepin *prep., conj.* except

cert, certie *in phr.* **my cert, my certie!** surely, certainly

chaamer *See* **chaumer**

chack *n.* chalk; chequered linen or calico

chackie *n.* farm worker's bag (T)

chackie-mull *n.* death-watch beetle

chackit *adj.* of a checked pattern; chequered

chad *n.* compacted gravel

chaddy *adj.* gravelly

Chae *pr. n.* deriv. of Charles

chaep *adj.* cheap

chaetry *n.* cheating

chaff *v.* chafe

chafts *n.* chops; cheeks

chaip-john *adj., n.* cheapjack

chairge *n., v.* charge

chairity *n.* charity

Chairlie *pr. n.* deriv. of Charles

chait *v.* cheat; *ppl.* cheated. *cf.* **chate**

chalder *n.* dry measure, of grain = 16 bolls

chancy *adj.* lucky, fortunate; safe

changefu *adj.* changeable

change-hoose *n.* alehouse, inn

chanter *n.* the part of the bagpipes on which the tune is played

chantie, chanty *n* chamber-pot

chap *n.* knock; *v.* to knock, to pound, mash; chop; (of clocks) strike; **the clockie chappit** the clock struck; **chappin** *ppl., n.* knocking

chape *adj.* cheap. *cf.* **chaep**

chapper *n.* utensil for mashing potatoes; **chappit tatties** mashed potatoes

chaps me *excl.* (when a person chooses a particular thing) give me…

charge *n.* oath

chate *n., v.* cheat. *cf.* **chait**

chatter *v.* shatter

chaumer *n.* chamber; best room; sleeping-place for farm workers in Banff and Buchan. In the Mearns, the bothy was more common. Unlike the bothy, no food was eaten in the chaumer (A, M1); *v.* to live in a chaumer

chaw *v.* chew

cheekie-for-chowie *adv.* cheek by jowl; side by side

cheena *adj., n.* china

cheenge *v.* change. *cf.* **chynge**

cheengeless *adj.* changeless

15

cheeper *n.* young or half-fledged bird

cheer *n.* chair

cheerman *n.* chairman

cheery-pyke *n.* tasty morsel, treat

chessel, chesset *n.* cheese vat or press

chief (wi) *adj.* intimate, friendly

chiel *n.* man; fellow

chik *n.* cheek

chilpit, chilpy *adj.* chilled

chim(b)ley, chimbly *n.* chimney

chimbley-chik *n.* hearth

chine *n.* chain

chine-gaird *n.* (on a bicycle) chain-guard

chingle *n.* shingle

chirm *v.* complain; fret (A); sing, murmur (C1)

chirr-wirrin *n.* chatting back and fore, chin-wagging (S)

chirry *n.* cherry

chitter *v.* tremble, shiver; **chittering-chow** bread eaten after open-air bathing; **chit-chow** good things to eat (B1)

chop *n.* shop

chouk *n.* cheek

choup *n.* a cheep; **didna get a choup oot o im**

chowks *n.* the jaws

chowter *n.* term of endearment, mostly for children (B)

chucken, chucknie *n.* chicken

chucken-hertit *adj.* faint-hearted

chuckenwort *n.* chickweed

chuckie-steen *n.* granite chipping; pebble

chuddy *n.* chewing-gum

chuff *adj.* chummy

chumla, chumlay *n.* mantel-shelf. *cf.* **chimbley**

chunner *v.* murmur plaintively

chuntie *n.* chamber-pot

chynge *v.* change. *cf.* **cheenge**

chyse *n.* cheese; *v.* choose

chyser *n.* team-picker in games

cla *n., v.* claw, scratch

clachan *n.* hamlet

claes *n.* clothes. *cf.* **clyse**

claggieleerum (T) *See* **claggum**

claggum *n.* treacle toffee

claik *n., v.* gossip, tittle-tattle. *cf.* **clash**

clair *adj.* clear; distinct; ready

claith *n.* cloth; **aa ae claith** all the same

claithe *v.* clothe

clam(b) *v. pt.* climbed

clamjamfrey, clanjamfry *n.* noisy crowd, mob; company of people

clamp *v.* walk noisily, as with hobnailed shoes

clap *n., v.* pat, fondle

clart *v.* daub, smear

clash *n.* gossip, tittle-tattle

clapper *n.* butter-hand

clashmaclavers *n.* idle discourse, silly talk

claught *v.* clutch, lay hold of

claw *v.* scratch; **clawed the caup** cleaned the dish (the last to rise in the morning had to clean the common bowl); *fig.* came to the end; **clawin post** scratching post for cattle, usually a stone (T)

clead *v.* clothe. *cf.* **claithe**

cleadin *n.* clothing

clean-lan *adj.* (field) cleared of turnips and ready for ploughing (T)

clear *adj.* undamaged, in good condition (S)

cleathin *n.* mould-board (F)

cleck *v.* give birth to young (of rabbits)

cleckin *n.* brood, litter

cled *adj.* clad

cleek, cleik *n.* hook; device to set gird spinning (S); golfing iron; *v.* seize (with the claws); hook, catch up by or fasten (on a hook)

cleekit shalt *n., ppl.* pony suffering from string-halt

cleg *n.* gadfly, horsefly

clench *v.* clinch, settle; limp (A2)

cless *n.* class

cleuch *n.* narrow glen, ravine

clew *v. pt.* clawed; *n.* ball of straw-rope used in thatching. *cf.* **cloo**

clim *v.* climb. *cf.* **sclim**

clink *n.* resounding blow; *v.* mend by rivetting; hammer; weld

clinker-biggit *adj.* (boat) built with planks overlapping. *cf.* **carvel-biggit**

clip *n.* pert girl; *v.* cut

clipe *n.* tell-tale; *v.* to tell tales. *cf.* **clype**

clish-ma-claver *n.* idle talk

clivver *adj.* clever; *n.* clover

clocher *v.* cough, wheeze

clockin *ppl., adj.* (of hen) brooding, broody

clod *v.* pelt

cloddie *n.* clod of earth; a peat

clog(gie) *n.* log; block of wood

clog-fit *n.* club-foot

cloo *n.* ball of rope, cord or wool, etc. *cf.* **clew**

clood *n.* cloud

clook *n., v.* claw

cloot *n.* cloth; blow; *v.* mend. *cf.* **clout**

clootch *v.* clutch (A)

clootie-dumplin *n.* sweet dumpling cooked in a cloth

clootie-rug *n.* rug made from old cloths

Cloots *pr. n.* the Devil

clort *n.* mud; anything soft and sticky; *v.* to besmear

clortit *ppl.* smeared

clorty *adj.* dirty; messy

close, closs *n.* enclosure; farmyard; passage; alley

close-han't *adj.* tight-fisted

closen-in *ppl.* closed in

clossach *n.* a mass; hoard of money

clour *v.* strike, indent

clout, cloutie *n.* a cloth

clout *n., v.* mend, patch *(e.g.* a kettle). *cf.* **cloot**

clout *n.* blow; *v.* beat, strike. *cf.* **cloot**

clouty-rug *See* **clootie-rug**

clum *v. pt.* climbed. *cf.* **clim**

clyack *n.* end of harvest; **clyack shafe** the last sheaf cut in harvest

clype *n.* tell-tale; *v.* to tell tales. *cf.* **clipe**

clyse *n.* clothes. *cf.* **claes**

clyte *n.* a sudden or heavy fall; **cam clyte** fell suddenly

coach *n.* pram

coal-coom *n.* coal-dust

coble *n.* pond for watering cattle

cock *v.* swagger, show off

cock-a-leekie *n.* chicken and leek soup

cockernony *n.* starched crown of a

17

woman's cap

cockit on *ppl., prep.* perched, mounted on

cockit up *ppl., prep.* dressed up showily

cockle-ee *n.* an eye with a squint (B)

Cock o the North *phr.* nickname for the Marquises of Huntly

coff *v.* buy (G1); *ppl.* **coft**

cog, coggie, cogue *n.* wooden pail for milking, or herring-guts

cog *v.* feed from the cog or pail

coggit *ppl.* fed from the **caufie's cog** (T)

colcannon *n.* dish of mashed potato and chopped cabbage served with meat

cole, coll *n.* haycock; *v.* to make haycocks

colleague (wi) *v.* associate, consort with

colleeginer *n.* student at college (A1)

collieshangie *n.* uproar (C)

collogue *v.* converse; *n.* intimate chat

come *in phr.* **come hairst** when harvest comes; **come ower** *v.* befall

commeenicant *n.* communicant

compleen *v.* complain

compleent *n.* complaint

concairn *n.* concern

concaited *adj.* conceited

condeeshun *n.* condition

conduck *n.* conduct

confeerin tae *ppl.* corresponding to, accordant with

confoon, confoun *v.* confound

congregat *v. pt.* congregated

connach *v.* spoil; destroy; **connacht** *ppl.* destroyed, wasted

conneck *v.* connect; *ppl.* **conneckit**

constiteetion *n.* constitution

conteena *v.* continue (B1); *v. pt.* **conteenit**

conteenwal *adj.* continual

conten *v.* contend

conter, contar *v.* contradict; *adj.* opposite. *cf.* **cwanter**

contermashious *adj.* contrary

contermin't *adj.* contradictory; contrary, perverse

contreebit *v.* contribute

convainience *n.* convenience

convoy *v.* convey, escort

coo *n.* cow; **coo's lick** hair overhanging the brow at one side

cooch *n.* dog's kennel (A)

coof *n.* coward (M)

coonjer *v.* scold; intimidate. *cf.* **counger**

coont *v.* count

coontenance *n.* countenance

coonter *n.* (shop) counter

coonter-louper *n.* shop-assistant

coontin *n.* arithmetic

coor *v.* cower

coord(ie) *n.* coward

coordy-lick *n.* coward's blow

coorie *See* **coory**

coorse *adj.* coarse; cruel (A); evil, bad (M1); *n.* course; **an coorse, of coorse** of course

coort *v.* court; *n.* cattle-court

coory *v.* cower, crouch

cooter *See* **couter**

corbie *n.* crow

core *n.* company, corps

corkit *adj.* constipated
corn *n.* oats; *v.* feed with oats
corn-laft *n.* grain-loft
corn-kist *n.* corn-chest
cornkister *n.* farm-workers' song
corn-yard *n.* stack-yard
corp *n.* corpse
correck *v.* correct
corrie *n.* circular hollow on mountainside; *v.* cower, crouch. *cf.* **coorie**
corrieneuchin *ppl.* conversing intimately
corter *n.* quarter; quarter of oatcake. *cf.* **korter**
cottar *n.* farm worker occupying tied cottage; *v.* to lead the life of a cottar
cottar-hoose *n.* farm worker's house
cotts *n. pl.* petticoats
counger *See* **coonjer**
coup *See* **cowp**
coup-the-ladle *n.* the game of see-saw
couper *n.* one who deals in horses or cattle
couple *n.* rafter (S). *cf.* **cupple**
couter *n.* coulter, iron cutter at front of plough; nose; **bleedy couter** nosebleed. *cf.* **cooter**
couthie, couthy *adj.* kindly; pleasant
covin-tree *n.* trysting tree; tree in front of an old mansion-house, where the laird met visitors
cow *v.* beat, outdo, surpass; **yon cows aa** that beats everything
cowe *n.* twig of a shrub or bush; *v.* to surpass

cower *v.* recover from, get over
cowk *v.* retch; vomit (A)
cowp *v. tr.* upset; *intr.* fall over, overturn; bargain, exchange; **cowp the creels** upset a plan; **cowpit sheep** overturned sheep. *cf.* **coup**
cowshus *adj.* cautious
cowt *n.* colt
coy *n.* heifer. *cf.* **quaik**
crabbit *adj.* bad-tempered, cross
crack *n.* talk, gossip; *v.* to chat
crackie *adj.* chatty, talkative
crackit *ppl., adj.* cracked
craft *n.* croft
craggin *n.* jar, pitcher
craig *n.* throat
craighle *v.* cough huskily
craighly *adj.* husky
craik *n., v.* croak
craiter, craitur *See* **cratur**
crame *n.* cream (S). *cf.* **ream**
crannie *n.* the little finger
cran-the-net, a *n.* a good catch
crap *n.* crop; bird's crop; throat; highest part of anything; **craw in his crap** annoy, give cause for regret; **shook their craps** expressed their grievances and feelings; **crap o the wa** highest part of an inside wall; *v.* crop land; *v. pt.* crept
crater, cratur *n.* creature; **the cratur** whisky
craver *n.* creditor; dun
craw *n.* crow; *v.* boast, exult; **a craw tae pluck** a bone to pick
creel *n.* basket for fish, used by fishwives
creenge *v.* cringe

creep doon *v.* shrink, bend with age
creepie *n.* low stool
creepin-eevie *n.* convolvulus; a very slow person (T)
creesh *v.* thrash, beat; *n.* fat, grease
creesis *n.* crisis
creetick *n.* critic
cries *n. pl.* banns (giving notice of impending marriage)
crine *v.* shrink; shrivel
criticeese *v.* criticise
crive *n.* enclosure (for poultry)
crochle *n.* disease in the hindlegs of cattle; *v.* limp
crochle, crochly *adj.* crippled
crockeneetion, crockaneeshin *n.* destruction; smithereens
crood *n., v.* crowd
crood-brakker *n.* curd-breaker (F)
croodit *adj.* crowded
croodle *v.* huddle together
croods *n. pl.* curds; **croods an fy** curds and whey
crook *n.* iron hook from which pots and kettles were hung by chain over fire; twist. *See* **links**
croon *n.* crown; the head; *v.* crown
croose *adj.* lively, bold, bright, confident; **croose i the craw** brisk and confident in conversation. *cf.* **crouse**
croup *v.* croak. *cf.* **crowp**
crouse *adj.* lively, bold, bright. *cf.* **croose**
crowdy *n.* meal and water mixed cold (M)
crowp *v.* croak; complain. *cf.* **croup**
cruisie *n.* old-fashioned oil lamp, with rush wick

crulge (doon) *v.* cower, crouch
crummie *n.* cow; cow's name
crunkle *v.* crease, crinkle
crusie *See* **cruisie**
cry in by *v.* visit briefly
cry on *v.* to call (on); visit; shout for
cry tee *v.* call in by (B)
crydit *n.* credit
crynt *adj.* stunted. *cf.* **crine**
cud *v.* could; **cudna** *v. neg.* could not
cuddy *n.* donkey
cuff *v.* winnow for the first time
cuffins *n. pl.* rough husks and hairs after first winnowing
cuist *v. pt.* cast, threw. *cf.* **ceest**
cuitikins *n.* gaiters. *cf.* **queetikins**
Cullen skink *n.* fish soup made with smoked haddock, onion and mashed potato
cupple *See* **couple**
curduddoch *adv.* close together (J)
curlie-wurlies *n.* hair in curl papers (B1)
curn, a *n.* a quantity; company; **a gweed curn** considerable number
currack *n.* coracle
curran *n.* currant; **curran daad** fruit slice
curran-bap *n.* currant bun
currieboram *n.* confused, noisy crowd
cushie (doo) *n.* wood-pigeon
cut *v.* reap; castrate
cutchack *n.* small blazing coal or peat fire; the clearest part of the fire; the side of the fire
cutter *n.* small whisky bottle

cuttins *n. pl.* encouragement; **ye'll get nae (short) cuttins fae him**
cuttit *v. pt.* cut
cutty *n.* short tobacco pipe; knife
cutty steel *n.* stool with short legs
c'wa *imp.* come away
cwanter *v.* contradict. *cf.* **conter**

cwanter-kine *adj.* contrary
cweel *adj., v.* cool
cwid *v. pt.* could
cyaard, cyaurd *n.* tinker
cyacks *n.* oatcakes
cyarn *n.* cairn

— **D** —

daachter *n.* daughter (A2). *cf.* **dother, dochter**
daar *adj.* dear, expensive
Daavit *pr. n.* David
dab *v.* poke; *in phr.* **let dab** give hint, give sign, let on; **dab han** skilled exponent
dacent *adj.* decent. *cf.* **daicent**
dachle, dackle *v.* hesitate, dawdle; (of the weather) let up; cause to hesitate, discourage (C)
dad *n.* lump; *v.* pelt; spatter. *cf.* **daud**
dae *v.* do *(gen. pro.* **dee**; *pro.* **day** by S, J); *ppl.* **daen**; **dae awa** do not so badly. *cf.* **dee, deen**
daff *v.* flirt (J)
daffie *n.* daffodil
daft *adj.* foolish; frolicsome
dag *v.* confound; **dag it** *excl.* confound it; **dag the bit** not a whit (B1); **dag the grain** not at all (B1)
daicent *adj.* decent. *cf.* **dacent**
daidle *v.* dirty (S)
daily-day *adv.* every day
dainner *n.* dinner. *cf.* **denner**
dairk *adj.* dark (J)
daith *n.* death

daivert *adj.* fatigued; confused; benumbed
dale *v.* deal
dall *n.* doll
dallies' cleysies *n. pl.* doll's clothes; coloured seaweed (B)
dambrod *n.* draught board
dammer *v.* confuse; astonish (R)
damn the bit *excl.* mild expletive
dander *n.* temper; **tae get yer dander up** to get angry
dandy *adj.* fine, light-hearted (J)
dane *ppl.* done. *cf.* **daen, deen**
dang *v. pt.* dashed down. *cf.* **ding**
dang *n., v.* used for *damn*
darg *n.* a day's work; *v.* work
darger *n.* a day-labourer; worker
darksome *adj.* melancholy, dismal
dask *n.* desk
dassint *adj.* decent. *cf.* **daicent, dacent**
dauchle *v.* dangle
daud *n.* stroke, blow; a large piece; **daud aboot** *v.* bump, bounce; jolt; pelt; spatter
daunder, dauner *v.* stroll
daur *v.* dare; **daurna** dare not; **daursna** dares not
daut *n.* caress. *cf.* **dawt**

daver *v.* stun, stupify; benumb

daw *n., v.* dawn

dawt *n.* caress; *v.* dote, fondle. *cf.* **dawt**

dawtie *n.* darling, pet

dazzle *n.* any fizzy drink

deave *v.* deafen; pester with entreaties. *cf.* **deeve**

dee *v.* do; die; **dee doon** do down; **dee wintin** do without. *cf.* **dae**

deece *n.* wooden seat or settle, which could be used as table or bed; turf seat out-of-doors; **haud doon the deece** rest, take it easy. *cf.* **deese**

deed *in phr.* **to be the deed o' t** to be responsible for (B); *adv.* indeed

deef *adj.* deaf. *cf.* **deif**

deegnity *n.* dignity

deelt (wi) *v. pt.* dealt (with)

deem(ie) *n.* a young girl; servant-girl

deen *ppl.* done; *adj.* exhausted; **caad himsel deen** wore himself out

deese *See* **deece**

deester *n.* (often contemptuous) doer; promoter; agent

deet *v. pt.* died

deeth *n.* death (A2). *cf.* **daith, deith**

deeve *v.* deafen; pester with entreaties. *cf.* **deave**

deevil *n.* devil; potato digger

deevilock *n.* imp, demon

defait *n., v.* defeat; *ppl.* defeated

defarred *v. pt., ppl.* deferred

defate *See* **defait**

defiet *v. pt.* defied

deft *adj.* bold; hard up

deg *See* **dag**

degraad *v.* degrade, *ppl.* **degraadit**

degraadin *ppl.* degrading

deid *adj.* dead

deidly *adj.* deadly

deid-thraw *n.* death-throe; **i the deid-thraw** between one state and another, undecided

deif *adj.* deaf. *cf.* **deef**

deil, Deil *n.* devil, Devil; *adv.* no, not, *e.g.* **deil-ma-care** no matter; **deil the bit** not at all

deist *See* **dyst**

deith *n.* death (J). *cf.* **daith**

deleebrate(ly) *adj., adv.* deliberate(ly)

deleer *v.* intoxicate; render delirious

deleerit *ppl.* demented, gone mad

dell *n.* goal or base in children's games; **nae great dell** no great shakes, not of great quality (T)

dell *v.* dig, delve; **dellt** *ppl.* dug

delt *v.* fondle, cuddle (M2)

delve *v. in phr.* **delve the bank** argue out the matter (B1)

dem *v.* dam

denner *n.* dinner; *v.* provide dinner. *cf.* **dainner**

denty *adj.* dainty (J)

dert *n.* dart

descrive, descryve *v.* describe

designtly *adv.* deliberately

deteen *v.* detain

deuk *n.* duck

devall *n.* a pause, ceasing; *v.* to cease, stop

deydie *n.* grandfather

deykon *n.* deacon. *cf.* **dykon**

dibber-dabber *n.* wrangle (B)

dicht *v.* clean; wipe up

diddle *v.* sing in a low tone without words; dandle a child (B)
didnin *v. neg. interrog.* didn't?
diffeekwalty *n.* difficulty (accent the second syllable) (A2)
dilet *adj.* stupid; crazed; confused. *See* **dylt**
dilse *n.* dulse, edible seaweed
dince *n.* dance (S)
dindeerie *See* **dundeerie**
ding *v.* beat, over-come, excel; (of rain, snow) to fall heavily
dinna *v. neg.* don't
din-raisin *adj.* quarrelsome, trouble-making; **din-raiser** trouble-maker
din-skinnt *adj.* weather-beaten, sunburned (T)
dip *v.* challenge; discuss
dipthairy *n.* diphtheria
dird *n.* a thud, thump, blow; heavy fall; *v.* beat, thump
dirdin *n.* onslaught
dirdum *n.* loud noise, uproar
dirk *n.* long dagger
dirl *v.* tingle; vibrate
dirler *n.* chamber-pot
dirrum-dicht *n.* vigorous wipe (B)
dirry *n.* ash on top of a pipe (T)
dirten *ppl.* dirtied; mean, contemptible
diry *See* **dyrie**
dis *v.* does
disadvise *v.* warn against (A1)
disappint *v.* disappoint
discoont *n.* discount
discoorse *n.* discourse
dish-cloot *n.* dish-cloth
disjaskit *adj.* downcast, dejected (J, M2)

disjeest *v.* digest
disna *interrog.* doesn't
disnint *interrog.* doesn't it?
dispeace *n.* trouble, discord
displenish, displinis *v.* disfurnish; to sell off goods and stock on leaving farm; **displenishing sale** *n.* sale by auction of farm stock etc.
dist *n.* dust; fine particles of meal and husk (F)
dister *n.* duster
districk *n.* district
dit *v.* close, shut up; shut the mouth
dite *See* **doit**
div *v. pr.* do (I, you, we, they **div**)
divert *n.* entertainment, diversion
divnin *v. neg. interrog.* don't?
divot *n.* piece of turf
dixie *n.* severe scolding (A); **she gya him his dixie** she gave him a dressing-down
dizzen *n.* dozen
doag *n.* dog (J). *cf.* **tyke**
dochter *n.* daughter (A1). *cf.* **daachter, dother**
dock *n.* buttocks; bottom. *cf.* **doke**
docken *n.* common dock plant
dockiment *n.* document
docknail, docknell *n.* mainpin; nail used to fix handle on a scythe or plough; very experienced farmservant
Dod *pr. n.* nickname for George
dodd *v.* to be, or be made, hornless
doddit *ppl., adj.* without horns
doddy mitten *n.* worsted glove without separate division for the four fingers
dog-birdie *n.* storm petrel (B)

dog-dirder *n.* whipper-in; kennel attendant

doit *n.* old coin of little value; **he caredna a doit**

doit *v.* to grow feeble in mind; **doitit** *ppl.* in dotage; stupid

dome *n.* press-stud

dominie *n.* schoolmaster

done *ppl.* outwitted

donal(ie) *n.* glass of spirits (from Donald)

donnert *adj.* in dotage; stupid

Dons, the nickname of Aberdeen football team

doo *n.* dove, pigeon

dooble *adj.* double; two-faced (A1)

dooble-jintit *adj.* double-jointed

dooble-legs *n. pl.* crutches

doocot *n.* dovecot

dook *n., v.* bathe

dooker *n.* bather

dool *adj.* sorrowful; *n.* woe; grief

doolsome *adj.* sad

doomsil *n.* domicile (B1)

doon *adv., prep.* down; *adj.* depressed, fed up; **doon i the moo** disconsolate, dejected

doonby *adv.* down yonder

dooncome *n.* fall

doonfa *n.* downfall

doonpoor *n.* downpour

doonricht *adj.* downright

doon-sit *n.* home (B1). *See below*

doon-sittin *n.* settlement, usually at marriage

doorie *n.* (small) door; a game of marbles played against a door

doosht *n.* bump, heavy fall or throw

doot *n., v.* doubt; **dootfu** *adj.* doubtful

dorb *(of birds) n.* a peck; *v.* grub, peck (R)

dorty *adj.* fastidious, hard to please, e.g. **dorty wi their maet**

dose *n.* large number of anything

doss *n.* bow, or knot

dossie *n.* small quantity in the form of a cluster or heap

dother *n.* daughter (A, M). *cf.* **daachter, dochter, douther**

dottle *n.* the unconsumed tobacco left in a pipe; *v.* become stupid and fretful; **dottelt** mentally confused; in dotage

douce *adj.* respectable, decent; gentle, kind; circumspect

Doup *pr. n.* nickname for village of Boddam

doup *n.* buttocks. *cf.* **dowp**

dour *adj.* grim, austere

dover (ower) *v.* doze (off)

dowf *adj.* melancholy, gloomy

dowie *adj.* sad; dismal

dowp *n.* buttocks. *cf.* **doup**

dozen *v.* to benumb, stupify, daze

dozent, dozin *ppl.* in a benumbed state; stupid

dozen't *excl.* confound it!

draaght *See* **dracht**

dracht *n.* a load; two or more cartloads brought at one time; draught, drink

draars *n. pl.* long underpants

draavers *n. pl.* long drawers for men

drabble *v.* make wet or dirty, to besmear

drabbly *adj.* (of weather) wet, disagreeable

drablich *n.* muddy person (B1)

draff-hurlie *n.* iron trolley filled with distillery draff for feeding cattle

draigon *n.* child's paper kite (J)

drap *v.* drop

drappie *adj.* rainy

drate *v. pr., pt.* defecate; *ppl.* **dritten**

draucht *See* **dracht**

drauchtit *ppl., adj.* (of a horse) harnessed for work

drauchts *n. pl.* draughts

dree *v.* endure; **dree yer ain weird** endure your fate

dreeble *v.* dribble

dreed *n., v.* dread. *cf.* **dreid**

dreel *n.* drill, small furrow for sowing seed; ridge with such furrow on top; scolding

dreep *n.* drip; dripping condition; *v.* drip; empty to last drop

dreepin *n.* dripping

dreepin-pen *n.* enclosure, where newly dipped sheep were held for dripping (T)

dreeve *v. pt.* drove

dregie *n.* refreshment given at a funeral

dreich *adj.* dull, wearisome

dreid *n., v.* dread. *cf.* **dreed**

dribble, driblach *n.* drop, usually of alcohol

dribbly *adj.* drizzly

drift *n.* driving or driven snow

drog *n.* drug

droggie, droggist *n.* druggist

drook *v.* drench

drookit *adj.* drenched

droon *v.* drown; **droont** drowned

drooth, drouth *n.* drought; thirst; drunkard, tippler. *cf.* **drucht**

droothy, drouthy *adj.* thirsty

drow *n.* fit of illness (A, A1)

drucht *n.* drought. *cf.* **drooth**; **druchtit** *ppl.* in a state of drought; dehydrated (G)

drucht *n.* drying effect of air; **a gran drucht** (B)

drucken *adj.* drunken

druckenness *n.* drunkenness

drumly *adj.* thick, muddy, gloomy (of water); sullen

drumster *n.* town drummer

drush *n.* peat dust (R)

dry-darn *n.* constipation

dryster *n.* man who dried the grain before grinding

dubs *n.* mud; **dubby, dubbit** *adj.* muddy

ducksie *adj.* dull; lazy (A)

duddie *adj.* ragged

duds *n. pl.* rags; clothes

Duffer *pr. n.* native of Macduff

dule *See* **dool**

dumfoonert *adj.* dumbfounded

dummie *n.* a mute

dumplin *n.* plum (or Christmas) pudding

dundeerie *n.* a great noise (M2)

dunderheid *n.* an outstanding fool

dune *ppl.* done. *cf.* **deen**

dung *v. pt.* (of **ding**) dash down, smash. *cf.* **dang**

dungers *n. pl.* dungarees

dunt *n., v.* thump; **the very dunt** the very thing needed

dursna *See* **daursna**

durstna *v. pt. neg.* did not dare

dusht *ppl.* struck dumb, silenced

dutch *n.* ditch (G, M1)

dwaal, dwall *v.* dwell; **dwallin-hoose** dwelling-house

dwam, dwaam, dwalm, dwaum *n.* a faint, fit of sickness; **tae tak a dwam**

dwebble, dweeble, dweebly *adj.* feeble

dweemly-dwamly *adj.* feeble (M1)

dwine *v.* languish, pine; waste away

dyester *n.* dyer

dyke *n.* wall of stone or turf; **dry stane dyke** made without mortar

dyker *n.* builder of dykes

Dyker *pr. n.* native of Cellardyke

dykon *n.* deacon

dylt *ppl.* wearied, fatigued

dyod *excl.* euphemism for God

dyow *n.* dew; **dyowie** *adj.* dewy

dyrie *n.* dairy

dyst(e) *v.* fall, sit down or throw with a thud or bump; go up and down bumping

dytit *ppl.* in dotage; stupid. *cf.* **doitit**

—— **E** ——

e, 'e *def. art.* the

each *n.* adze

ear, ear' *adj., adv.* early

ear, 'ear *n.* year

ear *v.* plough

earer *adj.* earlier

earin *n.* ploughing (A2)

Earl o Hell *pr. n.* the Devil; **blaik as the Earl o Hell's weskit**

earock *n.* a fowl of the first year

easedom *n.* ease; relief; comfort

easin *n.* eaves. *cf.* **eezen**

easin-gang *n.* row of sheaves projecting at the eaves of a stack to keep the rain off

easy *adv.* easily

easy-osy *adj.* easy-going

eave-raip *n.* rope around eaves of a stack

ebb land *n.* shallow soil

ebb-ploo *v.* to shallow plough (F)

echt *adj.* eight. *cf.* **aicht, aucht**

echt *v.* owe; own. *cf.* **acht, yacht**

echteen *adj.* eighteen

echty *adj.* eighty

edder, edderan *conj.* either (can be used at end of sentence as in Eng.)

edder *v.* to rope thatch with an edderin (F)

edderin *n.* shuttle-shaped ball of rope (F)

eddicat *adj., ppl.* educate

eddicashun *n.* education

edick *n.* edict

edifee *v.* edify; *ppl.* **edifeein**

ee *n.* eye; **hid a lang ee at** was attracted to (G). *See* **een**

eechie *n.* absolutely nothing (*in phr.* **eechie nor ochie**)

eediot *n.* idiot

eedle-oddle *adj.* easy-going, lacking character

eek *v.* add on or to; **eekin** *ppl.* adding to

eeksy-peeksy, -picksy *adj.* exactly equal

Eel *pr. n.* Yule. *cf.* **Eile, Yeel**

eel *adj.* dry, empty (used of cows which have stopped giving milk). *cf.* **yeld**

eely *adj.* oily

eemost *adj.* uppermost; **eemost wynin** upper part of field

eemur *n.* humour

een *n., numeral* one. *cf.* **ane**

een *n. pl.* eyes. *See* **ee**

eence *adv.* once. *cf.* **aince, ance; eence on a day** once upon a time, at one time

eenoo *adv.* just now. *cf.* **eyvnoo**

eeran *n.* errand

eesage *n.* usage; behaviour

eese *n. (pro.* **eece)** use; *v. (pro.* **eeze)** use; **eest wi't** used to it

eesefu *adj.* useful

eeseless *adj.* useless

eeshan *n.* small child (M2); small puny person (B1)

eeshich *n.* small, untidy person (B1)

eeswal(l) *adj.* usual; **eeswally** *adv.* usually

eevie *n.* ivy; **creepin eevie** convolvulus; a slow person

eezen(s) *n.* eaves. *cf.* **easin**

effeck *n.* effect

efter *prep., adv.* after; *adv.* afterwards; **efter-an-aa** after all. *cf.* **aifter**

efterhin *adv.* afterwards. *cf.* **efter**

efterneen *n.* afternoon (A1)

efternin *n.* afternoon (S)

egg shallies *n. pl.* egg shells; **aa egg shallies** feeling fragile, fretful (B)

eident *adj.* diligent; industrious

eik, eke *n.* addition; *v.* add; **eik him**

up egg him on (A2). *cf.* **eek**

Eile *pr. n.* Yule. *cf.* **Eel, Yeel**

eild *n.* old age; **eildit** aged

elbick, elbock, elbuck *n.* elbow; **elbick jam** runny jam

eld *n.* old age (C1). *cf.* **Eild**

eldritch *adj.* unearthly, uncanny

eleeven, eleiven *adj.* eleven. *cf.* **aleyven**

ell *n.* Scottish measurement, equal to 37.0578 inches

eller *n.* elder (of the church). *cf.* **elyer**

ellieson *n.* shoemaker's awl (B1). *cf.* **eshin**

ell-wan *n.* yardstick

elshin *n.* shoemaker's awl. *cf.* **ellieson**

elyer *n.* elder tree; church elder

emmers *n. pl.* embers

emmerteen *n.* ant

en *n.* end

enew *adj.* enough. *cf.* **eneugh**

engeen *n.* engine

enoo *adv.* just now

en-rig *n.* the land at the end of the furrow on which the plough is turned

enstinck *n.* instinct

enstrument *n.* instrument

enteetle *v.* entitle

enterdick *n., v.* interdict

enterfere *v.* interfere

enterin *adj.* favourable for beginning or entering on (S)

enterteenment *n.* entertainment

ere *prep., conj.* before. *cf.* **or**

errant *n.* errand (S)

erse *n.* arse, hind-quarters. *cf.* **doke**

esk *n., v.* hiccup; **tak the esk** get

hiccups
espeeshully *adv.* especially
ess *n.* ash, ashes. *cf.* **aiss**
essfu *adj.* useful. *cf.* **eesefu**
ether *n.* udder
etnach *n.* juniper (berry)
etsleel *n.* young child (B1)
etten *See* **aeten**
ettercap *n.* spider. *cf.* **nettercap**
ettle *v.* aim at, intend, be eager, to
begin
ettlin *ppl., adj.* intending, eager
even *n.* evening. *cf.* **een; at even** in
the evening
evendoon *adj.* sheer, downright
everlaistin *adj.* everlasting
excamb *n.* one piece of ground
exchanged for another; *v.*
exchange lands
exceesable *adj.* excusable
excep *prep.* except. *cf.* **'cep**
exerceese *n.* exercise; **exerceese-
beuk** exercise-book

exhibeetion *n.* exhibition
exkeesable *adj.* excusable
expairience *n.* experience
expeck *v.* expect; **expeckit**
expected
expoon(d) *v.* expound
exterordnar *adj.* extraordinary
eydent *See* **eident**
eyn *n., v.* end; *ppl.* ended; **the back
eyn** the end of harvest; late
autumn; **get eyns tae rug the
gidder** make ends meet. *cf.* **en,
eynt**
eynless *adj.* endless
eynrig *n.* end ridge
eyven *adj.* even, straight; **set yer tie
eyven** straighten your tie
eyvnoo, eynoo *adv.* just now. *cf.*
enew, eenoo
eyzle *n.* a live coal, hot ember;
eyzly ee't with eyes like burning
coals

—— **F** ——

fa, faa *pron.* who; *v.* fall, befall; *n.*
fall, fate; **faa clyte** fall heavily;
fa tee fall to, begin
faamous *adj.* famous
faar *adv.* where
faavour *n.* favour; **for ony
faavour!** for goodness sake!
faavrit *adj.* favourite. *cf.* **fauvrit**
faceable *adj.* likely to be true;
barely true (B1)
fack *n.* fact; *v.* make, shape, form
(B1)
fader, fadder *n.* father (A)

faddom *v.* fathom
fae *n.* foe (A); *prep.* from. *cf.* **frae**
faem *n.* foam
faik, fayich, fyaak *n.* plaid
fail-dyke *n.* turf wall. *cf.* **feal-dyke**
faimly *n.* family
fain *adj.* eager, anxious
fair *adj.* fair; **fair hornie** fair play;
adv. very, quite, completely
fair-furth-the-gate *adj.* honest and
straightforward (R)
fairin *n.* treat, present bought at a
fair

fairlie *See* **ferlie**

fairly *adv., excl.* quite, surely

fairm *n.* farm. *cf.* **ferm**

fairmer *n.* farmer

fairmhoose *n.* farmhouse

fairmin *n.* farming

fairm-servan *n.* farm-hand

fairn *n.* fern

fairrier *n.* farrier

faist *adj., adv.* fast. *cf.* **fest**

faisten *v.* fasten

faith *excl.* indeed!

faither *n.* father (C1, F). *cf.* **fader**

faithfu *adj.* faithful

Faithlie *pr. n.* Fraserburgh

fald *v.* fold

fan *adv.* when; *v. pt.* felt, found. *See* **fin**

fan, fanner *n.* winnowing machine

fancy *n.* fancy-cake

fang *n.* scamp; lout; large lump cut from something

fank *n.* sheepfold

fant *n.* fainting fit; *adj., v.* faint

fantoosh *adj.* very smart, grand

far *adv.* where. *cf.* **faur**

far *in phr.* **far ben wi** intimate with, esp. in favour with God

far-ben *adj.* in high favour

fardel *n.* a large piece (B1)

farder *adv.* farther

fardin *n.* farthing; butter biscuit, originally four a penny (B)

farever, farivver *adv., conj.* wherever

Farfar *pr. n.* Forfar

Farfar bridie *See* **bridie**

farlan *n.* a long box into which herrings are emptied for gutting

farrer *adj.* further; **farrest** furthest; **farrest ootbye** furthest out

fas, fast *n., v.* fast; **fast day** day in week preceding half-yearly Communion in Presbyterian Churches, treated as holiday, with service of preparation for the Sacrament

fash *n., v.* trouble; **dinna fash yer thoom** don't trouble yourself

fashious *adj.* fussy, hard to please

Fasten's Een, Faster's Even *etc.* Shrove Tuesday. *cf.* **Festeren's Eve**

fat *adj.* what; **fat o** what a lot of; **fatna** what sort of a

fatever *adj., pron.* whatever

fat-hen *n.* weed growing among turnips

fattal *adj.* fatal

fattrels *n. pl.* ribbon-ends (B1)

fatty-bannocks *n.* fat person

fat-ye-ca't *n.* what-do-you-call-it

fauch *v.* rub; scratch, claw (B1); plough or harrow fallow land

fauchie *adj.* sickly-looking

faugh *n.* fallow land. **Fairmers' faugh gars lairds lauch** (Proverb)

faul(d) *n.* fold; sheep-fold; *v.* fold; fold sheep; **faul yer fit** sit down (R)

faur *adj., adv.* where. *cf.* **far**; *v.* fare; **faur-ye-weel**

faur idder *interrog. adv.* where else?

faured, faurt *adj.* favoured. *See* **weel-faurt, ill-faurt**

fause *adj.* false

faut *n.* fault

fauvrit *adj.* favourite. *cf.* **faavrit**
fawmous *adj.* famous
fawvour *n., v.* favour
fawvourt *adj., ppl.* favoured
feal dyke *n.* wall built of sods
fear *n.* fright; *v.* frighten (Abdn. and coastal)
fear, for *conj.* in case (in neg. context)
fearna *v. neg.* have no fear
feart *adj.* afraid
feart things *n. pl.* superstitious beliefs (A1)
feathers *n. See* **ploo**
fecht *n., v.* fight
feck *n.* the majority
fecket *n.* waistcoat, under-jacket
feckless *adj.* weak, feeble; useless, incapable
feckly *adv.* chiefly, mostly
fedder *n., v.* feather
fee *n.* a farm-hand's wage; *v.* engage a farm-hand; **fee't man** *n. with ppl.* hired hand
feech *excl.* of pain or distress. *cf.* **feich**
feeder *n.* an ox fattened for market
feedle *n.* field (A, A2)
feein-fair, -mairket hiring-fair, market for farm servants
feel *n.* fool; *adj.* foolish; **feel's eeran** fool's errand. *cf.* **fule**
feelish *adj.* foolish
feelness *n.* foolishness
feem *n.* state of sudden heat, a sweat; *v.* fume
feenal(ly) *adj., adv.* final(ly)
feenish *n., v.* finish
feer *v.* to set up the first furrow, when ploughing a field

feerich *n.* bustle; state (of excitement); fit of enthusiasm; *v.* bustle
feerin *n.* furrow drawn out to mark the rigs before ploughing the whole field; **feerin pole** pole used as marker in setting up the first furrow (F)
feerious *adj.* furious; *adv.* (used intensively for exceedingly)
feeroch *See* **feerich**
feese *v. pt.* fetched
feesick *n.* medicine
feesickle *adj.* physical
fegs *excl. of surprise or emphasis* faith!
feich *excl. of disgust. cf.* **feech**
feingie *v.* feign
feint *See* **fient**
feish *v. pt.* fetched
fell *adj.* deadly; dangerous; *adv.* exceedingly; clever, shrewd (J); *v.* kill; stun; knock down
fell-thocht *v. pt.* reconsidered, had second thoughts (B)
femisht *adj.* famished
fence-fed *adj.* (of animals) fed with titbits at the side of the fence; pampered
fen(d)less *adj.* shiftless, without energy
fere *adj.* strong, sturdy; **hale and fere** thoroughly healthy
ferich *See* **feerich**
ferlie *n.* oddity, wonder
ferm *n.* farm. *cf.* **fairm**
fer-nothing *n.* dreadnought coat
fernyear *n.* last year; **fernyear was a year** the year before last
fern(y)-tickles *n. pl.* freckles
ferny-tickled *adj.* freckled

ferr *n.* fear (S)

fersell *adj.* forceful, energetic

fesh, fess *v.* fetch, bring; **fess back** bring to mind, recall; **fess up** bring up (children); **fessen in** *ppl.* established

fest *adj., adv.* fast

Festeren's, Festren's Eve *See* **Fasten's Een**

feth *n.* faith; *excl.* faith!

feuch *v.* smoke a pipe (R); *n.* smoke (B1)

fey *adj.* disordered in the mind; clairvoyant; behaving in an excited way, not oneself

feyther *n.* father (J). *cf.* **faither, fader**

fiars *n.* prices of grain legally fixed for the year

ficher *n.* slow awkward work; *v.* fiddle about

ficket *n.* woollen garment with sleeves and buttoned front, an undervest worn under shirt

fidder *conj.* whether. *cf.* **fudder**

fiddley *n.* hatchway on a drifter (B)

fidge *v.* fidget; be eager (B1)

fidgick *n.* tufted vetch; **fidgick piz** small peas growing at the roadside

fiedle *n.* field (A1). *cf.* **feedle**

fie na *excl.* not at all

fient *n.* fiend; the devil (used in strong negations); **fient a** not (a); **fient een** not one; **fient a fears** not likely; **fient haet** not a bit, the devil a bit. *cf.* **feint, fint**

Fiersday *n.* Thursday

fifeteent *adj.* fifteenth

fifety *adj.* fifty

fikie *See* **fykie**

file *conj., n.* while; **files** sometimes; *v.* dirty, soil. *cf.* **fool**

filget, filjit *n.* untidy, disreputable-looking person

filie *n.* a little while

filk *pron.* which

fillies *n. pl.* felloes of wheel

fin *adv., conj.* when

fin *v.* find; feel

Finechty *pr. n.* local name for the village of Findochty

fineerin *n.* fancy ornamentation

finger-eyns *n.* finger-tips

fingerin *n.* fine worsted from spun wool

fint *See* **fient**

fir, fir-candle *n.* pine-torch; **fir-yowes** fir-cones; **firwood** bog-wood, formerly used for candles

fire *v.* to discharge any missile

firehoose *n.* dwelling house (M); farmhouse

firewid *n.* firewood

firlit *n.* a corn measure, the fourth part of a boll

firry *adj.* resinous

first fit *n.* the first person to meet a marriage party or other procession (A2); the first visitor to cross the threshold on or after New Year's day

fisher-loon *n.* fisher-boy

fisher-quine *n.* fisher-girl

Fishie *pr. n.* village of Fetterangus, near Mintlaw

fist *v.* grasp with the hand (B1)

fit *n.* foot; *v.* to foot it; **first fit** first visitor of a new year; **fit-an-mou** foot-and-mouth disease

fit *adj., pron.* what; *rel. pron.* which (S); **fit like?** how are you?; **fit wye** how; why; **fit I leuch** how I laughed

fitba *n.* football

fit-socks *n. pl.* short socks; the feet of stockings

fitstep *n.* footstep

fite *adj.* white; *v.* whittle; **fite the idle pin** pass the time away (M). *cf.* **futtle**

fite-iron *n.* tin ware

fite-oot *n.* blinding snowstorm (S)

Fittie *pr. n.* Footdee. *cf.* **Futty**

fittie-fies *n. pl.* fault-finding; quibbles

fittit *v. pt.* footed

fittock *n.* sock with the leg cut off

fivver *n.* fever; **fivvert** *adj.* fevered

flacht *n.* flash, gleam, flash of lightning; **flacht o fire** streak of lightning; **get the flacht** suffer damage (B); flight. *cf.* **flaught**

flae *v.* flay, skin

flaesick *n.* spark from wood fire; wood-shaving. *cf.* **flezick**

flaff, flaffer *v.* flap, flutter

flag *n.* large snowflake; *v.* snow in big flakes

flagarie *n.* finery (esp. in dress); a gewgaw, piece of frivolity; dainty, delicacy

flaggit *ppl., adj.* (of floors) flagged

flake *n.* hurdle for penning sheep; hurdle used as a gate (M2)

flan *n.* a gust of wind; sudden down-draught in a chimney

flang *v.* flung

flannen *n.* flannel; **flannen broth** saps (T)

flap *n.* a rest; *v.* flop

flate *v.* scolded. *cf.* **flite, flyte**

flaught *See* **flacht, flocht**

flaughter-spaad *n.* two-handed spade for cutting turfs, peats

flech *n.* flea

flee *n., v.* fly; **flee aboot** dash about; **flee up** *imp.* get lost!

fleech *See* **fleetch**

fleed *n.* head ridge on which the plough is turned

fleein *adj.* wildly intoxicated

fleem *n.* fleam, lancet

fleep, flype *n.* lout

fleer *n.* floor; jeer (J)

fleerish *v.* flourish; **flint an fleerish** flint and steel, used to strike a spark

fleetch *v.* flatter

fleg *n.* fright; *v.* frighten; *ppl.* **fleggit**

flench *v.* flinch

fley *v.* frighten, scare

fleyed, fleyt *ppl., adj.* frightened (A1). *cf.* **fleggit**

flezick *See* **flaesick**

flicher *v.* flicker

flicht *n.* flight

flichty *adj.* flighty

flinrikin *n.* very thin cloth, a mere rag

flit *v.* leave a place, go elsewhere; move house

flite, flyte *v.* scold

flittin *n.* house removal

float *n.* lorry for carrying livestock

flocht *v.* excite, flurry; **flochtit** in a state of excitement, worked up

flooer, floor *n., v.* flower

floor *n.* (wheaten etc.) flour

floorish *n.* blossom

flow *n.* very small quantity of powdery substance, *e.g.* meal, dust

flucht *v.* agitate; **fluchtit** *ppl.* in a state of excitement

fluffert *n.* (of snow) a light shower (T)

flum(mer)gummery *n.* any useless thing or action; vain adornment, trimming (B1)

fly, fly-cup *n.* sly cup of tea (but taken ritually)

flype *v.* turn inside out

foalie *n.* foal

fob *v.* pant with heat or exertion; **fobbit yowe** ewe panting from exertion

fochen *ppl.* fought; exhausted; **fochen deen** worn out

focht *v. pt.* fought

fodderin, foddrin *n.* fodder

fog *n.* long grass left standing in winter; moss, lichen; *v.* gather wealth

foggie-bee *n.* yellow humble-bee

Foggieloan *pr. n.* Aberchirder, Banffshire

foggit *ppl., adj.* moss-covered; well off

foggy *adj.* wizened, dry, sapless; mossy

foifteen *adj.* fifteen (A2)

folk (G, M). *cf.* **fouk, fowk**

folla *n.* fellow

folm *n.* a billow of mist; *v.* overturn

fond *adj.* foolish; *n.* fund

foo *adj.* full; *adv.* how; why

foodge *v.* (in marble-playing) to take unfair advantage; cheat

fooever *conj., adv.* however

fool *adj.* dirty. *cf.* **file**

fools *n. pl.* fowls (*dim.* **foolies**)

foon(d) *n.* foundation. *cf.* **founs**

foon *ppl.* found (J)

fooner *v.* founder; *ppl.* **foonert** exhausted, worn out

foont *n.* fount

foord *n., v.* ford

foorich *v.* work in a flurried manner

foort *adj.* fourth

foorty *adj.* forty

foosh up *v. pt.* fetched up; brought up

foosion *See* **fushen**

foostie, fooshtie, fooshtit *adj.* fusty, mouldy

footer *n.* bungler; silly, useless person; troublesome, fiddling job; *v.* fiddle with

footers term of contempt

foraneen *n.* forenoon. *cf.* **forenin**

forby(e) *adv.* besides; *prep.* in addition to; compared with

forbyes *prep.* besides; far less; not to mention; *conj.* whereas

forcie *adj., adv.* active(ly), forceful(ly); (of weather) warm, dry, good for crops

fordal, fordel, fordle *n.* progress, advancement; a store; *v.* store up for future use; **get fordalt wi** get ahead with (G)

forder *adj., adv.* further

forebreist *n.* front seat of a gallery; front of a cart

forenicht *n.* interval between twilight and bedtime

forenin *n.* forenoon (S). *cf.* **foraneen**

foreshaida *v.* foreshadow

foreslings *n. pl.* for attaching harness at front of cart shaft

foresta *n.* manger

forfecht (yersel) *v.* overburden (yourself), overdo

forfochen *adj.* exhausted, worn out

forgaither *v.* forgather

forgat *v.* forgot

forgettle *adj.* forgetful

forgie *v.* forgive

forgieness *n.* forgiveness

forgya *v. pt.* forgave (A)

forhooie *v.* forsake; **forhooiet** *ppl., adj.* forsaken

forjeskit *adj.* fatigued, worn out

forkie(tail) *n.* earwig

forl *n.* whorl, small wheel on a spindle steadying its motion

forleithy *n.* surfeit (B1)

fornent *prep.* over against, opposite, facing

forquant *v.* acquaint; intimate

forrit *adv.* forward(s)

fort *adj.* fourth. *cf.* **foort**

fortiet *adj.* fortieth

fortig *n., v.* fatigue

fortin *n.* fortune

fortnat *adj.* fortunate

fortnicht *n.* fortnight

forty-faal *adj.* deceitful (B)

foryet *v.* forget, *pt.* **foryat**

fossy, fosy *adj.* (often used of rotten vegetables) soft, spongy. *cf.* **fozie**

fou *adj.* full, drunk; *n.* stone crop, saxifrage

fouk *See* **fowk**

foumart *n.* pole-cat; term of abuse

founs *n. pl.* foundations

fousome *adj.* foul

fower *adj.* four

fowk *n.* people (A, A1, A2, C, J, M, R). *cf.* **fouk, folk, fock**

foy *n.* farewell feast on leaving a place or finishing a job (B1)

fraacht *See* **fraucht**

frae *prep.* from (J). *cf.* **fae**

fraikie *adj.* coaxing, wheedling

fraise *v.* speak flatteringly

fraisie *adj.* given to flattery

frap *n.* predicament (B)

fraucht *n.* freight or load; what can be carried or carted at one time (two pails-full, cartloads)

fraughty *adj.* liberal, generous

Freday *n.* Friday

freely *adv.* particularly; **freely fine** remarkably fine

freen *n.* friend

freest *n., v.* frost

freet *See* **fret**

freevolous *adj.* frivolous

fremt, fremmit *adj.* foreign; **the fremt** *n. pl.* strangers

fresh *adj.* (of weather) thawing; cold; open

fret *n.* superstition

freuch *adj.* brittle, dry

frichen *v.* frighten. *cf.* **frichten**

fricht *n.* fright

frichten *v.* frighten

froon *n., v.* frown

front shelvin *adj. with n.* movable board on front of box-cart

frost *v.* to fit frost nails (F)

frost-hole *n.* frost nail hole (F)

frostit *adj.* inflamed by cold

fry *n.* parcel of fish taken home by workers in the fishing industry

fu *adj.* full, tipsy; *adv.* very. *cf.* **fou**

fucher *See* **ficher**

fudder *v.* move hurriedly; run in excited or aimless fashion; *conj.* whether

fuffer *v.* (M1) prob. **fuffle** walk awkwardly, hobble, shuffle

fugie (*rhymes with budgie*) *n.* truant from school

fugle *v.* deceive (B1)

fuish *v. pt.* fetched, brought. *cf.* **feish, foosh**

ful, full (*rhymes with gull*) *adj.* full; puffed up, conceited; *v.* fill; **ful (up)** replete after food

fulage *adj.* foolish (B1)

fule *n.* fool. *cf.* **feel**

full *See* **ful**

fullt *ppl.* filled

fulp *n.* whelp

fulpie *n.* puppy, whelp

fummle *v.* fumble

fun, funn *n.* whin; **fun mull** whin mill for bruising whins for food for horses etc.

fun *v. pt., ppl.* found. *See* **fin**

fun *v.* to do something for fun; joke

fund *v. pt.* found (S)

fung *v.* throw

funk *n.* a breath (of wind) (B); *v.* sulk (B1)

funtain *n.* fountain

funtainheid *n.* fountainhead

fup *n., v.* whip; **fup-han** whip-hand. *cf.* **whup**

fur, furr *n., v.* furrow

fur-beast *n.* horse for walking in furrow. *cf.* **furrer**

furhooied *See* **forhooie**

furl *v.* whirl; **furly** whirly

furliefaa *n.* showy ornament(ation)

furligorum *n.* showy ornament (G)

furm *n.* form, bench without a back

furnitur *n.* furniture

furrer *n.* horse walking in furrow

furth *adv.* forth, away

furth, the *n.* the open air

furth-the-gait *adv.* honestly

fushach *n.* loose, untidy bundle; **I carena a fushach**

fushen, fushon *n.* pith, vigour

fushenless *adj.* lacking vigour

fusion *See* **fushen**

fuskers *n. pl.* whiskers

fuskert *adj.* whiskered

fusky *n.* whisky

fusome *adj.* disgusting. *cf.* **fousome**

fussle *n., v.* whistle

fut *pron.* what; **fut for nae** why not. *cf.* **fat, fit**

futher *conj.* whether. *cf.* **fudder**

futlie (beelin) *n.* whitlow

futrat, futtrat *n.* weasel; small, thin, hatchet-faced person

futtle *n.* short gutting knife; *v.* whittle

Futty *pr. n.* Footdee. *cf.* **Fittie**

fy *n.* whey

fyaach *v.* fidget. *cf.* **fyke**

fyaak *n.* plaid. *cf.* **faik, fayich**

fyke *n.* fuss; difficulty; *v.* fidget

fykie *adj.* troublesome, tricky; restless

fyle *n., v.* while; **fyles** now and then; *v.* to soil, make dirty

fyou, fyow(e) *adj.* few

fyower *adj.* fewer

— **G** —

gaad, gad *n.* goad, wand

gaager *n.* exciseman. *cf.* **gauger**

gaan *v.* go (coastal); *ppl.* going. *cf.* **gaun**

gaan-aboot hen *adj., n.* free-range hen

gaar *n.* oozing vegetable matter; **green gaar** growth seen on piers and low on the walls of houses (B)

gab *n.* prattling talk; one who talks incessantly; the mouth; *v.* to chatter, prate

Gab o Mey *phr.* the last days of April anticipating the weather of May

gabbin *n.* chattering

gaberlunzie *n.* beggar

gad *n.* goad for driving horses or cattle. *cf.* **gaud**

Gadie *pr. n.* stream at the hill of Bennachie, Aberdeenshire

gadsman *n.* person who drives horses or cattle with a gad; or uses gad to direct corn to the scythe (B1) or binder. *cf.* **gaudsman**

gae *v.* go (A, A1, A2, J, M, R). *cf.* **gyang, gang, ging**;

gae *v. pt.* gave (A2, M)

gaed *v. pt.* went; **gaed worth** became as nothing

gae-lattin *ppl.* letting go; *n.* the verge of bankruptcy

gaff *v.* laugh loudly, guffaw. *cf.* **gauff**

gager *n.* exciseman

gaidy *n.* the arm (A)

Gaimrie *pr. n.* local name for the village of Gardenstown; **Gaimrie knottie** biscuit

Ga'in *pr. n.* Gavin

gaird *n., v.* guard

gairden *n.* garden

Gairtly *pr. n.* Aberdeenshire village of Gartly

gait *See* **gate**

gaither *v.* gather. *cf.* **gedder, gether, gidder**

gaitherer *n.* one who gathers grain to make sheaves. *cf.* **lifter**

gaivel *n.* gable. *cf.* **gavel**

gale *n.* gable (M)

galliart *adj.* bright, gaudy (B1)

galluses *n. pl.* trouser braces

galore *adv.* in abundance

galshachs, galshochs *n. chf. in pl.* sweets, titbits; treats, goodies; junk foods

gamey, gamie *n.* gamekeeper

gane *v.* gone

gang *v.* go (A2, M, M1, R); **gang yer gait** go your way. *cf.* **gyang, ging, gae**

gangrel *n.* vagrant, tramp

ganjie *See* **gansey**

ganner *n.* gander

gansey *n.* guernsey, a seaman's jersey. *cf.* **ganjie**

gant *v.* yawn

gapus *adj.* stupid; *n.* fool

gar *v.* compel, cause to

garron *n.* small horse

gartens *n.* garters; **green gartens** given by girl to her elder sister if marrying before her

gash *adj.* ghastly, gruesome

gast *n.* fright; shock

gat *v. pt.* got

gate *n.* way, route; **the richt gate** properly; **dee the richt gate** do the right thing; **some gates** in some places

gatefarrin *adj.* presentable; comely

gate-ganger *n.* wanderer, tinker

gaud *See* **gad**

gaudsman *See* **gadsman**

gaun *v.* go (coastal) *ppl.* going. *cf.* **gaan**

gaup *v.* gape; eat voraciously (A1)

gavel *n.* gable. *cf.* **gaivel**

gawk, gawkie *n.* silly, clumsy person

gawkit *adj.* stupid, clumsy

gawkitness *n.* stupidity; uncouth silliness

gavel *n.* tail of sheaf (F)

gean *n.* wild cherry tree

gear *n.* property, wealth

geck *n.* disdainful toss of head; *v.* toss the head in scorn; turn the head in a foolish or coquettish way; **geck-neck(it)** (having) a twisted neck

gedder *v.* gather; **geddert** *v. pt., ppl.* gathered; *adj.* well-to-do. *cf.* **gaither, gether, gidder**

gedderer *n.* (usually female) gatherer in the harvest field

gee *n.* sullenness; stubbornness; **tak the gee wi** take offence at someone; whim, foolish notion;

gee up *imp.* forward! (command for a plough-horse in Buchan)

geed *adj.* good (F)

Geery *pr. n.* Garioch (a district in Aberdeenshire). *cf.* **Gerry**

geet *n.* child

genteelity *n.* gentility

Geordie *pr. n.* deriv. of George

Gerry *pr. n.* Garioch (a district in Aberdeenshire). *cf.* **Geery**

gether *v.* gather (R). *cf.* **gaither, gedder, gidder**

get on tae *v.* scold, *e.g.* **dinna get on tae them**

gey *adj.* great, considerable

gey, geyan *adv.* very, somewhat, rather

geylies *adv.* rather; nearly; pretty well

ghaist(ie) *n.* ghost

gheelie *n.* man or boy attending sportsman

gibbles *n.* wares

gid *See* **gaed, gied**

gidder *v.* gather. *cf.* **gaither, gedder, gether**

gie *v.* give; **gie intae trouble** scold

gied, gid *v. pt.* gave

gif *conj.* if (B1). *cf.* **gin**

gilgal *n.* (hard g) hubbub; uproar (B1)

gillieperous, gileepris *n.* (hard g) fool; rough, ungainly person (B1, T)

gilp *See* **jilp**

gimmer *n.* ewe from one to two years old; or not yet having borne young

gin *conj.* if, whether; if only (M2); than, by the time that; *prep.* (used

of time) by
ginch-breid *n.* gingerbread
ging *v.* go (A, S). *cf.* **gyang**
ginkmen (B1) *See* **ginkum**
ginkum *n.* trick, dodge
gird *n.* child's hoop
girdin *n.* girthing, *e.g.* to secure saddle, or lash a load to a cart
girdle *n.* circular iron plate with bow handle for baking oatcakes, etc.
girn *n.* snare; whimper; fretful fault-finding; *v.* complain peevishly, grumble; snarl
girnal, girnel *n.* meal chest
girnie, girnin *adj.* peevish
girse, girss *n.* grass
girse-hyeuk *n.* metal strut on scythe
girssy *adj.* grassy
gizzen *v.* dry up; shrivel; **gizzent** *adj.* parched; shrivelled; warped
glack *n.* fork of a tree; ravine; point where two things branch off
glaid *adj.* glad. *cf.* **gled**
glaik *n.* gleam
glaiket, glaikit *adj.* senseless; stupid
Glaisga *pr. n.* Glasgow
glammach, glammoch *n., v.* grasp, grab; **lat glammach at;** *n.* morsel
glamour, glamourie *n.* magic
glaur *n.* mud; ooze
gled, gledsome *adj.* glad
gled, gleed *n.* kite (bird of prey)
gleebrie *n.* large piece of (waste) ground
gleg *adj.* keen, sharp; eager; *n.* gadfly
glegsome *See* **gleg** *adj.*
glen *n.* narrow valley

glent *n.* glance
gless *adj.* glass; *n.* mirror
glesses *n.* spectacles
gley *n., v.* squint; **gleyed ee** eye with a squint
gliberal *n.* large piece of waste ground (B1). *cf.* **gleebrie**
gliff *n.* shock, scare (B1)
glint *n.* glimpse (M)
glive *n.* glove (A2)
gloam, gloamin, gloomin *n.* twilight
glorious *adj.* highly stimulated by alcohol (M2)
glowe *n., v.* glow
glower *n., v.* scowl
gluff *n.* shock; inhalation of air; *v.* eat greedily (B)
glumf *v.* to look sulky
gnap *n.* bite, mouthful
gnappin *in phr.* **in gnappin earnest** in dead earnest (B1)
gnauve *v.* gnaw
gnipper *n. in phr.* **gnipper for/and gnapper** the very smallest particle (deriv. from sound of mill when grinding); every bit
go-ashores *n. pl.* fishermen's dress for going ashore (B)
gobbinfae *See* **gowpenfu**
gock *n.* cuckoo; fool. *cf.* **gowk**
gockit *adj.* foolish
gog *n.* nestling (S). *cf.* **gorbel**
gollach, goloch *n.* beetle; **hornie-gollach** earwig
gollar *v.* shout incoherently
gomeril *n.* fool, blockhead
good al meggins! *excl.* probable euphemism for God Almighty
goodman *n.* husband (A2). *cf.*

guidman
goodwife *n.* wife (A2). *cf.* **guidwife**
goon *n.* gown
goor *n.* mud; slime
goranichy *adj.* complaining feebly (B1)
gorbel, gorblin *n.* unfledged bird. *cf.* **gog**
gorbellt *adj.* state of egg with young bird partially formed
goshie *excl.* gosh!
goup *v.* gawp, stare. *cf.* **gowp**
govie-dick(s) *excl. of surprise* (M1)
gow *n.* seagull (Buckie); *v.* induce, persuade; gull (A2). *cf.* **goy**
gowan *n.* daisy
gowd *n.* gold; **gowden** *adj.* golden
gowdie *n. in phr.* **heels ower gowdie** head over heels
gowf(f) *n.* ruin, destruction; golf
gowf(f)er *n.* golfer
gowk *n.* cuckoo; fool. *cf.* **gock**
gowkit *adj.* foolish. *cf.* **gockit**
gowp *v.* gawp, stare. *cf.* **goup, gype**
gowpenfu (fae) *n.* as much as two cupped hands can hold
gowsty *adj.* pale, sickly
gowt *v. pt., ppl.* got
goy (ower) *v.* allure, entice; convince (B1). *cf.* **gow**
graavit *n.* scarf; cravat. *cf.* **grauvit**
graen, grain *n., v.* groan
graip *n.* large fork used in farming; *v.* fork
graith *n.* accoutrements, harness; substance, riches; clothes
graivel *n.* gravel
gralloch *v.* disembowel the carcass of a deer
gran *adj., adv.* grand

granda *n.* grandfather
grane *v.* groan. *cf.* **graen, grain**
gran'eur *n.* grandeur
granfadder *n.* grandfather
Granny's John *n.* coddled boy
grape *v.* grope (J)
grat *v. pt.* wept; **roared an grat** wept noisily. *cf.* **greet**
grauvit *n.* cravat; scarf
grease *n.* disease affecting horses' legs
great-hertit *adj.* overcome by emotion; having a full heart
gree *v.* agree
green *n.* lawn; grassland
green (efter) *v.* long, yearn (for) (B1)
green-hoose *n.* greenhouse
greenichtie *adj.* greenish
greep *n.* open drain in cowshed; middle part of byre
greeshach *n.* flameless fire of red-hot embers (A1)
greet *v.* weep; **greetin fou** in an advanced stage of intoxication
greff *n.* grave (A)
greybeard *n.* earthenware bottle
grieve *n.* farm overseer
grimmy *n.* Grimsby boat or fisherman (B)
grindie, grindie tocher *n.* small greenish crab found in sea-shore pools (B)
grinsteen *n.* grindstone
grippit *adj., ppl.* seized with pain; hard up, pressed for cash (R)
grippy *adj.* stingy, tight-fisted
grizzelt *ppl.* turning gray (G)
grofe *adj.* coarse, rough
groncie *n.* anything large or fine of

its kind

groo *v. See* **grue**

growe *v.* grow; **growin shoorie** light rain good for plants and crops (T)

growthe *n.* growth; vegetation

growth-midden *n.* compost heap

growthy *adj.* (of weather) conducive to growth; (of a season) of good growth

grozart *n.* gooseberry

grubber *Eng. n.* agric. implement clearing ground of roots etc.

grubbit *ppl.* (land) cleared with a grubber

grue *v.* shudder

gruggle *v.* to render sub-standard by much handling; **grugglt** creased

grumlie *adj.* grumbling, fault-finding

grummle *v.* grumble

grun *n.* ground

grunny *n.* grandmother

grun offisher *n.* manager of an estate (A2)

grunter *n.* fisher word for the pig, where the word pig is taboo. *cf.* **Sandy Campbell**

gruntle *v.* grunt

grup *v.* grip

grutten *ppl.* wept; *adj.* tear-stained

gryte *adj.* great; **gryte lins** heavy fishing lines (B)

guaird *n., v.* guard. *cf.* **gaird**

Gude *See* **Gweed**

guddle *v.* catch fish with the hands by groping below the banks of a stream

gudge *n.* small, thickset fellow

guff *n.* smell

guffa *n.* guffaw

guid *adj.* good. *cf.* **gweed**

guid-brither *etc. See* **gweed-brither**

guidman *n.* master, head of household; husband (J)

guidwife *n.* female head of house, the mistress; wife (J)

guidwillie *adj.* generous (R)

guise *v.* to go mumming, masquerade. *cf.* **gyse**

guiser *n.* mummer; child in disguise who goes round doors at Hallowe'en offering entertainment in return for gifts or money

guizard *n.* mummer (J)

gull *n.* haze, mist

guller *n.* gurgling sound in throat

gullie *n.* large knife

gumbile *n.* gumboil

gumfleers, gumfloors *n. pl.* artificial flowers for ladies' bonnets (B1)

gumption *n.* common-sense

gundy *n.* candy; toffee

gunpouther *n.* gunpowder

Gurdon *pr. n.* Gourdon

gurk *n.* a short fat person

gurl *n., v.* growl

gurlie, gurly *adj.* (of weather, sea) stormy, threatening

gurr *n.* growl; drive, spirit; *v.* to growl

gurron *n.* strong, thickset person

gushet *n.* gusset; triangular piece of land; corner of a building

gutsy *adj.* greedy

gutter(s) *n.* mud, mire (S)

gutter *v.* work untidily, dirtily

g' wa *imp.* go away

gwana *n.* guano fertiliser

Gweed *pr. n.* God; **Gweed kens!** goodness knows!; **Gweed keep's aa** God keep us all; **Gweed preserve's** God preserve us!; **Gweed send** God grant

gweed *adj.* good; **gweed fegs** *excl.* good faith

gweed *n.* good; **tak the gweed o** take advantage of

gweed-brither, -breeder *n.* brother-in-law

gweed-dother *n.* daughter-in-law

gweed-father *n.* father-in-law

gweedlie *adv.* godly

gweed-mither *n.* mother-in-law

gweed-nicht *int.* goodnight

gweed-sin *n.* son-in-law

gweedwife *n.* wife

gweed-words *n. pl.* prayers

gweed-wull *n.* goodwill

gweed-wully *adj.* good-hearted; generous (B1). *cf.* **guid-willie**

gwestie, gweeshtie, gweeshtens *excl.* goodness!

gwite *n.* a narrow rocky inlet

gya *v. pt.* gave (A)

gyad(-sakes) *excl.* of revulsion, usually over food

gyana *v. neg.* did not give

gyang *v.* go (A, A1); *n.* a gang; row; **gyang forrit** attend Communion

gyangrel *See* **gangrel**

gyaun, gyaan *ppl.* going; **a-gyaun** going about

gyke-neckit *adj.* descriptive of someone whose neck is held slightly to one side (B). *cf.* **geck-neckit**

gype *n.* a fool; *v.* stare foolishly. *cf.* **gowp**

gypery *n.* foolishness, silly talk

gypit *adj.* foolish

gyse *See* **guise**

gyte *adj.* mad, crazy

—— H ——

ha *n.* hall

haach *n.* phlegm; *v.* hawk, clear the throat

haar *n.* (sea) mist

haaver *n.* half share; *v.* divide in two. *cf.* **halver**

habber *v.* stutter, stammer

hack *n.* chap, the effect of severe cold; notch

hack(ie) *n.* a certain amount, a bit; **a hackie langer**

had *v.* hold; **haddin hame** going home. *cf.* **hud**

haddie *n.* haddock

hae *v.* have; **haed** *v. pt.* had; *ppl.* **haen** had; **haena** *v. neg.* have not. *cf.* **hinna**

haffets *n.* temples; sides of the head

hag *n.* brushwood

hagger *n.* wound (A)

haibit *n.* habit

haik *n.* rack for fodder; **living at haik and manger** living extravagantly; **on the haik for**

on the look-out for. *cf.* **hake**

hail, haill *adj., n.* whole. *cf.* **hale**

haill *v.* heal

haill Eel *n.* the old Christmas season which extended from Dec. 25th to Twelfth Night; *in phr.* **tae haud haill Eel** to make merry, to celebrate with abandon

haimal(t), haimil(t) *adj.* homely, plain; without ceremony

haimle *See* **haimal(t)**

haimmer *n., v.* hammer. *cf.* **hemmer**

haims *n.* curved pieces of iron attached to horse's collar; **pit the haims on** (*fig.*) bring someone into line

hain *v.* save, husband; hoard; **a great hainin** a great saving; *v.* spare

hair *in phr.* **nae a hair o't** not a bit of it

hairbour *n.* harbour. *cf.* **herbour**

hairm *n., v.* harm

hairmless *adj.* harmless

hairrial *n.* something that impoverishes, costly expenditure. *cf.* **herrial**

Hairry *pr. n.* Harry

hairse *adj.* hoarse

hairst *n.* harvest

hairt *n.* heart. *cf.* **hert**

hairth *n.* hearth (J). *cf.* **ingle**

hairy-tatties *n.* hash made with potatoes and dried, salted fish (B)

hait *n.* atom, particle; **fient hait** not a bit

haith *excl.* (of surprise) faith!

haive *v.* heave, throw

haiveless *adj.* careless; unmannerly (A2)

haiver *v.* talk nonsense. *cf.* **haver**

haivers *n.* nonsense. *cf.* **havers**

hake *n.* wooden frame for drying fish. *cf.* **haik**

hale *adj.* whole; **hale an fere** whole and entire. *cf.* **hail**

halesome *adj.* wholesome

half-hung-tee *adj.* irresponsible (T)

halfie *n.* half-holiday

halflin *adj.* half-grown; *n.* half-grown boy, youth; farm- or stable-boy

half roads *adv.* half-way

halla *adj.* hollow (C). *cf.* **boss**

halver *v.* divide in two. *cf.* **haaver**

hallyrackit *adj.* boistrous, romping

hame *n.* home; **fae hame** away from home

hame-drauchtit *adj.* selfish

hame-fairm *n.* home farm

hamel *adj.* belonging to home. *cf.* **haimal(t)**

hameowre, -ower *adj.* homely, humble

hamesick *adj.* homesick

hamespun *adj., n.* homespun

hameward *adv.* homewards

hamewith, -wuth *adv.* homewards

hammer *v.* work or walk in clumsy, noisy way

hamsh *v.* eat noisily, voraciously

han *n.* hand; **at aa hans** at every opportunity; **tak throw han** deal with, discuss

han-breed *n.* hand-breadth

hane *ppl.* had. *cf.* **haen**

hanfu *n.* handful

hangie *n.* hangman; a soft cheese (F); **hangman cheese** curds in cloth, salted and hung to dry (T)

hank *v.* fasten, secure; tie tightly, constrict

hankey *n.* handkerchief

hanle *n.* handle

han-leem *n.* hand-loom

hanlin *n.* going-over, critical assault (A1); hand fishing line (B)

hansel *n.* handsel; first money received (B1); *v. tr.* handsel

hantle *n.* large quantity or number

hap *v.* hop; cover; **happit** *ppl.* covered; *n.* cover

hape *n.* heap (S)

hap in/up *v.* cover over

happer *n.* basket or container, esp. of seed for sowing

hap-warm *n.* a warm wrap or covering

harassment *n.* fatigue (A2)

hard *v. pt.* heard

harden *(adj.), n.* (of) very coarse cloth made of **hards**

hards *n. pl.* the coarse refuse of flax or hemp separated by heckling

hard-vrocht *adj.* hard-worked

hare-shard *n.* hare-lip (B1)

harigals *n. pl.* animal entrails

harken *v.* listen

harle *v.* rough-cast a wall with mix of mortar and small gravel

harlin *n.* rough casting

harn *n.* coarse cloth, sackcloth

harns *n.* brains; **harn pan** the skull

harp *n.* (a mason's) wire screen for cleaning sand or gravel

harra *n.* harrow

harry *v.* plunder bird's nest, bee's bike. *cf.* **herry**

hash *v.* slice, cut up; work at high pressure, hustle; **hasht** *ppl.* pressed, harrassed

haste-ye-back *phr.* come back soon. *cf.* **hist**

hat *v. pt.* hit

haud *n., v.* hold; **haud awa** go on; **haud in wi** keep in with; **haud oot** maintain; **haud ootower** keep away; **haud redd o** keep clear of (R); **haud yer tongue** be quiet; say no more; **haud yer wheesht** be silent; **nae tae haud nor bin'/bin** not to be held down, out of control

haud *v.* continue, to go on

haud awa fae *prep. phr.* except for

hauden-doon inhibited, constrained (of husbands) hen-pecked

hauden in aboot *ppl.* constrained

haudin *n.* (small)holding (A, M)

hauf *adj.* half

haugh *n.* low-lying ground beside a river; clearing of throat

hauld *n.* stronghold

hault *See* **hult**

haumer *v.* stamp about noisily

haved *v. pt.* heaved

haveral *n.* half-witted person; fool; garrulous person

haw *adj.* bluish-gray or pale green

haythen *adj., n.* heathen

heapie-on, a *n.* boy's game

hearken *v.* listen

hearthsteen *n.* hearthstone

heater *n.* glazed, sugared bun

hech *v.* pant (J)

heck an manger, to live at to live extravagantly. *cf.* **haik**

hed *v. pt.* had (A2)

hedder *n.* heather

heediepeers *n. pl.* people of the same height

heelabalow *n. var.* of hullabaloo

heeld *v.* held; (of time) spent (A1)

heelster-gowdie *adv.* head over heels

heelster-heid *adv.* head first

heely, heely *excl.* of correction slowly! or wait!

heemlin *ppl., adj.* humbling

heepocreet *n.* hypocrite

heerican *n.* hurricane (G)

heerin *n.* herring

heese, heeze *v.* heave; lift; exalt; intensify

heesh *int.* make hissing sound to drive animals away. *cf.* **hish**

heepochondreech *adj.* listless, gloomy (B1)

heepocrat *n.* hypocrite

Heeven *pr. n.* Heaven (C)

heft *n.* haft, knife handle; *v.* lift up; carry aloft; **heftit coo** unmilked cow with full udder

heich *adj.* high; *adv.* aloud

heichen *v.* heighten

heicher, heichest *adj.* higher, highest

heich-heidit *adj.* haughty

heicht *n.* height. *cf.* **hicht**

heid *n.* head; headmaster; **ower the heids o** because of

heid-bummer *n.* leader

heid-hurry *n.* busiest time

heid-, heidin-shafe *n.* last sheaf on top of a stack

heidie, heidy *adj.* clever; head-strong; opinionative

heidiepeers *n.* (young) people of exactly the same height

heidmaister *n.* headmaster

heid-rig *n.* head ridge

heid-stall *n.* head-stall, part of halter

heir *v.* inherit

heirskip *n.* heirship, inheritance

heist *v.* lift with effort

helpender, helpener *n.* assistant; minister's assistant

helter *n.* halter

hemmer *n.* hammer

hems *See* **haims**

hench *v.* to launch missiles by striking the hand against the thigh

hennie *n.* familiar name for a henwife

henny-hertit *adj.* timid, faint-hearted

henshine *n.* party for females

henwife *n.* woman in charge of poultry

herbour *n., v.* harbour. *cf.* **hairbour**

herd *n.* herdsman, -boy, one who tends cattle or sheep; *v.* tend cattle, sheep

heretick *n.* heretic

herp *n.* harp

herrial *n.* means of harrying; cause of ruin. *cf.* **harrial**

herrin *n.* herring; **herrin fivver** herring fever, condition caused by poor fishing (B)

herry *n.* plunder; *v.* plunder, rob birds' nests. *cf.* **harry**

hersel *pron.* herself; *pred. adj., adv.* by herself, alone

hert *n.* heart; **hert oot** *v.* build up heart of a stack or cart-load of grain. *cf.* **hairt**

hertnin *n.* encouragement; strengthening

hertsca(u)d *n.* heartburn; a disappointment (B1)

hesp *n.* hasp

het *adj.* hot; *v. pt.* heated (A1); **het fit** hot foot

heth *excl.* faith!

heugh *n.* a crag; rugged steep

heuk, heuck *n.* hook; reaping-hook, scythe. *cf.* **hyeuk**

hey *n.* hay

hey-hoose *n.* hay-shed (S)

hey-makker hay-maker

hey-ruck *n.* haystack

hey-soo *n.* haystack

hi! *imp.* turn left! (instruction for a plough-horse in Buchan) (T)

hicht *n.* height. *cf.* **heicht**

hid *n., v.* hold (S)

hid *v. pt.* had; **hidna** had not

hie *adj.* high (S); **hier** higher. *cf.* **heich**

hielan *adj.* highland

Hielander *n.* Highlander

hielant *adj.* Highland

himpen *adj.* hempen

himsel *pron.* himself; *pred. adj., adv.* by himself, alone

hinch *n.* haunch

hinder-, hinner-en *n.* latter or final part, the extremity; the end; death; the remains of anything; **at the hinder-en** in the end

hindmost *adj.* last. *cf.* **hinmaist**

hine *adv.* far; **hine awa** far off, far away. *cf.* **hyne**

hing *v.* hang *(tr., intr.)*

hing in *v.* get on with something, persevere

hingin *n.* a hanging

hingin-luggit *adj.* having drooping ears; disappointed

hinmaist *adj., n.* last

hinna *v. neg.* have not. *cf.* **haena**

hinner *v.* hinder

hinny *n.* honey

hin-shelvin *n.* movable board on back door of box cart (A2)

hin-slings *n. pl.* part of **britchin**, for attachment to rear of cart shaft (F)

hint *n.* the end; **hint o' hairst** end of harvest

hippen, hippin *n.* baby's nappy

hippen-towie *n.* rope for hanging nappies

hippit, hip-grippit *adj.* having stiff hip-joints and lower back

hire *v.* hire; engage oneself as an employee; season food

hirehoose *n.* farm labour or service; the place or house where servant is engaged to go

hirple *v.* limp; hobble

hirsel *n.* flock of sheep

hirstle *v.* to move with grazing or friction (M). *cf.* **hurschle**

hir't *ppl.* hired; seasoned

his *v.* has; **hisna** has not

hish *v.* drive animals, esp. poultry. *cf.* **heesh**

hist *n.* a great number; *v.* haste; **hist ye back** come back soon

hit *pron.* it

hiv *v.* have; *n.* hoof

hive *v.* swell, cause to swell

hivven *n.* heaven

hiz *pron.* us

hize *See* **hyze**

45

hizzie *n.* housewife; hussy

hoast *n., v.* cough; **a kirkyaird hoast** severe cough

hobble *n.* predicament; swarm of any kind

hobblet *adj.* perplexed

hoch *n.* lower part of human thigh; hind-leg joint of animal

hod *v.* hide; *pt.* hid; **hodden** *ppl.* hidden

hodden *n.* homespun cloth of wool of the natural colour

hodden-grey *n.* grey homespun

hodge *v.* move or walk awkwardly or jerkily

hoffin *n.* clumsy, awkward person

hog, hogg *n.* young sheep before first shearing

Hogmanay *pr. n.* New Year's Eve

hollach (aboot) *v.* lark (about)

hoo *adv.* how; why. *cf.* **foo**

hooch *n.* dance (S); loud cry esp. when dancing; *v.* shout when dancing

hooer *n.* whore. *cf.* **hure**

hoodie *n.* the hooded crow

hoodie-craw *n.* hooded or carrion crow

hooever *adv., conj.* however. *cf.* **hoosomever**

hooick *n.* small rick of corn or hay (T). *cf.* **scroo**

hooie *v.* barter, exchange (incl. knives between boys)

hoolet *n.* owl. *cf.* **howlet**

hoomble *adj.* humble

hoose *n.* house; **hoosefu** houseful

Hoose, the *n.* the laird's house

hoosebrakker *n.* burglar

hoose-room *n.* house-room

hoosewifeskip *n.* housewifery

hoosomever, hoosomediver *adv.* however

hoot(s) *excl.* of doubt, contempt, irritation; **hoot awa wi** down with; **hoot ty** oh, yes

hooze, the *n.* disease in sheep and cattle

horn-en, -eyn *n.* best room in two-roomed cottage

hornie *in phr.* **fair hornie** fair play

Hornie *pr. n.* the Devil

horny-gollach *n.* beetle; earwig

horrifie *v.* horrify

horseman's wird *n.* code word revealed on joining horsemen's secret society

horse-troch *n.* horse-trough

hose *n.* stocking; **hose an sheen** (*lit.* shoes and stockings) exaggeration (B)

hotch *See* **hodge**

hotchin *adj.* infested, seething, overrun

hotter *v.* simmer, sputter; *n.* a seething mass; the noise or motion of the crowd; jolting movement; the sound this produces; **gie a vrang hotter** make a wrong move

hottle *n.* hotel

hough *n.* thigh

houk *v.* dig. *cf.* **howk**

houp(ie) *n.* mouthful of food or drink. *See* **howp**

hoven *ppl., adj.* swollen, blown out

howder *n.* sudden gust of wind; *v.* bluster

howdie *n.* midwife; **at howdie haste** at high speed

howdie-wifie *n.* midwife (S)
howe *n.* hollow, valley
Howe o the Mearns *pr. n.* valley of the Mearns
howe-backit *adj.* hollow-backed
howff *n.* a place of resort, or evil repute; a haunt
howfin *n.* clumsy, senseless fellow
howk *v.* dig. *cf.* **houk**
howlet *n.* owl (G1). *cf.* **hoolet**
howm *n.* holm (J)
howp *v.* hope; **howpfu** hopeful
hubber *v.* stammer. *cf.* **habber**
hucky-duck *n.* team game for boys (S)
hud *v.* hold; **hud in wi** keep in with. *cf.* **haud**
hudden *ppl.* held
hudd(e)ry *adj.* unkempt, dishevelled
huick *See* **hooick**
hull *n.* hill
hullick, hullock *n.* hillock, heap
hull-run *adj.* uncouth
hult *v.* halt
hummel, hummle *adj.* without horns
hummel-doddie *adj.* hornless
hummel-doddies *n. pl.* woollen mittens without fingers
hummel-thrummy mittens *adj., n.* unknown, perhaps synonym for above
humoursome *adj.* affably disposed
humph *n.* hump, curvature of the back or spine; *v.* carry, lug, lift something heavy
humphie-backit *adj.* hunchbacked
humsh *v.* eat noisily and greedily, munch. *cf.* **hamsh**

hunger *n.* (**ng** pronounced as in singer) hunger; a mean or avaricious person
hungert *adj.* hungry
hungry *adj.* mean; avaricious; **hungry Angus** mean person
hunker *v.* squat down on the haunches; *n. pl.* the haunches resting on the heels; **doon on yer hunkers**
hunker-slidin *n.* evasive behaviour
hunkit *See* **hank**
hunner *adj., n.* hundred
hunnerwecht *n.* hundredweight
hup *adv.* up
hurb *n.* clumsy, awkward fellow; displeasing person; good-for-nothing
hurdies *n. pl.* the buttocks
hure *n.* whore. *cf.* **hooer**
hurl *n.* lift on a vehicle; the sound of laboured breathing due to phlegm in the throat; **hurl in the throat** (when **r** is pronounced gutturally)
hurlie *n.* barrow; handcart
hurlie-bed *n.* low bed on castors, stored under the box-bed
hurschle *v.* move along a seat without rising (A). *cf.* **hirstle**
huz *See* **hiz**
hyaave *adj.* sallow; grey
hyeuk *See* **heuk**
hyne *See* **hine**
hyow(e) *n., v.* hoe
hypal *adj.* crippled (B1)
hypothec, hale *phr.* whole concern
hyse *See* **hyze**
hyste *v.* hoist, lift
hystergowdie *adv.* head over heels

47

(T). *cf.* **heelster-gowdie**
hyter *v.* walk unsteadily; stumble
hyze *n.* banter; frolic, sport; a
practical joke; **tae hae a hyze wi**
to play a trick on

— I —

I *pron. (pro.* **aa**) I. *cf.* **A, Aw**
i *prep.* in
ice-tangle *n.* icicle
idder *adj., n., pron.* other
idelty *n.* idleness; *in pl.* idle frolics
idleset, idleseat *n.* idleness
ile *n.* oil
ile-cake *n.* oil cake (for cattle)
ile-skin *adj., n.* oil skin
ilk, ilka, ilky *adj.* each, every
ill *adj.* ill; bad, *e.g.* **ill widder**;
  wicked; unkind, cruel; hard,
  difficult; *adv.* badly; **the ill pairt**
  hell. *cf.* **ull**
ill-aff *adj.* badly off
ill-deen *adj.* unkindly done
ill-eese *v.* ill use, abuse
ill-farrant *adj.* unpleasant in
  behaviour; bad-mannered
ill-fashence *n.* curiosity
ill-fashioned *adj.* inquisitive
ill-faured, -faurt *adj.* ugly;
  unbecoming
ill-gatit, ill-gettit *adj.* badly
  behaved, perverse
ill-gruntit *adj.* ill-natured
ill-guide *v.* maltreat
ill-hung *adj.* (of the tongue)
  impudent, sharp
ill-naturt *adj.* ill-natured
ill-pairt, the *pr. n.* Hell
ill-pairtit *ppl.* badly shared out
ill-peyt *adj.* extremely sorry

ill-shakken-up *ppl.* disordered,
  untidy
ill-teen *n.* bad mood
ill-thochtit *adj.* suspicious; ill-
  disposed
ill-tongue *v.* abuse
ill-trickit *adj.* mischievous
ill-tricks *n.* mischief
ill-willer *n.* adversary; one who
  wishes you harm
ill-willie *adj.* ungenerous
ill-win *n.* abusive language (A2);
  scandal, slander
ily-lamp *n.* oil lamp. *cf.* **crusie**
imaagine, imaigin (A1) *v.* imagine
imaiginashun *n.* imagination
immediantly *adv.* immediately
immis *adj.* variable (B1)
impident *adj.* impudent
impreevement *n.* improvement
impruv *v.* improve
in aboot, come *v. with prep.*
  approach
in-by(e) *adv.* inside; (with verb of
  motion) from outside to inside
inch, insch *n.* island; stretch of
  higher ground in the middle of a
  plain
inchie *n.* small amount
income *n.* ailment of unknown
  cause
indraacht *n.* suction of air, breath
induck *v.* induct

inflooensie *n.* influenza
ingan, ingin *n.* onion
ingine *n.* engine
ingle *n.* fire; hearth, fireside; chimney-corner
ingle-cheek *n.* fireside
ingle-lowe *n.* blazing fire
ingle-neuk *n.* chimney corner
in-haudin *adj.* currying favour with one, fawning
inklin *n.* inclination
inower *prep.* in and over
inquar *v.* inquire
inquary *n.* inquiry
In'rurie *pr. n.* Inverurie
insnorl *v.* entangle, entrap
interaistin *adj.* interesting
intil, intill *prep.* into; **intill't** into it
intimat *adj.* intimate

intimmers *n. pl.* intestines; inner workings of anything
intoon *n.* land nearest the farm-house
inveet *n.* invitation (A); *v.* (A1)
inveetor *n.* inventory; value of goods inventoried
I'se *pron. with v.* I shall
I'se warn I'll warrant you, I guarantee
isna *v. neg.* is not
isnint *v. interrog.* is it not?
ither *adj.* other
itmost *adj.* utmost
iv(v)er *adv.* ever
iverleevin *in phr.* **at the iverleevin gallop** at high speed (T)
ivnoo *adv.* just now

—— J ——

jaa *n.* jaw; talk, chatter. *cf.* **jaw**
jabb *v.* fatigue, exhaust; **jabbit** *ppl., adj.* exhausted
jaicket etc. *n.* jacket
jalouse *v.* guess; suspect; imagine
jamaica *n.* seizure, as in the *phr.* **he jist aboot hid a jamaica**
Jamie *pr. n.* deriv. of James
jamph *v.* mock, sneer, jeer
jamphin *n.* mockery
jandies, the *n.* jaundice
jannie *n.* school janitor
jant *n., v.* jaunt
Janwar, Janiwar *n.* January
jassamine *n.* jasmine
jaud *n.* a jade
jaup *v.* fatigue, weary; **jaupit** *ppl.*

weary
jaw *n.* chatter; abusive talk; (at sea) wave; *v.* talk; chatter. *cf.* **jaa**
jaw-hole *n.* sink; hole in the wall for dirty water
jee *v.* to move, stir. *cf.* **gee**
jeedge *v.* judge
jeedgement *n.* judgment (B1)
jeel *adj.* cold as ice; *v.* freeze; congeal
jeely *n.* jam; **jeely pigs** jam jars
Jeems *pr. n.* deriv. of James
jeesty *adj.* normally used in the *neg.*; **nae jeesty** no joking matter
jeho(y) *v.* cease, give over
jelly *adj.* jolly
jibble *n.* small quantity of liquid

(contemptuous term)

jibble ower *v.* brim or spill over

jile *n.*, *v.* jail

jilp *v. tr.* spill, cause to splash; *intr.* splash about; *n.* a splash of liquid

jimp *adv.* scarcely

jine *n.*, *v.* join. *cf.* **jyne**

jine-on *n.* playground game

jiner *n.* joiner, carpenter. *cf.* **jyner**

jing-bang *in the phr.* **the hale jing-bang** the whole party or affair

jings *excl.* gosh

jink *n.* sudden turn; *v.* elude; dodge; cheat

jinkie *adj.* jaunty (R)

jinnip(e)rous, jinipperous *adj.* trim, spruce; ingenious; natty; finicky, over-particular

Jinse *pr. n.* Janet

jint *n.* joint

jip *n.* pain (sometimes retributive)

jipperty *n.* jeopardy

jist *adv.* just. *See also* **jyst**

jivvle *n.* a gaol; house as uncomfortable as a gaol

jo *n.* sweetheart (J)

job *v.* prick; **jobby** prickly; **jobby nickles** stinging nettles (B)

Jock *pr. n.* John

Jocktober *n.* October (T)

joco *n.* jovial

Johnny Groatie *n.* small cowrie shell (B). *cf.* **kysie**

joog *n.* jug

joogle *v.* joggle, jerk repeatedly

joost *adv.* just (A2). *cf.* **jist**

joostice *n.* justice (A2)

jorum *n.* whisky jug

jot *n.* job; piece of work; **a jot wark** a job of work

jougs *n. pl.* instrument of public punishment, sometimes in church, consisting of iron collar attached to wall and placed around offender's neck

jouk *v.* dodge, duck, swerve; **jouk an lat the jaw gae by** yield to circumstances

joukerie pawkery *n.* trickery, roguery

jow *n.* sound of bell; *v.* move with a rocking motion; ring

jummle *n.*, *v.* jumble

junny *n.* wrench; severe jolt

jyne *v.* join

jyner *n.* joiner, carpenter. *cf.* **jiner**

jyst *n.* joist

—— K ——

(The initial *k* is usually pronounced before *n*)

kail *n.* colewort; **kail runt** kail stalk; also term of abuse; **caul kail het** *(fig.)* a stale story; **kail throu the reek** severe criticism or scolding

kaim, kame *n.*, *v.* comb

kebbuck *n.* round of cheese

keckle *v.* cackle, chuckle

keeble *See* **kibble**

keech *See* **kich**

keek *n.*, *v.* peep

keek-a-bo *n.* the game of peep-bo

keel *n.* any marking substance *(e.g. for sheep)* (M2)

keeng *n.* king

keengdom *n.* kingdom

keeperin *n.* the work of a game-keeper

keepit *v. pt.* kept

keep tee *v.* keep up

keer *n., v.* cure

keeriosity *n.* curiosity

keerious *adj.* curious, strange; keen, desirous

keest *v. pt.* cast. *cf.* **ceest**

kell *n.* caul; the puckered part of a woman's **mutch** which rises over the back part of the head

ken *v.* know; **kenna** don't know

kenle, kennle *v.* kindle; **kennelt** ablaze with colour

kennlin *n.* kindling

kenspeckle *adj.* easily recognised

kep *n.* cap; *v.* meet, catch, intercept; **kep the win** keep the wind out

kerridge *n.* carriage

keuk *v.* cook. *cf.* **kyeuk**

kibble *adj.* strong, sturdy; well-built; active; agile

kich *n.* excrement; *v.* defecate

kil(l) *n.* wooden tripod round which hay- or cornstack is built

kilt *v.* tuck up (skirts, sleeves etc.)

kiltimmer *n.* term of abuse for a woman of doubtful character; a rough woman; virago

kiltit *adj.* kilted

kimmer *n.* a gossip; married woman; wife

kin' *adj.* kind; *n.* kind, nature, sort; *adv.* rather; **caal kin'** rather cold

kinallie *n.* (Fr. *canaille*) mob

kindlin *adj.* blushing, ruddy (J)

kine *v.* cattle (A)

kinlin *n.* kindling

kinkhoast *n.* whooping cough

kinsh *v.* twist; wind (a rope)

kire *n.* choir. *cf.* **kyre**

kirk *n.* church

kirkit (to be) *ppl.* (to be) at church

kirkton, -toon *n.* village or hamlet with parish church

kirk-yaird *n.* churchyard

kirn *n.* butter churn; mess, state of confusion; *v.* churn butter; stir, mix up; work in slovenly manner

kirsen *v.* christen

kirsenin *n.* christening

kist *n.* chest; coffin; *v.* to put in a coffin

kitchie *n.* kitchen; seasoning, an addition to plain fare; **tak a piece an mak kitchie o yer egg**

kitchie-deem *n.* kitchen-maid

kite *n.* stomach. *cf.* **kyte**

kitlin *See* **kittlin**

kittle *v.* tickle; anger, annoy; upset; *adj.* skilful; (of a person) touchy; (of a task) tricky, difficult, not easily managed; (of an issue) controversial, sensitive

kittlesome *adj. See* **kittle**

kittlet (up) *adj., ppl.* excited

kittlie *adj.* tickly; ticklish

kittlin *n.* kitte*n. cf.* **kitlin**

kittly *See* **kittlie**

klyack *See* **clyack**

knablich *n.* small hillock (A2)

knablick *adj.* nobbly

knack *v.* to knock

knag *n.* knob or pin

knap *n.* knoll; *v.* knock; snap with

the teeth; starve (B1); **knap-at-the-win** a mere bite (ref. to stray dog) (M2)

knapdarloch *n.* dung-matted hair or hide on the hind-quarters of cattle or sheep

kneef *adj.* healthy and active

kneevlick *n.* a big lump (of cheese, beef etc). *cf.* **knyte**

kneggum *n.* sharp or disagreeable smell or flavour

kneip on *v.* press on

knibloch *n.* clod of earth; lump (used as mild insult)

knicht *n.* knight

knotty-tams *n.* dish of boiled milk with meal

knowe *n.* knoll, steep field; head

knowe-heid *n.* top of a hillock

knowpert *n.* crowberry

knyte *n.* large piece, lump

korter *n.* quarter; quarter of oatcake. *cf.* **corter**

kowe *See* **cowe**

kowk *v.* retch; vomit

kwintra, kwintry *n.* country

kwite, kwyte *n.* coat; oilskin skirt with bib worn by women in the herring curing yards (B)

kyaaks *n. pl.* cakes (usually oatcakes); **kyaak o breid** round of oatcakes

kyaard *n.* tinker; *v.* abuse; **kyaard-tonguet** given to loose or unwholesome talk

Kyack *pr. n.* nickname for the village of Pitsligo

kyarn *n.* large heap, cairn. *cf.* **carn**

kye *n. pl.* cows

kyeuk *n., v.* cook. *cf.* **keuk**

kyp(i)e *n.* scooped out hollow in ground for use in game of marbles

kyre *n.* choir. *cf.* **kire**

kysie *n.* small cowrie shell (B). *cf.* **Johnny Groatie, calfie's mooie**

kyte *n.* stomach. *cf.* **kite**

kythe *v.* show, display, reveal (B1)

— **L** —

laad *See* **lad**

lab *v.* lap

lab(b)ach *n.* long story about nothing (R); small quantity to drink (B1)

labster *n.* fisher term for lobster. *cf.* **partan**

lacer *n.* shoe-lace. *cf.* **pint**

lach *n., v.* laugh. *cf.* **lauch**

lachter *n.* laughter; a sitting of eggs. *cf.* **lauchter**

lad *n.* lad; boy-friend; sweetheart;

in phr. **a bit o a lad** rascal; lady's man; **lad o pairts** clever lad from small country school

laddie *n.* small boy

lade *n.* canal carrying water to a mill; load; lead (metal) (S)

ladle *n.* small wooden box with long handle, formerly in use in collecting offerings in church

laft *n.* loft; upper storey; church gallery

lagamachie *See* **lamgamachie**

laich, laigh *adj.* low
laich-in *adv.* in a low voice
laichy-braid *n.* short, stocky person or animal
laid *n.* load
laid *ppl.* (of a crop) flattened
laidle *See* **ladle**
laig *v.* talk idly. *cf.* **lyaag**
laigh *n.* stretch of low-lying ground
laimiter *n.* a cripple
lair *n.* mud, mire; burial place reserved in graveyard; *v.* sink in bog or mud
laird *n.* squire; landowner
lairdskip *n.* lordship; right as proprietor
lairge *adj.* unrestrained in talk
lairn *v.* learn; teach. *cf.* **leern**
lairnin *n.* learning (J). *cf.* **lear**
lair-stane *n.* gravestone
laist *adj., v.* last. *cf.* **lest**
laiteran *See* **lettrin**
lallan *adj.* lowland
lame *n.* crockery, earthenware; shard of earthenware
la(m)gamachie *n.* anything long and loose in movement; rigmarole
lamikie *n.* little lamb
Lammas *n.* beginning of August, a Scottish term
lammie *n.* lamb
lan *n., v.* land
lane *pred. adj., adv.* alone. *cf.* **leen**
lang *adj., v.* long
lang acre *adj., n.* grass verge at roadside (T)
langer *n.* languor, tedium; **haud oot o langer** keep from boredom, amuse
lang-gane *adj.* long-gone

lang-heidit *adj.* intelligent; shrewd
langidge *n.* language; words
lang-leggit *adj.* long-legged
lang-nebbit, -nibbit *adj.* prying; critical; acute in understanding; (of words) difficult to pronounce or understand
langsome *adj.* wearisome
langsyne *adv.* long ago
lanner *n.* land-side horse
lanside *n.* side of the plough next the unploughed land
lanstell *n.* parapet of a bridge
lant *v.* jeer
lanter (wi) *v.* leave in the lurch (with) (B)
lap *v. pt.* leaped
lapper *v.* (of water) lap
larrie, larry *n.* long, flat low wagon, horse-drawn or motorised; lorry
lass(ie), lassock *n.* girl
lassikie, lassockie *n.* young girl
lat *v. pr., pt.* let. *cf.* **leet, loot**
latch *adj.* slow; tardy; lazy (M2)
latten *ppl.* let; **latten be** let alone
latter-oot *n.* the letter-out, the one who feeds in the straw in rope-twisting (F)
lauch *v.* laugh; **lauchen at** laughed at
lauchter *See* **lachter**
lave *n.* the rest; the remainder
lave *v.* leave (S). *cf.* **lea, ley**; *v.* ladle out (B1)
laverock, lavrock *n.* skylark. *cf.* **livrock**
lawbor, lawbour *n.* labour
lawfu *adj.* lawful
lawin *n.* tavern-bill; reckoning

lawlands *n. pl.* lowlands
lawvyer *n.* lawyer
lay *v.* to put more iron on a sock or coulter
lay-aff *n.* harangue; rigmarole; *v.* talk volubly, spout
lay on *v.* work hard; beat severely
lea *v.* to leave (A1). *cf.* **ley, lave**
lead *v.* cart in the corn from the field (A1)
leadin *n.* carting hay, straw (S)
leal *adj., n.* loyal; **leal-loved** well-loved
leam *n.* gleam
lean *in phr.* **lean yersel doon** take a seat
lean-tee *n.* lean-to, shed
lear *n.* learning
leasure *n.* leisure. *cf.* **leesure**
leavie-oh *n.* catching game
ledder *v.* thrash, belabour
lee *n.* lie
leear *n.* liar
leeberary *n.* library
leeberty *n.* liberty
Leebie *pr. n.* deriv. of Elizabeth
leebral *adj., n.* liberal
leed *n.* lead
leeft *v. pt., ppl.* left
leefu-lane *adj.* all alone
leein *ppl., n.* lying
lee-lang (day) *adj.* livelong (day)
leems *n. pl.* implements; apparatus
leen *adj.* alone; **ma leen** by myself; **himleen** by himself; **themleen** by themselves
leenity *n.* lenity, mercy
leepie *n.* measure of oats; wooden box-shaped measure for horse's feed of corn

leerie(-man) *n.* lamp-lighter
leern *v.* learn; teach. *cf.* **lairn**
leernin *n.* learning. *cf.* **lear**
leernt *adj.* learned
leery-bows *in phr.* **tae gang by the leery-bows** (B1) to do mischief
leese-me-on *phr.* expression of pleasure in, or affection for someone/thing; **leese-me-on the Enzie fowk** (C)
leeshens, leeshins *n.* licence
leesome *adj.* pleasant
leesure *n.* leisure. *cf.* **leasure**
leet *n.* list; *v. pt.* let (A1); **leet at him** assailed him. *cf.* **lat, loot**
leeterary *adj.* literary
leethe *n.* a shelter. *cf.* **lythe**; *in phr.* **in the leethe o ye** through your influence (B)
leetiny *n.* litany
leevin *n.* living being; person
lefts-an-richts *n.* soup made from turnip and potato
leg *v.* to walk quickly; *pt.* **leggit**; **draw ma leg** pull my leg
leid *n.* language; dialect
len *n.* loan; *v.* lend; **tak a len o** take advantage of (M2)
lench *v.* launch
lenth *n.* length
lerb *n.* lick, mouthful of fluid (A1); *v.* lap with tongue
lest *adj., n., v.* last. *cf.* **laist**
let off *v.* break wind behind
leuch *v. pt.* laughed
leuk *v.* look
ley *n.* lea, unploughed land; grassland; **ley-corn** oats grown on ploughed-up grassland; *v.* leave (S). *cf.* **lea, lave**

lib *v.* castrate
lichen *n.* fog
licht *adj., n.* light; *v.* light, alight; **licht on** *v.* land on; **let licht that** let it be known that
lichthoose *n.* lighthouse
lichtlifie *v.* to make light of; belittle
lichtnin *n.* lightning
lichts *n. pl.* lungs (human/animal)
lichtsome *adj.* pleasant
lick *n.* smack, blow; **at a gweed lick** at high speed; *v.* thrash
lickened (wi) *ppl.* likened (to)
lickin *n.* thrashing
lickly *adj., adv.* likely
licky *adj.* lucky
lie-in *n.* the part of an attic room lying under slope of roof
lie-money *n.* money retained by employer for lie-time
lie-time *n.* the time before pay day for making up accounts, in which work has been done but payment remains or lies over till next pay day
lift *n.* sky
lifter *n.* one who gathers grain to make sheaves. *cf.* **gaitherer**
liftit *adj., ppl.* elevated; overjoyed
lig *v.* (literary) lie, recline, rest
like, likein *adv.* (used at the end of sentences to modify or intensify) that's to say; do you mean?
likein *ppl.* as; *adv.* like as; for example
liken tae *adj.* apt to
liket, likit *v. pt.* liked
limerin *n.* thrashing
limmer *n.* woman of loose morals; playful or *derog.* term applied to

a female; rascal
linder, linner *n.* woollen or flannel undershirt
ling *n.* long thin grass (J)
linga *n.* lingo
linglairy *n.* long story, rigmarole (B)
link *v.* walk hand-in-hand, arm-in-arm; **link at** work vigorously
links *n. pl.* chain by which a pot hung over a fire from the **crook**
linn *n.* precipice over which water falls; the cascade of water
linth *n.* length. *cf.* **lenth**
lintie *n.* linnet
lip *v.* to be full to the brim; brim over
lippen *v.* trust; depend on
lippie *n.* fourth of a peck
lirk *n.* crease, fold. *cf.* **lurk**
list *v.* enlist
lit *v.* let. *cf.* **lat**
litchie *adj.* light-headed
lith *n.* joint; segment
little ane, littlin *n.* small child
liveliheid *n.* livelihood
liver *v.* unload a ship's cargo
livrock *n.* skylark. *cf.* **laverock**
loaf *n.* bread
loan *n.* a small common; uncultivated land about a homestead
loaning(s) *n.* village common green
lochan *n.* small loch
locker *n.* small compartment in the end of a chest
lod *excl.* Lord!
lodesteen *n.* magnet
lodomy *n.* laudanum
loe *v.* love

lood *adj.* loud
loon *n.* lad; boy
loonikie *n.* little boy
loose *n.* louse
loosie *adj.* lousy
loot *v.* bend, bow, make obeisance; let; *v. pt.* permitted, let; **loot ye doon** sit down
loo-warm *adj.* lukewarm
lordlifu *adj.* sumptuous; extravagantly liberal
losh *excl.* euphemism for Lord
loshins *excl. of surprise* (A)
loshtie (be here) *excl. of surprise*
loshtie-goshtie guide's *excl.* good Lord guide us!
loss *v.* lose. *cf.* **tine**
loup *v.* leap. *cf.* **lowp**
Lourenkirk *pr. n.* Laurencekirk (S)
low door *adj., n.* entrance at ground floor level
lowe *n., v.* glow, flame, blaze; **sweer blue lowes** swear vehemently
lown *adj.* sheltered, unfrequented; (of weather) calm, still
lowp *n.* leap; *v.* leap. *cf.* **loup**
lowrie *n.* long, heavy, steel hook used on the market floor
Lowrin *pr. n.* Lawrence
lowse *v.* unyoke, leave off work; loose, loosen; *adj.* loose
lowser *n.* one who cuts bands on sheaves during threshing
lowsin-shooer *n.* heavy shower of rain putting a stop to out-door work on farm (T)
lowsin-time *n.* the end of the day's

work; the time for unyoking horses
lowss *adj.* suffering from diarrhoea
lowssen *v.* loosen
lozen *n.* window-pane
luckpenny *n.* sum of money given for luck, *e.g.* returned by the seller to the buyer as discount
lucky daddy *n.* grandfather (A2)
lucky minnie *n.* grandmother (B1)
ludgement *n.* a place to rest
luft *v.* lift
lug *n.* ear; handle
lug-babs *n.* earrings; knot of ribbons over the ears
luggie *n.* small wooden vessel with handles, for table use
lum *n.* chimney
lum-hat *n.* black tile hat
lumbaga *n.* lumbago
lundies, landies *n.* double ropes for skipping
lunt *n., v.* smoke, draw
lurk *n.* fold, crease. *cf.* **lirk**
lut *v.* let; **lutten** *ppl.* let. *cf.* **lat**
luve *n.* love
lyaach *adj.* low. *cf.* **laich, laigh**
lyaag *v.* to talk idly and at length. *cf.* **laig**
lyart *adj.* streaked with grey
lyen *ppl.* lain
lyin-holes *n.* patches of corn or barley flattened by heavy rain and unsuitable for the binder (T)
lyin-shafts *n. pl.* main beams under box cart (F)
lyter *v.* loiter
lythe *n.* shelter; *adj.* sheltered

— **M** —

ma *pron.* me; my
maa *n.* seagull. *cf.* **maw, myaave**
maasie *n.* knitted jersey
mackerels' backs an meers' tails
 phr. high cirrus clouds (B)
mad *adj.* angry
madden-dreem *n.* madness; folly;
 mad pranks (B1)
maet *n.* food; **aff o's maet** off his
 food; *v.* feed; **maetit** fed
maet-haill *adj.* able to take one's
 food
mager *prep.* in spite of; *v.* act in
 spite of; master (B1). *cf.* **mauger**
Maggie Rennie *in phr.* **a different**
 Maggie Rennie a different kettle
 of fish (B)
maggot *n.* whim, caprice, fancy
maggotive *adj.* full of whims,
 moody
maiden *n.* designation once given
 to farmer's eldest daughter
maik *n.* halfpenny
maikst *n.* a halfpennyworth
maillyer *n.* the quantity of oatmeal
 received from the mill at one time
main *n., v.* moan
mainners *n.* manners. *cf.* **menners**
Mains o Backchines *pr. n.*
 fictitious farm representing an
 inferior fee (T)
mair *adj.* more
Mairch *n.* month of March
mairch *n.* boundary; *n., v.* march
mairch-dyke *n.* boundary wall
mairket *n.* market. *cf.* **mercat**

mairrage *n.* marriage; wedding. *cf.*
 mairritch
mairritch *n.* marriage; wedding. *cf.*
 mairrage
mairry, mairry on (to) *v.* marry;
 ppl. **mairret, mairrit**
mairt *n.* ox killed at Martinmas for
 winter use (A). *cf.* **mart**
mairt *See* **mart**
maist *adj.* most; *adv.* **maistly**
maister *n.* master; stale urine used
 as detergent; **maister-pig** jar
 containing such urine; *v.* master
mait *See* **maet**
maitter *n.* matter
mak *v.* make. **mak nae odds** make
 no difference; **maksna, disna**
 mak does not matter; **mak yer**
 feet yer freen it's best to go
maker, makker *n.* poet
makins (o) *n.* makings (of)
mak on *n.* pretence; *v.* pretend
malagruze *v.* bruise
mallie *n.* fulmar
mammy *n.* mother
man *n.* husband; man
mang *v.* long for eagerly; **mangin**
 tae dying to
mannie *n.* man; *pl.* **mannies**. *cf.*
 mennies
mannikie *n.* little man; term of
 endearment for small boy
mant *n., v.* stammer
mappie *n.* rabbit (used on board
 ship to avoid taboo word, *rabbit*)
mardle *n.* crowd

Marget *pr. n.* Margaret
markness *n.* darkness (A2)
marless *adj.* not matching
maroonjus *adj.* harsh; outrageous
(A)
marra-been *n.* marrowbone
marra, marrow *n.* match, equal
marrowless *adj.* unmarried
mart *n.* ox killed at Martinmas;
market; building used for
agricultural auctions; such a sale.
cf. **mairt**
Martimas *n.* Martinmas
masel(lie) *pron.* myself; *pred. adj.,*
adv. by myself, alone
mashlie *n.* mixed grain, peas and
oats
mask *v.* infuse (tea)
mason's mear *n.* trestle
mauger *prep.* in spite of (M). *cf.*
mager
maumie *adj.* mellow
maun *v.* must; **mauna** *v. neg.* must
not
maut *n.* malt; **the maut was abeen
the meal** (leading to
intoxication)
mavis *n.* thrush (M)
maw *n.* mouth; seagull (M1); *v.*
mow, cut with a scythe
mawkin *n.* hare (A, M). *cf.*
myaakin
mawmie *See* **maumie**
maxie *n.* a maximus, the gravest
error in Latin prose composition
maze *n.* state of amazement
meal *n.* oatmeal; **meal-an-ale**
mixture of oatmeal, ale, sugar and
whisky, traditional fare at harvest-
home celebrations; the celebration

itself
meal-bowie *n.* barrel for oatmeal
meal-bunk (S) *See* **meal-kist**
mealer (S) *See* **meal-kist**
mealie puddin *n.* oatmeal pudding
meal-kist *n.* meal-chest in which
farm servant stored meal and
other eatables
mealock *n.* crumb of oatcakes etc.
mealy-mou't *adj.* mealy-mouthed
meangie *adj.* tight with money,
mingy
mear *n.* mare. *cf.* **meer**
meat *n.* food (J). *cf.* **maet**
mebbe *adv.* perhaps
meelyin *n.* million
meelyinaire *n.* millionaire
meen *n.* moon. *cf.* **mune**
meen *v.* pity
meeninit *n.* mignonette
meenister *n.* minister. *cf.* **minaister**
meenit *n.* minute
meenlicht *n.* moonlight. *cf.*
munelicht
meent *ppl.* meant
meer *n.* moor. *cf.* **muir**; *n.* mare. *cf.*
mear
meesic *n.* music
meesic-fan *n.* musical instrument
meet *in phr.* **meet the cat** have a
spell of bad luck (B)
meeve *v.* move
meggie-monyfeet *n.* centipede
meggins alive *excl. of surprise*
(M1)
megreem, megrim *n.* migraine
megstie me *excl. of surprise* (M1)
meikle *adj.* big, large, great. *cf.*
muckle
mell *n.* mallet, heavy hammer; *v.*

mix; meddle
melt *n.* the spleen
mengyie *n.* crowd, huddled mass (A)
menner *n.* manner; *pl.* **menners** manners; **weel-mennert** well-mannered
mennies *n. pl.* men (A1). *cf.* **mannies**
mense *n.* common-sense
mensefu *adj.* courteous, respectful; well-bred
menseless *adj.* rough, unmannerly
mercat *n.* market. *cf.* **mairket**
merch *v.* march. *cf.* **mairch**
merchan *n.* shopkeeper, retailer
merciment *n.* mercy; tolerance
merdle *n.* confused crowd of people or animals. *cf.* **mardle**
Merry Dancers *pr. n.* aurora borealis. *cf.* **Northern Lights**
mertyreese *v.* torture as a martyr
mervel *n.* marvel
messages *n. pl. in phr.* **go the messages** do the shopping
Mey *n.* month of May
micht *n.* might
michty me *excl. of surprise*
midden *n.* dunghill
midden-bree *n.* moisture from dunghill
midden-plunk *n.* wooden plank up which barrowload of dung could be wheeled up midden
midden-tap *n.* top of the dunghill
midder *n.* mother. *cf.* **mither**
middle *v.* meddle
middlin *adj., adv.* middling; fair(ly), moderate(ly), semi-
midgeck *n.* midge

midgie *n.* midge
midrig *n.* mid ridge
mids *n.* middle, midst; the open furrow between two ridges; a halfway point; *adv.* halfway
mildyow *n.* mildew
milk-broth *n.* dish made with milk and barley
milker *n.* milk cow
milkness *n.* the business of preparing milk (A2)
mill *See* **mull**
millert *See* **mullart**
milt *n.* spleen of an ox
mim, mim-like *adj.* prim
mim-mou'd *adj.* prim
min *n.* man (used as form of address); **hey, min!**
minaister *n.* minister (A2)
mind, min' *n.* mind; *v.* remember; remind
mink *n.* noose
minna *v. neg.* might not. *cf.* **mithna**
min(n)eer, mineerum *n.* great noise; fuss
minnie *n.* mother; pet name for a mother
minnon *n.* minnow; any small fresh-water fish
minse *See* **mense**
mint *n.* aim, intention; *v.* attempt, endeavour; *ppl.* **mintit** (C)
mirk *n.* darkness
mirky *adj.* smiling; merry
mirles, the *n. pl.* measles
mirra-hine, merry hyne *int.* off you go and good riddance
misca *v.* speak ill of; abuse; slander
mischeef *n.* mischief
miscomfit *v.* displease, offend;

disappoint (B1)

misdoot *v.* doubt, disbelieve

misfortnat *adj.* unfortunate

mishachlt *adj., ppl.* deformed; misshapen (B)

mishanter *n.* accident

mislippen *v.* neglect (A); mismanage; deceive (M); distrust (A2)

missaucre *v.* destroy, hurt severely

missie *n.* teacher

missionar *n.* missionary

mistaen *ppl.* mistaken

mistak *n.* mistake

misthrive *v.* fare badly; *ppl.* misthriven

mith *v.* might; **mithna, mithnin** might not. *cf.* **minna**

mither *n.* mother (A); **mither wit** native wit. *cf.* **midder**

Mither Tap *pr. n.* a peak of the hill, Bennachie

mitten *v.* grab hold of, seize

mixter *n.* mixture

mixter-maxter *adv.* in a state of confusion; *n.* mixture

mizzer, mizzor *n., v.* measure

mizzerment *n.* measurement

moch *n.* moth

moch-aeten *adj.* moth-eaten

moch-baas *n. pl.* moth balls

mochie *adj.* muggy, misty, damp; moth-eaten

moderate *v.* to preside at a Presbyterian Church court or at the election, calling or ordination of a minister

moderator *n.* one who presides at a Presbyterian Church court

modren *adj.* modern

moggan, moggin *n.* stocking (sometimes used as purse); footless stocking

moleskins *n. pl.* trousers of thick cotton

molie *n.* molecatcher

'mon *prep.* among

Monanday *n.* Monday (A)

moniment *n.* a spectacle

mony *adj.* many; **mony een** many a one

monyfaulds *n. pl.* entrails (consisting of many folds), intestines

moo *n.* large rick of hay or corn; **moo-bag** feeding-bag for horses; **moofae** mouthful; **moo o hairst** opening of harvest. *cf.* **mou**

moo-ban *v.* utter, articulate; mention (B1)

moocher *n.* scrounger

moold *n., v.* mould

mools *n. pl.* moulds; earth of a grave

moose *n.* mouse

moosewob *n.* cobweb

morn, the *adv.* tomorrow; **the morn's nicht** tomorrow night

mornin *n.* morning dram

mortifiet *adj., ppl.* humiliated

moss *n.* moor where peats are dug

mossin *n.* peat-cutting

mou *n.* mouth; **moufu** *n.* mouthful

moulter, mouter *n.* multure, miller's fee for grinding corn

mowdie(warp), mowdiewart *n.* mole

mowse *adj.* used in neg. **nae mowse, nae a mowse concairn** no joking matter; not safe; **nae**

mowse job no easy job
mowser *n.* moustache
moyen *n.* influence, means; *v.* accomplish by means; allure
muck *n.* dung; dirt; refuse; *v.* to clean a byre or stable; **muck the line** clear putrid bait from fishing line
muck-barra *n.* manure barrow
muckit *adj.* dirty
muckle *adj.* large; *adj., n., adv.* much
muckle-boukit pregnant (B1); burly; bulky
muddim *n.* madam
mudgeon *n.* facial expression; **he gied nae mudgeons he heard** (M2)
muggy, muggly *adj.* (of weather) drizzly and foggy
muir *n.* moor. *cf.* **meer**
muir-cock *n.* moorcock
muirlan *n.* moorland
muldoan, muldoon *n.* the basking shark
mulfa *n.* tinful *(deriv.* from **mill** a tin) (R)
mull *n.* meal- or threshing-mill; *n.* snuff-box; tin box with a lid; **snuff mull** snuff box. *cf.* **mill**
mullart, muller(t) *n.* miller

mullart's wird *n.* supposed secret password among millers
multiteed *n.* multitude
mum, mummle *v.* mumble
mump *v.* grumble
mune *n.* moon. *cf.* **meen**
munelicht *n.* moonlight
munsie *n.* the knave in cards; someone in a fix (B1); contemptible figure (A2)
munt *v.* mount
murgeon, murjin *n.* grimace. *cf.* **mudgeon**
murky *adj.* dark
murle *v.* crumble; **murly tuck** oatcakes crumbled into milk
murlin *n.* basket fitting into top of the fish-wife's creel
murn *v.* mourn
murnins *n. pl.* mourning clothes
musaeum *n.* museum
mutch *n.* woman's cap
mutchkin *n.* liquid measure equal to English pint
muther *n., v.* murder
muv *v.* move (B1). *cf.* **meeve**
myaakin *n.* hare. *cf.* **mawkin**
myaave *n.* seagull (Fraserburgh) (B)
myowte *n.* sound; whisper; murmur

— N —

na *adj., adv.* no. Also used to turn verb *neg. e.g.* **cudna, camna**
naarhan *adv.* nearly. *cf.* **nearhan**
nab *v.* seize; steal; take into custody
nabal *See* **nabble**

nabble *n.* churlish person; *adj.* ill-natured, churlish; grasping
nace *adj.* destitute
nackety *adj.* neat; *n.* a neat person
nacky *adj.* dexterous, adroit, skilful

nae *adj.* no, not; **nae een** no one;
  nae weel not well, ill
naehandy *pred. adj., adv.* a lot of;
  of great size; **there wis cyaaks
  naehandy, a queue naehandy**
naet *adj.* neat
naether *conj., pron., adj.* neither.
  cf. **nether, naither**
naething *n.* nothing
naewye *adv.* nowhere; on no
  account (S)
naftie, naphtie *n.* liquor (from Eng.
  naphtha)
nain, nown *adj.* own; **haud yer
  nain** hold your own; **yer nainsel**
  one's own self
nairra *adj.* narrow
nairra-myn(d)it *adj.* narrow-
  minded
naisty *adj.* nasty
naither *conj., pron., adj.* neither. *cf.*
  nether, naether
naithmost *adj.* undermost;
  naithmost wynin lower part of
  field (F)
naitional *adj.* national
naitral *adj.* natural
naitur *n.* nature
naitur-girss *n.* natural herbage
nakit *adj.* naked. *cf.* **nyaukit**
nammle *adj.* enamel (B)
nane *adv., pron.* none
napkin, naipkin *n.* pocket
  handkerchief
napper *n.* head
napron *n.* apron (B1)
nar *adj., adv.* near(ly); mean (B1)
na-say *n.* denial; refusal; *v.* deny,
  refuse
natheless *adv.* nevertheless

natur, Natur *n.* Nature. *cf.* **naitur**
navus-bore *n.* knot-hole in wood
near-beg(y)aun *adj.* miserly
near-beg(y)aunness *n.*
  niggardliness
nearhan *adv.* nearly; close by. *cf.*
  naarhan
neb *n.* beak; nose
necessar *adj.* necessary
nedder, nedderin *pron., conj.*
  neither
neebour *See* **neiper**
Neebra *pr. n.* village of Newburgh
  near Ellon
needcessity *n.* necessity, need
needsna *v. neg.* does not need
neen *pron.* none; *adv.* at all; **nae
  neen pleased**
neep *n.* turnip; *v.* to feed turnips
neep-click *n.* tool for pulling
  turnips (F)
neeper *See* **neiper**
neep-hasher *n.* implement for
  slicing turnips for fodder
neep-heid *n.* fool
neep(ie)-lantrin *n.* turnip-lantern
neep-pluck *n.* tool for pulling
  turnips (F). *cf.* **neep-click**
neep-reet *n.* land cleared of turnips
  for grain crop to follow (F)
neep-rinner *n.* old fashioned
  imple-ment for hoeing turnips
neep-rinnin *n.* turnip-hoeing
neep waatch *n.* turnip watch
neer-dee-weel *n.* ne'er-do-well
ne'er *adv.* never
neest, neesht *adj.* next. *cf.* **neist**
neffy *n.* nephew
negleat *v.* neglect (B1)
negleck *v.* neglect

neibour *See* **neiper**

neibourheid *n.* friendly relations between neighbours

neiper, neipor *n., v.* neighbour. *cf.* **neebour, neibour, neeper**

neiper-like *adj.* neighbourly

neist *adj.* next. *cf.* **neest**

neive *n.* fist; **neivefu** fistful; **steekit neives** clenched fists. *cf.* **nieve, niv**

nep *adj.* hairy (B)

nepkin *n.* napkin

nerra *adj. See* **nairra**

nervish *adj.* nervous

nether *conj., pron., adj.* neither. *cf.* **naither**

nettercap *n.* spider. *cf.* **ettercap**

neuk *n.* corner

neukit *adj.* having corners, crooked

new *adv.* newly

new-fangelt *adj.* newly invented; innovatory

newlins *adv.* newly, recently

news-gizzent *adj.* news-starved

news(e) *n., v.* chat

newsy *adj.* chatty; full of news

nib *n.* nose, beak. *cf.* **neb, niz, nob**

nibawa *adj.* snappy, crusty

nicher *n.* (of horses) neigh, whinny

nicht *n.* night

nicht-boun *adj.* overtaken by night

nick *n.* notch; *v.* make pregnant (B). *cf.* **bairn**

Nick, Aul *pr. n.* the Devil

nicket *adj.* disappointed

nickum *n.* mischievous boy

Nicky Cloots *pr. n.* the Devil

nicky-tams *n. pl.* buckled leather straps worn below the knee by farmworkers. *cf.* **waal-tams**

niev(e) *n.* fist. *cf.* **neive**

niffer *v.* to barter, bargain; exchange

nimp *n.* a very small part

nip *n.* advantage; speed; **deil a nip** not a bit (M2)

nippit *adj.* tight-fitting; curt in manner

nippock(ie) *n.* very small piece

nirl *v.* cause to shrink or shrivel; **nirlt** *ppl.* shrivelled

niv *See* **neive**

niver, nivver *adv.* never; **nivver een!** *excl.* certainly not!

niz *n.* nose (A). *cf.* **nib, nob**

nizzin *n.* drubbing; sharp reception

no *adv.* not (C1, G1, S). *cf.* **nae**; (used as interrogative after positive statement) isn't he, hasn't it etc. (A2)

nob *n.* nose (A). *cf.* **nib, niz**

nocht *n.* nought, nothing

nochtie *n.* puny in size. *cf.* **noughtie**

nominat *ppl.* nominated

non *n.* name given in mid 18th century to non-intrusion section of the Church of Scotland

noo *adv.* now; **noo an than** now and then; *also* **noo an aan, noos an aans**

nooadays *adv.* nowadays

nor *conj., quasi-prep.* than

norlan *adj.* northland

Noroway *pr. n.* Norway

noshun *n.* notion, idea; **noshun o** romantic fancy for; liking for

nosy-wax *n.* simpleton (B1)

not, nott *v. pt., ppls.* needing, needed; had to; **notna** did not

need
notice *v.* take care of (A1)
notionate *adj.* opinionative
noughtie *adj.* puny, trifling. *cf.*
  nochtie
nown *adj.* own
nowt *n.* (collective) neat, cattle;
  (sing.) an ox, steer (A1)

nummer *n.* number
nyaakit *adj.* naked. *cf.* **nyaukit**
nyatter *v.* speak fretfully, angrily;
  grumble (A, M1)
nyattery *adj.* peevish, grumbling,
  ill-tempered
nyaukit *adj.* naked. *cf.* **nyaakit**
nyod *excl.* euphemism for God

— O —

o, o' *prep.* of; on; **o' the tae han, o'
  the tither** on the one hand, on
  the other
obaidient *adj.* obedient
objeck *n., v.* object
obleege *v.* oblige
occupee *v.* occupy
och *excl.* oh
ocht *n.* aught, anything; *v.* **ought**;
  ochtna ought not
od *excl.* God
odder *adj., n., pron.* other. *cf.* **ither**
odds *n.* difference
o'ercome *n.* burden of a discourse
o'erleuk *v.* overlook
oes *n. pl.* grand-children (M)
o'ertak *v.* overtake
offeeshyat *v.* officiate
offen *v.* offend
offisher *n.* officer
oilie *n.* fisherman's oilskin frock
  (B); oil lamp
'oman *n.* woman. *cf.* **umman**
on *conj.* (used with *pt. ppl.*)
  without; **on-been** without being;
  on-hed without having; **on-deen**
  without doing
on *prep.* **on aboot** talking about;

on for keen on; in the mood for;
  far on, weel on tipsy
on- *prefix.* un- (C). *See* **oon-**
on-cairry *n.* carry-on
ondeemas *adj.* extraordinary
onding *n.* a heavy fall of rain or
  snow
ongaun *n.* activity; *in pl.*
  proceedings
ongauns *n.* goings-on
ongrutten *adj.* without shedding
  tears
onleet *adv.* without a word of a lie
onless *conj.* unless
onmynit (o) *adj.* unmindful (of)
ontill, oontill *conj.* till; *prep.* on to
ontirin *adj.* untiring
onwal *adj.* annual
onwuttin *adj.* unaware, abstracted
ony *adv., pron.* any; *adv.* at all; **gin
  it's ony weet** if it's wet at all
onybody *n., pron.* anybody
onyeen *n., pron.* anyone
onyroad *adv.* anyway
onything *n., pron.* anything
onywye *adv.* anyway; anywhere;
  anyhow
oo *n.* wool

oof *n.* Moray Firth name for the
monkfish. *cf.* **caithick**
ook, ouk *n.* week
ool *v.* treat harshly; *ppl.* **oolt**
oolet *n.* owl (A)
oonbapteest *adj.* unbaptised
ooncanny *adj.* uncanny; dangerous
ooncarin *adj.* uncaring
oonchancie *adj.* uncanny; risky, not
safe to meddle with
ooncommon *adj.* uncommon
oonder *prep.* under. *cf.* **ooner**
oondergrun *adj., adv.* underground
oondevallin *adj.* unceasing
oondisjeestit *adj.* undigested
oondootitly *adv.* undoubtedly
oonendin *adj.* unending
ooner *prep.* under. *cf.* **oonder**
oonerstan *v.* understand
oonertakin *n.* undertaking
oonexpeckit *adj.* unexpected
oonfashed *adj.* untroubled
oonfeelin *adj.* unfeeling
oonfersell *adj.* lacking energy
oongrutten *adj.* not wept over
oonhandy *adj.* unhandy
oonhappy *adj.* unhappy
oonheedin *adj.* unheeding
oonhonesty *n.* dishonesty
oonjustice *n.* injustice
oonkent *adj.* unknown
oonlawfu *adj.* unlawful
oonless *conj.* unless
oonmynit o *adj.* unmindful of
oonnaitral *adj.* unnatural;
supernatural
oonprenciplt *adj.* unprincipled
oonrichteous *adj.* unrighteous
oonslockened *adj.* unquenched
oonstable *adj.* unstable

oontill *conj.* till
oontirin *adj.* untiring
oonwaashen *ppl., adj.* unwashed
oonweel *adj.* unwell
oonwullin *adj.* unwilling
oonwuttin *adj.* unaware, abstracted
oor *n.* hour; *adj.* our
oorie *adj.* eerie; dismal
oorlich *adj.* (of people) miserable-
looking from cold, hunger etc; (of
weather) dull and cold;
melancholy; *n.* starved-looking,
stunted person
oorly *adv.* hourly
oors *pron.* ours
oorsels *pron.* ourselves; *pred. adj.,
adv.* by ourselves, alone
oot *adv., prep.* out; **oot amint** out
of things; **oot amon** *prep.* out of;
oot the door facing ruin; **oot o
han** beyond control; **oot wi** out
of favour with; **oot-win** wind off
the sea; **oot o yer box** out on the
tiles
ootbrak *n.* outbreak
oot-by *adv.* outside; out in the
fields; out and a little way off;
adj. out of the way; distant
oot-cry *v.* protest
ootfeedle *n.* outfield
ootgang *n.* outgoing, departure *e.g.*
from a tenancy at end of season
oothoose *n.* outhouse
ootlat *n.* outlet; expression
ootlay, ootlie *n.* outlay
ootlin *n.* stranger; outcast
ootmaist *adj.* outmost
ootower, -owre *prep.* out and over;
out of; **ootower the cairt**
oots-an-ins *n. pl.* hairpins

oots wi *v.* take(s) out
ootwith, -wuth *adj., adv.* outward;
 adv. outwardly, fully
opeenion *n.* opinion
opingan *n.* opinion
or *conj., prep.* before; until
ordeen *v.* ordain
ordinar *adj.* ordinary
orpiet *adj.* peevish, querulous (A2)
orra *adj.* odd; idle, worthless;
 shabby
orra-beaster *n.* the man who
 worked the odd horse on a farm
 (T)
orra loon *adj., n.* boy who did odd
 jobs on farm
orrals *n.* anything left over, refuse
orra man *adj., n.* man who did odd
 jobs on farm; wire-tightening
 lever (F)
orra wark *adj., n.* odd jobs
ou *excl.* oh
ouk *n.* week; **this day ouk** a week
 today. *cf.* **ook**
ousel *n.* blackbird (M)
overly *adj.* incidental

ow awa *excl. of sympathy*
owdience *n.* audience
ower, owre *adv., prep.* over; **ower
 the heids o** because of
owercassen *adj.* (of the weather)
 overcast
owercome *n.* a frequently repeated
 phrase or theme; burden or
 message
owergaan *n.* severe reproof; close
 examination
owergae *v.* go over; pass (through
 or over)
owergeen *adv.* (of time) past
owerlay *v.* overlay, cover over
owernicht *adv.* overnight
owersman *n.* person with authority
 over others
own *v.* admit
owse *n.* ox; *pl.* **owsen**
owthereese *v.* authorise
oxter *n.* armpit; bosom; *v.* embrace;
 oxterfu, oxterlift *n.* armful
oxter-pooch *n.* inside pocket
oxter-staff, -stav *n.* crutch

— **P** —

paal *n.* mooring post or bollard
Pace *See* **Pase**
pack-merchants *n. pl.* small
 scudding clouds
paewae *adj.* sickly, unwell (T)
pailace *n.* palace
pair, pairie *n.* pair of horse
pairis *n.* parish
pairl *n.* pearl
pairt *n.* part; *v.* part; divide; **pairt
 oot** *v.* share-out (S)
pairtin *n.* share-out; parting; *ppl.*
 parting
pairtner *n.* partner
pairtrick *n.* partridge (M, C). *cf.*
 paitrick
pairty *n.* party
paitrick *n.* partridge (S, M1). *cf.*
 pairtrick
palaiver *n.* (of a person) show-off

palin *n.* paling, stake fence

pammer *v.* walk about aimlessly, saunter; stamp around noisily. *cf.* **paumer**

pang *v.* cram

pan loaf *adj.* loaf with hard crust; *fig.* affected way of speaking

pap *n.* teat; sea anemone

Pape *n.* the Pope

park *n.* field (A). *cf.* **fiedle**

parley *n.* period of truce in games, after the cry **parleys-on**

parritch *n.* porridge (J)

partan *n.* the common crab

parteeclar *adj.* particular

Pase *n.* Easter. *cf.* **Pess, Pesch**

pass *n.* passage

passin *prep.* more than

pat *n.* pot; small ball of butter; *v. pt.* put; **pat tee** put by, put aside

patcher *n.* turnip-seed sowing device (F)

Patie *n.* deriv. from Peter

pattren *n.* pattern

pawky *adj.* shrewd; sly

pawmie *n.* a stroke on the palm with a **tawse** or cane (J)

pawrent *n.* parent

pawtron *n.* patron

pawtronage *n.* patronage

pawtronise *v.* patronise

peanny *n.* piano

pech *v.* pant

peek *v.* cheep; complain; **peekin-eevie** discontented girl

peel *n.* pill; pool

peel-an-aet tatties *n. pl.* potatoes boiled in their skins and peeled just before eating

peelie-wally *adj.* sickly

peelin *n.* skin; thrashing

peen *n.* pane of glass

peenge *v.* complain, whine

peenie *n.* pinafore

peer *adj.* poor. *cf.* **puir**

peerie *n.* spinning top

peer(s)-hoose *n.* work-house

peerman *n.* holder for fir candle

peer-man *n.* wire-tightening lever in fencing (F)

peer wi *v.* match, equal

peesie(weep) *n.* lapwing (S). *cf.* **pee-weet**

peetifu *adj.* pitiful

peetrol *n.* petrol

peety *n., v.* pity

pee-weet *n.* lapwing (M, R). *cf.* **peesie**

pelt *n.* trash, rubbish

peltin-pyock *n.* worthless rag

pend, pen(n) *n.* arch; arched passageway or entry, esp. one leading from the street into a back court

penner *n.* penholder

pensy *adj.* (would be) stately

pent (rhymes with hint) *n., v.* paint

perjink *adj.* precise; neat in appearance; prim; fussy

perlyaag *n.* rubbish; mixture of odds and ends, esp. rubbishy food; goodies (B1)

pernickety *adj.* very particular; over-fastidious

perswaad *v.* persuade

perteen *v.* pertain

Pesch (A1) *See* **Pase, Pess**

peshifie *v.* pacify (B1)

Pess *n.* Easter (M1). *cf.* **Pase**

peter *in phr.* **pit the peter on** bring

to a sudden stop, bring up short

pey *n., v.* pay

peyed-thankless *adj.* ungrateful (B)

peymen *n.* payment

phizog *n.* face

physeeshun *n.* physician, doctor

picher *n.* nervous excitement (B1)

picht *n.* Pict; small person

pick *n.* small quantity

picker *n.* lever for removing staples

pickiesae *n.* hat similar to deerstalker (T)

pick-mirk *adj., n.* pitch-dark

pickthank *adj.* ungrateful. *cf.* pykethank

picter, pictur *n.* picture

piece *n.* portable snack

pig(gie) *n.* pitcher; earthenware jar; stone hot-water bottle

pike *n.* frost-nail. *See* **pyke**

pilget *n.* fight, struggle, plight; **in a pilget wi pain** (B1)

pilk *v.* pilfer

pilla *n.* pillow

pilpert *n.* cold, badly fed child (B1)

pin *n.* clothes peg

pine *n.* pain. *cf.* **pyne**

pint *n., v.* (near rhyme with hint); paint; *v.* (rhyming with Eng. pint) point; *n.* (rhyming with Eng. pint) shoe-lace. *cf.* **pynt**

pint stoup *n.* drinking vessel with a handle containing a Scots pint

pirl *v.* poke, stir; trifle; *intr.* ripple

pirn *n.* reel on which yarn or thread is wound

pirn-taed *adj.* pigeon-toed

pirr *n.* sudden burst of activity; **on the pirr**

pirr-winnie *n.* breeze

pish *v.* urinate

pit *v.* put; *ppl.* **pitten; tae pit past** put away; **pit, pitten oot** put out, discomfitted, worried (A1); **tae pit aboot** to inconvenience

pitawtie *n.* potato (B1)

piz *n. pl.* peas

piz-meal, pizzers *n.* pease-meal

place *n.* laird's residence

plack *n.* small coin (J)

plaid *n.* long piece of woollen cloth with chequered or tartan pattern, outer article of Highland dress, worn over the shoulder; as above, used as a blanket

plaik *n.* plaything (M1)

plaise *v.* please (S)

plaised *adj.* pleased (C1, G1, S)

plaister *n.* plaster

planesteens *n.* pavement

plank *v.* place, lay

plantin *n.* plantation

plashie, plash fluke *n.* plaice

playgreen *n.* playground

playgrun *n.* playground

pleast *adj.* pleased. *cf.* **plaised**

pleece *n.* police

pleege *v.* plague (B1)

pleesint *adj.* pleasant

pleesur, pleesure *n.* pleasure

pleiter *See* **plowter**

plenish *v.* furnish a house; stock a farm

pleuch *n.* plough (A, M1). *cf.* **ploo**

pleura *n.* pleuro-pneumonia

plicht *n.* plight

plisky *n.* mischievous trick; plight (B1)

plivver *n.* plover (A1)

plizzant *adj.* pleasant

ploiter *n., v. See* **plowter**

ploitery *adj.* wet; muddy

ploo *n.* plough; **ploo-feathers** projecting wing on the share of a plough, which cuts out the furrow; **ploo-sock** ploughshare; **ploo-stilts** plough handles, sock of plough which cuts out the furrow

plook *n.* pimple

plooky *adj.* pimply

plooman *n.* ploughman

plot *v.* scald; burn, scorch

plottin *adj.* very hot

plowt *n.* blow, punch

plowter *n.* act of working or walking in mud or water; *v.* splash in mud or water, squelch; work messily; potter. *cf.* **pleiter, ploiter**

ploy *n.* frolic, escapade

pluff *v.* shoot (peas) through a tube

plump-churn *n.* plunge churn (F)

plunk *n.* plank of wood

plunkie *n.* homemade sweetmeat made with treacle or syrup and flour (A2)

plyaak *n.* toy (A1, A2)

plype *v.* fall *plump* into water

plyper *v.* walk in mud or water

pock, poke *n.* bag. *cf.* **powk, pyock** pocket (J). *cf.* **pooch**

poddick *n.* frog (G). *cf.* **puddock**

points *n. pl.* shoe-laces. *cf.* **pints**

poleetics *n.* politics

politeeshun *n.* politician

pollis *n.* police (J)

pom-pom *n.* the Field Marshall diesel tractor, the nickname deriv. from sound of engine

pooch *n., v.* pocket

poochle *See* **puchal**

pooder *n.* powder; **lattin oot the pooder** divulging the secret

pooer *n.* power; **pooer o pot an gallows** the old feudal power to hang or drown (A2)

poond *n.* pound sterling (J). *cf.* **pund**

poopit *n.* pulpit

poor *v.* pour

poortith *n.* poverty

pooshan, pooshin *n., v.* poison. *cf.* **pushion**

pooshinous *adj.* poisonous

poother-deevil *n.* primitive home-made firework

porritch *n. pl.* porridge *(takes pl. v.). cf.* **pottich**

port *n.* lively tune on the bagpipes

poseetion *n.* position

postie *n.* postman

potestatur *n.* prime

pot fit *n.* one of the feet of a cauldron; **stick oot like a pot fit** stick out like a sore thumb

potterlow *n.* ruined condition; unsightly mess; **geen tae potter-low** gone to pot, completely spoiled

pottich *n. pl.* porridge (A1); **he made his pottich an suppit them.** *cf.* **porritch**

pottiestattur *etc. See* **potestatur**

pottit-heid *n.* dish made from head of ox or pig, boiled to a jelly

poun *n.* pound sterling

pow *n.* poll; head

powk *n.* bag. *cf.* **pock, poke;** *v.* poke

powster *n.* posture; position, situation

practeese *v.* practise

praisent *n.* present

pran *v.* crush; hurt severely or fatally

preceese(ly) *adj., adv.* precisely

precent *v.* lead the psalmody in a Presbyterian church

precunnance *n.* condition; footing

pree *v.* taste; experience

preef *n.* proof. *cf.* **pruif**

preen *n., v.* pin

preen-heidit *adj.* pin-headed; unintelligent

preevilege *n.* privilege

prefairrance *n.* preference

prefar *v.* prefer

prejudeece *n.* prejudice

prence *n.* prince

prenciple *n.* principle

prent *n., v.* print

press *n.* wall-cupboard

prick *v. intr.* (of cattle) to stampede, to escape insect bites

pridefu *adj.* proud (J). *cf.* **prood**

prig *v.* plead

'Prile *n.* April; **'Prile eeran** April (fool's) errand

prile *n.* three cards of equal value, *e.g.* **a prile o queens** (B)

primpit *adj.* prim (R)

prob *v.* to pierce, prod; release gas from stomach of cattle by piercing

prodeegious *adj.* prodigious

projeck *n.* project

pron *n.* residue of oat husks and oatmeal left over after the milling process, bran

prood *adj.* proud

prop *n.* ploughing marker (F); landmark or memorial

prophesiet *v. pt.* prophesied

proteck *v.* protect

protick *n.* rash or idle adventure; bit of mischief

protty *adj.* pretty; **a protty penny**

proveesions *n. pl.* provisions

pruif *n.* proof. *cf.* **preef**

pruv, pruve *v.* prove

pu *v.* to pull

puchal, puchil *adj.* reserved, proud; self-important (A2). *cf.* **poochle**

puckle *n.* a small quantity, some

puddle *v.* play with hands or feet in water

puddick, puddock *n.* frog; flat wooden platform for transporting heavy loads on farms

puddock's eggs *n. pl.* nickname for sago or tapioca pudding

puddock-steel *n.* toadstool

puggled *ppl.* worn out

puir *adj., n.* poor

pule *n.* seagull (Gardenstown) (B)

pul-throwe *n.* cord with which cleaning rag is pulled through rifle

pultice *n.* poultice

pump *v.* break wind behind

pumphel *n.* pen for cattle; square church pew

pun, pund *n.* pound (in weight)

punctwal *adj.* punctual

purchase *n.* a hold or grip

purpie *adj.* purple

pushion *See* **pooshan**

putt *v.* push, shove; **ae putt an row**

a hard struggle
putten *ppl.* put; sent
pye *n.* a counting-out rhyme in children's games and the serving of food; **say a pye**
pyke *v.* pick; steal; **pyke their pooch** cost them a lot; *n.* spike (of a railing etc). *cf.* **pike**
pykethank *See* **pickthank**
pykit *ppl.* spiked
pykit weer *n., ppl.* barbed wire (F).

cf. **barbit-weer**
pyne *n.* pain. *cf.* **pine**
pyner *n.* animal suffering pain (M2)
pyocher *n.* troublesome cough; *v.* to clear the throat
pyock *See* **poke** *etc.*
pyooch *v.* cough
pyot *n.* magpie
pyshon *See* **pooshan**

— Q —

quaet *adj.* quiet. *cf.* **quait**
quaetness *n.* quietness, peace
quaich *n.* drinking cup with two handles
quaikin-aish *n.* aspen
quait *adj.* quiet. *cf.* **quaet**
quake, quaik *n.* heifer
quarterer *n.* tramp with quarters on the farm in exchange for farm work (F)
quat *v.* quit; stop what one is doing
queed *n.* cud
queeger *n.* mess, muddle; mixture
queel *adj., v.* cool
Queenie arabs *n. pl.* inhabitants of the Queenie (Keith Inch) in

Peterhead (B)
queet *n.* ankle
queetikins *n.* gaiters. *cf.* **cuitikins**
quern *n.* stone hand-mill
queyn, quine *n.* girl
quig *n.* mix up
quigger *n.* mess, muddle; mixture
quile *n.* coal; burning coal
quine *n.* girl
quinkins *n. pl.* something of no value
quirky *adj.* tricky
quisson *n.* question
quite *See* **quyte**
quo *v.* quoth
quyte *n.* coat; petticoat. *cf.* **kwite**

— R —

raa *adj.* raw
raan *n.* fish roe
rackle *n.* chain of tin pipe-lid
rackon *v.* reckon
rade *v. pt.* rode. *See also* **redd**
rael *adj., adv.* real; really

raelly *adv.* really
raeper *n.* reaper; **tiltin-raeper** reaping-machine, requiring a man to knock off the sheaves with a rake
raff *n.* riff-raff

raffy *adj.* plentiful (M); *n.* a rank growth (A1)

ragie *adj.* raging; scolding

raggit *adj.* ragged

raggit-robin *n.* (flower) *lychnis flos-cuculi* (S)

raiffle *See* **reffle**

raik *v.* to rake; roam about; reck, care; **fat raiks?** what does it signify? (A2). *cf.* **rake**

raikins *See* **rakins**

raip *n.* rope. *cf.* **rape**

raise *v.* excite, infuriate, madden; **raise din** make trouble; **raise him wull** drive him crazy

raise *v. pt.* got up

raise-o-the-win *n.* a stroke of good luck (T)

raist *adj.* excited, angry

raith *n.* quarter of a year; term at school

raither *adv.* rather. *cf.* **redder**

raivel *v.* entangle; wander in speech

raivelt *adj.* tangled; mentally confused

raiverie *n.* rumour (M2)

rake *n.* great energy; **cam mair rake** worked faster, with more energy; *v.* search; range, stray; roam, wander

rakins *n.* gathering of loose hay or strands of corn which escape the reaping-machine

rally (on) *v.* scold; speak angrily to

rammack *n.* rough piece of wood; worthless article

rammy *n.* uproar

rampauge *n.* fury, rage; *v.* to rage

ramsh *adj.* hasty, rash

ramshackle *adj.* disorderly; un-methodical; thoughtless; head-strong

ranagant *n.* wild, loose-living person (B1); good-for-nothing

ran-dan *n.* carouse; rumpus (A); **oot on the ran-dan**

randy *n.* virago; loose-tongued woman

ranegill *adj.* renegade; rough character; criminal

rank *v.* get ready, esp. dress to go out

rank oot *v.* bring out, look out in preparation

rant *n.* lively tune

ranter *v.* mend, stitch; put together

rantletree *n.* the beam across the chimney from which the **crook** is suspended

rantree *n.* rowan tree, mountain ash

rape *n.* rope, esp. of straw. *cf.* **raip**

rare *adj.* excellent

rase *v. pt.* rose

rash *n.* rush

rauchle *adj.* noisy, clamorous

rave *v. pt.* tore. *cf.* **rive**

raw *n.* row

rawn-tree *n.* mountain ash. *cf.* **rowan, rodden, raantree**

rax *v.* stretch; hand

readin-sweetie *n.* conversation lozenge

ream *n.* cream; *v.* foam; buzz (of thoughts); overflow; **reamin fu** brimming

rebat *v.* retort; speak again

recaipt *n.* recipe

reck *v.* to take heed of

recreet *v.* recuperate

redd *v.* clear out, to rid; **redd yer**

throat clear your throat; **redd yer crap** get something off your chest

redd up *v.* clear up; (a person) criticise

redd *ppl., adj.* rid; **wun redd o** get rid of

redd *adj., adv.* read(il)y, willing(ly); **as redd wark as nae**

reddance *n.* riddance

redder *adv.* rather. *cf.* **raither**

rede *v.* advise (J)

red-lan *n.* ploughed land

ree *n.* enclosure; hen run

reed *adj.* red. *cf.* **reid**; *n.* rood by measurement

reed-het *adj.* red-hot

reef *n.* roof; **reef a ditch** roof a ditch, vacate your home with no other to go to (T)

reek *n., v.* smoke. *cf.* **rik; reek-bouk** belch of smoke (R)

reek-hen *n.* a hen exacted for every reeking chimney or inhabited house

reem *n.* cream

reemis(h) *n.* resounding crash, din, clatter; *v.* rummage

reemishin *v. n.* uproar; clatter

reenge *v.* range, roam

reerie *n.* row; **kick up a reerie**

reesle, reeshsle *v.* rustle; hustle noisily

reest *n.* roost; *v. intr.* roost; sit; refuse to move; *v. tr.* arrest; bring to a halt; **reest the fire** bank up the fire. *cf.* **reist**

reet *n.* root; **the reet an the rise o't** beginning and end of it (M2); the whole story, affair

reeve *v. pt.* tore. *cf.* **rive**

reevin *adj.* (of wind) high, strong; (of fire) burning brightly

reeze *n.* high praise; *v.* praise

refar *v.* refer

refeese *v.* refuse

reffle *v.* ransack

regaird *n., v.* regard

reglar *adj.* regular

reid *adj.* red; **a reid een** a new net (B); **reid fish** the salmon (this being a taboo word at sea). *cf.* **reed**

reid-biddy *n.* mixture of cheap red wine and methylated spirit or other alcohol

reid-cheekit *adj.* red-cheeked

reid-heidit *adj.* red-headed

reid-kaimed *adj.* red-combed

reist *v.* roost; sit; bank up a fire. *cf.* **reest**

reistin *adj.* restive

reive *v.* to plunder

releegion *n.* religion

releegious *adj.* religious

remeid *n.* remedy

remis *See* **reemis**

remorse *v.* express regret about; repent (A2)

repoort *n., v.* report

repree *v.* reprove

requar, requair *v.* require

respeck *n., v.* respect

retour *n.* a renewal, replacement

reuch *adj.* rough (J). *cf.* **roch**

revarse *n.* reverse

reverie (B1) *See* **raiverie**

reyn *n.* rain. *cf.* **ryne**

ribbet *n.* rabbit (S). *cf.* **rubbit**

richt *adj., n., v.* right; **richtit**

righted

richteous *adj.* righteous

rickle *n.* loose heap or stack *(e.g.* of peats set up to dry)

rickmatick *n.* concern, affair; collection

riddel *n.* sieve

rideeclous *adj.* ridiculous

riever *n.* thief

rift *n., v.* belch

rig *n.* ridge; section of a field; practical joke; **play a rig** play a trick; *v.* to dress

riggin *n.* ridge, roof; head, skull; **riggin o the nicht** middle of the night

riggit-oot *adj.* all set; equipped (S)

rig-lamb *n.* male lamb with only one descended testicle (T)

riglin *n.* animal with testicle undescended

rig oot *n.* outfit; *v.* prepare (a ship for the fishing season) (B)

rik *n.* smoke. *cf.* **reek**

rime *n.* hoar-frost

rim-rax *n.* a good feed (B1)

rin *v.* run; (of a cow) be in heat (F)

rine *n.* rein. *cf.* **ryne**

ringel-een *n.* wall-eyes

rink *v.* clamber; range about noisily

rinnins *n.* main outlines

rin oot *n.* urination

rint *n.* rent

rin-the-wuddie *n.* fugitive from the gallows

rin-watter *n.* natural flow of water, esp. one which will drive a mill-wheel without a dam; *fig.* just enough money to pay one's way

ripp *n.* a handful of unthreshed corn or hay

ripper *n.* hand-line for catching cod

ripper-yole *n.* yawl used for ripper-fishing

rippit *n.* uproar (M, B1)

rise *n.* joke at someone's expense; **hae a rise oot o, tak the rise o** play a trick on

risp *v.* rasp

rist *n.* rest

rive *n.* tear; bite, large mouthful; *v.* pull forcibly; burst asunder; tear; **rivven** *ppl.* pulled apart

rizzar *n.* redcurrant

rizzon *n.* reason

rizzonable *adj.* reasonable

roadit *adv.* on the road, on one's way; **get roadit** set off

roasen, roassen *ppl.* roasted; *adj.* roasting hot

Rob(bie) *pr. n.* dim. of Robert

robsorby *n.* a make of scythe, synonymous with the implement (T)

roch *adj.* rough

roch an richt *phr.* rough in manners

rock *n.* distaff

rockin *n.* evening gathering of neighbours with **rock** and spindles; a spinning-bee (M)

rocky-on *n.* sea-shore game involving a stone cairn (B)

rodden *n.* mountain-ash (berry)

rodden-, roddin-tree *n.* mountain ash or rowan

rogie *n.* little rogue, term of endearment for a child

rone *n.* a slide

Room *pr. n.* Rome (A2)

room, the *n.* the best room in a small house

roon *adv., prep.* round

roon-shoodert *adj.* round-shouldered

roose *v.* rouse (to anger); salt herring

rooser *n.* watering-can

Roosian *n.* rabbit (Russian)

roosin-tub *n.* tub in which herring were salted

roost *n., v.* rust

roosty *adj.* rusty. *cf.* **rousty**

rosit *n.* resin; **rositie** resinous; **rositie eyn** resined thread used for sewing leather

rottack *n.* useless, discarded object; *pl.* lumber, junk

rottan *n.* rat

rounder *n.* an ungutted fish

roup *n., v.* auction

roup oot *v.* sell up by auction

roupy *adj.* hoarse

roust *v.* roar, bellow (also of animals)

roust *v.* rust. *cf.* **roost**

roustin *adj.* rusting;

rousty *adj.* rusty. *cf.* **roosty**

routh (o) *n.* plenty (of); *adj.* abundant. *cf.* **rowth**

rowe *v.* roll; wheel (a barrow)

rowie *n.* a morning roll

rowle *n., v.* rule

rowler *n.* ruler

rowt *v.* (of cattle) bellow, roar (G1)

rowth (o) *n.* plenty (of). *cf.* **routh**

royd, royt *adj.* (of children) wild, unruly, capering

rozet *n.* resin; cobbler's wax. *cf.* **rosit**

rubbit *n.* rabbit

ruck *n.* rick, stack; **het ruck** steaming stack built before crop has dried out; **thackit ruck** stack thatched for the winter; **wattert ruck** badly built and porous (T)

ruck-foon *n.* stack foundation

ruck-ledder *n.* stack ladder

ruck-post *n.* wooden support for off-centre stack

rug *n.* high profit, bargain perhaps to the seller's disadvantage (A1); tug; *v.* pull sharply, tug

rumigumshun (A1) *See below*

rum(mil)-gumption *n.* common sense (M1)

rummle *v.* rumble; *ppl.* rummlin

runch *n.* wild radish (F)

rung *n.* heavy staff

runk *n.* old, outworn animal; contemptuous term for a woman of ill repute

runklt *ppl., adj.* wrinkled. *cf.* **wrunklt**

runt *n.* withered hag, m. or f.

runtit (o) *ppl., adj.* having lost all (as in the game of marbles); completely deprived of

ryne *n.* rein. *cf.* **rine**

rype *v.* ransack, rifle; steal

— S —

's *pron.* his; **aff o's maet** off his
food
sa, saa *v. pt.* saw
saabre *n.* sabre
saach *n.* willow. *cf.* **sauch**
saadist *n.* sawdust
saan *n.* sand
saar *n.* savour
saarless *adj.* tasteless, insipid. *cf.*
saurless
sab *v.* sob
sae *adv., conj.* so
saeven *adj.* seven. *cf.* **seyven**
saeventy *adj.* seventy
saff *adj.* safe
saft *adj.* soft; weak; simple
saftie *n.* weak(-minded) person;
slipper (G). *cf.* **softie**
saftness *n.* softness
saick *n.* sack; **a saickfu o sair
beens** a hiding
saicret *n.* secret
saiddle *n.* saddle
saiddler *n.* saddler
sailary *n.* salary
sair *adj., n.* sore; *adv.* sorely, badly;
very much, greatly; **sair aff**
badly off, hard up; **sair awa wi't**
worn out; in a bad state; **sair
come at** far gone, worn out; **sair
dung** hard-pressed; **sair fecht**
hard struggle; **sair heid**
headache; **sair hert** sad heart;
sair made hard pressed; **sair on**
hard on (clothes etc.)
sair *v.* serve; satisfy (esp. with

food/drink) (M1); satiate, sate;
sair maetit well-fed (A1); **weel-
sairt** well satisfied with food or
drink; **ill-sairt** not having had
enough; **sick sairt** satiated. *cf.*
ser
sairgint *n.* sergeant
sair-heidie *n.* sponge-cake in paper
cup
sairin *n.* serving, helping; deserts;
fill; **she got her sairin o't**
sairious *adj.* serious. *cf.* **sarious**
sairly *adv.* badly
sairs *n.* ailments
Saiterday, Setturday *n.* Saturday
saitisfie *v.* satisfy, *ppl.* **saitisfiet**
saiven *adj.* seven
sal *See* **saul**
sall *v.* shall. *cf.* **saul**
salvenda (B1) *See* **solvendo**
sang *excl.* blood!
sang *n.* song
san-gless *n.* hour-glass
sanna *v. neg.* shall not
sanshach *adj.* saucy; disdainful;
irritable
sant *n.* saint
santifie *v.* sanctify
santly *adj.* saintly
sappy *adj.* moist, full of juice;
heavy in the water, laden with
fish (B); **sappy sodjers** ball
game
saps *n.* bread with milk and sugar
sarious *adj.* serious. *cf.* **sairious**
sark *n.* shirt; chemise

sarket, sarkit *n.* undershirt; shirt or jersey
sate *n.* seat
satteral *adj.* stiff; tart
sattle *v.* settle
sauchen *adj.* unsociable
saugh *n.* willow; **saugh-wans** willow wands. *cf.* **saach**
saughy *adj.* abounding in willows
saul *n.* soul; also used as *excl.*; *ppl.* sold
Sauners *pr. n.* Alexander
saurless *adj.* tasteless; spiritless
saut *n.* salt; **wirth saut till his kail** worth his salt
saut-backet *n.* salt-box
sauter *n.* salter; one who can do severe things
sautie *adj.* tasting of salt
sautie-bannocks *n.* oatmeal pancakes
saut-lick *n.* salt brick for cattle (T)
saw *n.* salve, ointment; *v.* sow (S)
Sawboth *n.* Sabbath
sawer *n.* sower
sawna *v. pt. neg.* did not see
Sawney *pr. n.* deriv. of Alexander
Sawtan *pr. n.* Satan
sax *adj.* six; **sax-pair toon** farm with six pairs of horses
saxpence *n.* sixpence
saxteen *adj.* sixteen
saxty *adj.* sixty
say-awa *n.* discourse, narrative, monologue
scaa *n.* barnacle. *cf.* **scaw**
scaad *v.* scald
scabbie *adj.* scabbed
scabbit *adj.* scabby; shabby
scadden *n.* person of spare figure;

contemptuous term for person or thing
scaffy *n.* street-sweeper
scaith *n.* injury; damage
scalder *n.* stinging jellyfish
scam *n.* singe, scorch; scald slightly. *cf.* **scaum**
scance *v.* scan; *n.* a look
scarecraw *n.* scarecrow
scart *n., v.* scratch (A). *cf.* **scrat**
scashle *n., v.* quarrel
scaul *v.* scold; *n.* a scold; scolding
scaum *v.* singe, scorch, scald slightly. *cf.* **scam**
scaup *n.* thin, poor soil; bank of mud or soil exposed at low tide
scaur *n.* bare place on side of hill; cliff
scavie *n.* mishap (B1)
scaw *See* **scaa**
schaim *n.* scheme
scholar *n.* school pupil
schule *n.* school (J)
scienteefic *adj.* scientific
sclaff *n., v.* stroke
sclaffert *n.* a stroke with the palm of the hand; slap
sclait *n.* slate. *cf.* **sklate**
sclaive *See* **sclave**
sclap *v.* walk in flat-footed or shuffling way. *cf.* **sclaup**
sclarry *v.* daub, smear (J)
sclaup *See* **sclap**
sclave *n.* gossip, scandal-monger; *v.* spread a story by gossip
sclaver (M2) *See* **sclave** *v.*
sclim *v.* climb. *cf.* **clim**
scob *v.* put in splints
scomfish *v.* suffocate (A1)
scoof *n.* quick swig; *v.* swallow

food or drink quickly. *cf.* **scowf**

scool *v.* scowl

scoon(e)ral *n.* scoundrel

scoor *v.* scour

scoorin-buird *n.* scrubbing-board

scooshle *v.* shuffle

scoot *n.* term of contempt applied to
man or woman

scooth *n.* scope. *cf.* **scowth**

score, over the *phr.* beyond what is
reasonable

scorie-hornt *adj.* calloused (G)

scouf *See* **scoof**

scoug *n.* shelter; pretence; ruse

scouk *n.* evil look; *v.* skulk. *cf.*
skook

scouth *n.* freedom of movement,
elbow-room, scope

scouth-an-routh *phr.* freedom to
range and plenty of food

scowff *v.* scoff at, mock (R)

scowth *n.* freedom to move; scope.
cf. **scouth, scooth**

scraich *n., v.* shreik

scrat *n.* shallow furrow; scratch; *v.*
scratch (M). *cf.* **scart**

scrauch *n.* screech

scran *v.* scavenge for

scrath *n.* cormorant

screed *n.* long piece of writing

screef *n.* surface of water

screeve, screive, scrive *v.* write

screeve *n.* a large scratch; *v.*
scratch, scrape

screid *See* **screed**

scrie *v.* cry; proclaim

scries-buird *n.* announcement
board (at church)

scriffan *n.* membrane, film, thin
cover. *cf.* **striffin**

scrog *n.* stunted bush

scronach *n.* shrill cry; fuss, outcry
(A2)

scroo *n.* small rick of corn or hay.
cf. **hooick**

scruff *n.* raff-raff

scrunt *n.* anything stunted in
growth

scry *v.* cry; proclaim, advertise

scud, the *n.* slap with a **tawse** on
the open hand

scuddle *v.* mess about at domestic
work; **scuddlin claes** second-best
clothes

scuddy *adj.* niggardly

scudge *v.* do rough, menial work.
cf. **skudge**

scuff *v.* touch lightly in passing

scuff o rain *n.* sudden, passing
shower

scull, skull *n.* shallow wicker
basket. *cf.* **skull**

scunner *n., v.* disgust; **scunnert o**
or **wi** *ppl. adj.* disgusted; bored,
fed up, sick of; **tae tak a scunner
till** to go off something

scunnerashun *excl., n.* offensive
sight or thing

scunnerfu *adj.* disgusting,
loathsome

scurry *n.* seagull (Peterhead) (B)

scurry-waster *n.* seagull (M1)

scushle *v.* shuffle

scutter *n.* messy or difficult work;
nuisance; *v.* potter, work messily,
awkwardly; **scutter aboot** mess
about

scutterie jobbie *adj., n.* messy or
trifling job

scypal *n.* rascal, rogue. *cf.* **skypal**

scythe-brod *n.* sharpening board for scythe

seagoo *n.* seagull (A1, R)

seama(w) *n.* seagull (M1)

search *n.* milk strainer (F)

seck *n.* sack. *cf.* **saick**

seck-apron *n.* sackcloth apron. *cf.* **harn-apron**

seck-lifter *n.* hand-barrow (F)

sedarin *n.* scolding, dressing-down

seddle *See* **saiddle**

seek *adj.* sick (S)

seek *v.* look for; ask for; invite; desire; **fit are ye seekin?** what do you want, what are you looking for?

seekener *n.* sickener, something which upsets

seelence *n.* silence

seelent *adj.* silent

seely *adj.* blessed; happy

seelyhoo *n.* the caul rarely found on the head of a new-born child and thought a good omen

seen *prep.* since; *adv.* soon; ago

seenit *n.* Synod

seer(ly) *adj.* sure(ly) (A, B1)

seerup *n.* syrup

seet *n.* site; building-ground

seetivation *n.* situation

seg *v.* sag; **seggit** *ppl., adj.* sagged, sunk down

seg(g)s *n.* sedge; the yellow iris

seiven *adj.* seven

seiventeen *adj.* seventeen

seiventy *adj.* seventy

sel *n.* self

seleck *v.* select

sell *n.* chain to bind cattle (F)

sellfitness *n.* selfishness

selt *v. pt., ppl.* sold

semmit *n.* undershirt

sen *n.* messenger sent ahead of a bridegroom to summon the bride; *v.* send

ser *v.* serve. *cf.* **sair**

ser'in *See* **sairin**

serve's *excl.* preserve us!

set *v.* lease, let

set tee *v.* begin

settin *n.* clutch of eggs a hen sits on to hatch

settril *adj.* slightly stunted in growth

sey *n.* sieve; *v.* strain through a sieve, strain milk. *cf.* **sye**

seyven *adj.* seven (A1). *cf.* **saeven, saiven**

shaave *v.* sow. *cf.* **shauv**

shacklebane, -been *n.* wrist-bone

shadda, shaeda *n.* shadow

shaef, shafe *n.* sheaf. *cf.* **shaif; the croonin shafe** the last straw, the tin lid

shafter, shaftit weskit *n.* sleeved waistcoat (F)

shaif *n.* sheaf. *cf.* **shaef, shafe, shave**

shair *adj.* sure (S)

shak *n., v.* shake; **the Big Shak** the near-ruinous shaking of barley by high winds one night in the 1960s

shakker *n.* part of a threshing mill which shakes out the straw

Shakkin Briggie *pr. n.* bridge across the River Dee at Cults near Aberdeen

shakkin-spoot *n.* wooden chute conveying corn to the elevator lifting it to the corn loft

shakky *adj.* shaky
shakky-doon *n.* make-shift bed
shall *n.* shell; **shall san** shell sand, used as grit for hens (T)
shallie o tay old term for a cup of tea (B)
shally *adj.* abounding in shells
shalt(ie) *n.* pony
shalt-loon *n.* farm-boy looking after the shalt (F); groom
shammelt *adj.* uneven, irregular
shan-dre-dan *n.* any old rickety vehicle
shangie *n.* fight; scrimmage
shank *v.* to knit; *n.* stocking being knitted; the leg; **to shank it** to walk; **shanks' meer** shanks' pony
shankless *adj.* having no leg(s)
shapit *ppl.* shaped
shargart *ppl.* stunted
sharger *n.* a stunted person or animal; lean, scraggy person
sharn *n.* cow-dung; **sharn-bree** liquid cow-dung
sharny *adj.* dung-covered; dirty
sharp *n.* frost-nail; *v.* sharpen
sharrie *n.* quarrel; fight
shauchle *v.* shuffle in walking
shauv *v.* sow (S). *cf.* **saw**
shauven *ppl.* sown
shave *n.* sheaf. *cf.* **shaif**
shaven *ppl.* shaved
shaw *n.* green leaf; small wood (J); *v.* sow; show
shear *v.* reap
sheath *n.* holder for needles during knitting
sheave *n.* slice of bread
shed *v.* part the hair or sheep's wool

shee(n) *n.* shoe(s). *cf.* **shoon, shune** *v.* to shoe
sheel *n., v.* shovel; *v.* to shell
sheelock *n.* corn husk; unfilled ear of corn
sheelter *n.* shelled mussel (B)
sheemich *n.* person or thing of no value
sheen *n., v.* shine; *pl.* of **shee**
sheers *n.* scissors
sheet *v.* shoot
sheet-iron *n.* corrugated iron
sheilin *n.* temporary dwelling for shepherds
shelt, sheltie *n.* pony. *cf.* **shult**
shelvin *n.* movable board on box cart, to increase capacity
sheugh *n.* ditch; furrow; hollow, trench
shew *v.* sew. *cf.* **shoo**
shewin-machine *n.* sewing-machine
shiel *n.* shovel; scoop for fish
shillans *n.* grain freed from husks
shilpit *adj.* feeble
shim *n.* horse-hoe, small plough for weeding
shine *n.* party. *cf.* **henshine**
shippie *n.* steam drifter (B)
shirra *n.* sheriff
shirrameer, shirramineer (B1) *n.* tumult, uproar
shirry *n.* sherry
shiv, shive *v.* shove, push
shochle *v.* waddle
shog, shoggle *n., v.* shake. *cf.* **shoogle**
shoggly, shoogly *adj.* shaky
shoggly-wullie *n.* a table jelly
shoo *v.* sew. *cf.* **shew; shooin**

sewing; *v. pt.* sowed. *cf.* **shaw**

shooder *n., v.* shoulder; **shoodrin** *ppl.* shouldering. *cf.* **shouder**

shooderheid *n.* shoulder joint

shooer *n.* shower

shoogle *v.* to shake. *cf.* **shoggle**

shoogly *adj.* unsteady (of a table etc.)

shoon *n.* shoes. *cf.* **sheen, shune**

shoorie *n.* light shower

shoot *n., v.* suit

shoppie *n.* small shop

short *adj., in the phr.* **short i the trot** quick-tempered; irritable

shortcomes *n.* shortcomings

shortsome *adj.* amusing, making the time seem short

shot *n.* the shooting of a fishing net; the catch

shottie *n.* turn

shoud, showd *n., v. tr., intr.* swing

shouden-boats *n.* swing-boats at carnival

shouder *n., v.* shoulder. *cf.* **shooder**

shouther *See* **shouder**

shouther-the-win *(adj.), n.* (having) one shoulder higher than the other

shrood *n.* shroud

shud *v.* should

shue *v.* sew. *cf.* **shoo**

shuit *v.* suit. *cf.* **shoot**

shullin *n.* shilling

shult *See* **shelt**

shune *n. pl.* shoes. *cf.* **sheen, shoon**

shuner *adv.* sooner (S)

shunner *n.* cinder; **harn bags an shunners** sackcloth and ashes

shyve *n., v.* throw (of rope or fishing line only) (B)

sib *adj.* closely related, akin

sibness *n.* relationship

sic, siccan *adj.* such; **sic-an-sic** such-and-such

siccar *adj.* secure, certain; dependable, reliable

sich *n.* sigh

sicht *n.* sight; **a sicht for sair een** a welcome sight

sick lamb *n.* pet lamb brought up on the bottle, drawn by the call 'sick'

siclike *adj.* such-like

siclikes *n.* things like that; *prep.* just like

sid *n.* seed; *v.* should. *cf.* **sud; sidna** shouldn't

sidelins *adv.* sideways

siderig *n.* side ridge

side-shelvin *n.* movable board on side of box-cart

sidiewyes *adv.* sideways

sids *n. pl.* oat husks, used for **sowans**

siftin riddle *adj., n.* riddle for small seed

signaatur *n.* signature

sik *v.* seek; desire; **nae sikken't** don't want it. *cf.* **seek**

sile *n.* sand-eel (B). *cf.* **sunnel**

siller *n.* silver; money

silly-made-up *adj.* (of a child) mischievous

simmer *n.* summer

simmer-hoose *n.* summer-house

sin *n.* son; sun; *prep.* since; **sin, seen, sinsyne** since then

sinacle *n.* vestige, trace (B1)

sin-brunt *adj.* sun-burned

sinder, sin'er, sinner *v.* separate, sunder

sindoon *n.* sundown, sunset
single *v.* hoe turnips
sing-sang *n.* singsong speech
sinker *n.* weight for fastening horse in stall (F)
sinny *n.* senna
sinry *adj.* sundry
sinsyne *adv.* since then
sipper *n.* supper
siree *n.* soirée
sitiwat *ppl.* situated
sit saft *v., adv.* enjoy an easy life (B)
sitt *n.* soot
siven *adj.* seven
sivven *n.* raspberry
size *n.* chives
sizzon *n., v.* season
skaalie *n.* slate pencil. *cf.* **skeily**
ska(i)ken *v.* feel disgust at, be nauseated by (food); **ska(i)kent wi't.** *cf.* **skechan**
skaikit *ppl.* bedaubed; besmeared
skail *v. tr.* spill; *intr.* disperse (school pupils etc); *v. tr.* dismiss. *cf.* **skale**
skaillie *n.* slate-pencil. *cf.* **skaalie**
skaillies *n. pl.* something spilt or scattered
skaim *v.* scheme. *cf.* **skem**
skaith *n.* harm
skale *n.* school (S). *cf.* **skweel**
skale *v. tr.* dismiss; spill; *intr.* scatter. *cf.* **skail, skel**
skalie, skallie *n.* slate pencil. *cf.* **skaalie, skeily**
skance *n.* glance
skate *n.* jade (term of contempt)
skech *v.* go about in a silly, vain way

skechan *See* **skaiken**
skeel *n.* skill; **skeely** skilful
skeily *n.* slate pencil. *cf.* **skaalie**
skel *v.* spill. *cf.* **skale**
skelb *n.* splinter
skelf *n.* shelf; thin flat fragment or slice; splinter esp. lodged in skin
skellach *n.* wild mustard, charlock
skelp *n.* smack, whack; chunk, slab, sizable area; *v.* dash, run
skelve *n.* shelf (B1); *v.* laminate (B1). *cf.* **skelf**
skem *v.* scheme. *cf.* **skaim**
skep *n.* beehive; *v.* handle bee-hives
skew *adv.* askew
skew-fittit *adj.* splay-footed. *cf.* **skyow-fittit**
skice *v.* to run off quickly. *cf.* **skyce**
skichent *adj.* showing contempt. *cf.* **skech**
skicy *adj.* mean, unfair
skiff *v.* rain, snow, hail lightly
skiffin *n.* light fall (of rain, snow)
skiffie *n.* scivvy (S)
skiken *See* **skaiken**
skink *n.* shin or knuckle of beef from which soup may be made
skinnymalink *n.* a thin person
skip *v.* slide on ice
skirl *n., v.* scream
skirl(ie) *n.* squall of wind with rain or snow
skirlie *n.* oatmeal cooked with onions, dripping and seasoning; a very small quantity (A1)
skirp *n., v.* splash; *n.* fragment
skirt *v.* hurry off (A)
skiry *adj.* gaudy. *cf.* **skyrie**
Skite *pr. n.* nickname of Drumlithie
skite *v.* slip or slide suddenly; run

off quickly; rebound, ricochet; squirt, splash; *n.* slip or skid; a squirt of liquid; small amount of liquor, a dram

skitie *adj.* slippery

skitter(s) *n.* diarrhoea

sklaik *n., v.* lick, smear with the tongue. *cf.* **slaik**

sklate *n.* slate

sklater *n.* slater

sklent, sklint *v.* slope, slant; glance

sklype *n.* derog. term for someone of dirty habits

sklyte, sklyter *v.* slip awkwardly, fall heavily; *n.* a heavy fall; expanse (G)

skook *v.* skulk. *cf.* **scouk**

skowf *v.* quaff; drink off. *cf.* **scoof**

skraich *v.* screech

skreefer *n.* skimmer for surface soil and weeds (F)

skreek o day *n.* dawn

skrie *v.* shriek, cry; proclaim

skudge *v.* do rough menial work. *cf.* **scudge**

skull *n.* shallow wicker basket. *cf.* **scull**

skum *v.* skim

skurken *v.* dry out; shrink, shrivel

skwaal *v.* squall, scream

skweel *n.* school. *cf.* **squeel**

skweenge *v.* scrounge (of dogs and people)

skwyle *v.* squeal. *cf.* **squile**

skyce *v.* scurry. *cf.* **skice**

skycie *adj.* unsporting, ungenerous

skyow *v.* to go askew; **skyow-fittit** splay-footed. *cf.* **skew-fittit**

skypal *n. (var. of* **skybald**) rascal, rogue. *cf.* **scypal**

skyre *v.* shine or glitter gaudily. *cf.* **skire**

skyrie *adj.* gaudy; showy

skyte *See* **skite**

slabber *n.* mud; slush; slop

slack *v.* slake or quench thirst

slaik *v.* lick, smear with the tongue. *cf.* **sklaik**

slammach *n.* gossamer, webs of small spiders

slap *n.* opening, gap in wall or fence

slater *n.* woodlouse

slauchter *n., v.* slaughter

slauchter-hoose *n.* slaughter-house

slaw *adj., adv.* slow

slee *adj.* sly; **sleely** *adv.* slyly

sleed *v. pt.* slid (S)

sleek *n.* alluvial deposit of mud left in tidal rivers. *cf.* **slich**

sleekit *adj.* smooth, glossy; sly, sneaky

sleepit *v. pt.* slept; **sleepit in** overslept

sleicht *n.* sleight

sleumin *n.* hint; surmise

slewie *v.* walk with heavy, swinging gait (B1)

slich *See* **sleek**

slicht *adj., n.* slight

sliddery *adj.* slippery

slider *n.* retaining rod for cattle-binding; harness fitment on cart shaft; ice-cream between two wafers

slip *n.* loose frock or pinafore

slip the timmers *v.* die (M)

sliv(v)er *n., v.* slaver

slivvery-doctor *n.* harmless jellyfish (B)

Sloch, the *pr. n.* village of Portessie
slocher *v.* (of a pig) wallow in mud
slock, slocken *v.* slake thirst
slorach *n.* wet or dirty, disgusting
mess (B1)
slubber *v.* sip noisily
slung *n.* a low fellow
slype *n.* worthless fellow
sma *adj.* small; **sing sma** say little
(as matter of discretion); **sma
drink** of no consequence; **sma
lins** small fishing lines; **sma
watter** calm waters (B); **sma
weet** a soft drizzle
smad *n.* blemish, smudge
smachrie *n.* hotch-potch of foods,
esp. sweets
smarrach *n.* confused crowd. *cf.*
swarrach
smatchet *n.* pert, impudent person
smeddum *n.* intelligence;
shrewdness
smeeky *adj.* smoky (G1)
smeerich *n.* a kiss. *cf.* **smoorich**
smeerless *adj.* lacking spirit,
energy, sluggish; handless (B1)
smeeth *adj.* smooth
smeirless *See* **smeerless**
smert *adj.* smart
smiddy *n.* blacksmith's shop
smiler *n.* small rake
smird *n.* smut, smudge. *cf.* **smad**
smirr *n.* drizzle, fine rain
smit *v.* infect; **smittin** infectious
smith *n.* blacksmith
smoocherin *n.* fine rain
smoor *v.* smother (J). *cf.* **smore**
smoorich *n.* kiss. *cf.* **smeerich**
smore *v.* smother
smout *n.* term of endearment for a
young animal or child
smucht *v.* choke
smuchter *v.* smoulder
smyteral *n.* collection of small
objects
sna, snaave, snaw *n.* snow. *cf.*
snyaave
snap-an-rattle *n.* dish of oatcakes
crumbled into milk (F). *cf.*
murly-tuck
snapper *n., v.* (of a horse) stumble
snappus *adj.* testy, snappy (A2)
snavie *adj.* snowy (S)
snaw *n.* snow. *cf.* **sna**
snaw-bree *n.* melted snow; slush
snaw-fite *adj.* snow-white
sneck *n.* latch; *v.* sneak
sneck-drawin *adj.* crafty, sly (A2)
sneck-harl *v.* rough-cast a wall
with mortar
sned *n.* scythe handle; *v.* cut, prune
sneeshin *n.* snuff
sneevil *v.* snivel
snell *adj.* (of the wind) cold, sharp
snicher *v.* snigger, laugh up one's
sleeve
snifter *v.* sniff, draw air through the
nose
snipe *See* **snype**
snippet *adj.* having a white streak
down the face
snocher *v.* sniff; breathe noisily;
snore
snod *adj.* tidy; neat; *v.* tidy up (C)
snod-in-aboot *n.* haircut (T)
snoot *n.* snout, nose; peak of a cap
snootit *adj.* (of a cap) peaked
snoove *v.* move smoothly, glide
snorl *n.* tangle, difficulty
snotter *n.* nasal mucus; *v.* let mucus

run from nose; snuffle; blubber

snowk *v.* (of an animal) smell about

snype *n.* rebuff; reverse of fortune; setback, let-down, loss by cheating; *v.* cheat, defraud; **snypit o** cheated by

snyte *v.* blowing the nose with finger and thumb

sober *adj.* weakly; of spare figure

socht *ppl.* sought. *cf.* **seek**

sock *n.* ploughshare

sodger *n.* soldier

softie, soft biscuit *n.* a kind of plain floury bun

some *adv.* rather, to some extent; **some caul** rather cold

some-ane, -een *n., pron.* someone

son-afore-the-father *n.* flowering currant (the blossom appearing before the leaves)

sonsy *adj.* plump and pleasant

soo *n.* sow; rectangular stack of hay or straw; **soo-moo't** having projecting upper-jaw

sooch *See* **souch**

sooder *n., v.* solder

sooie *n.* dough trimmed off edges of oatcake before baking

sook *v.* suck

sooker *n.* tree sucker; cow suckling calves

sookin caafie *adj., n.* suckling calf

soom *n.* sum; *v.* swim (C)

soon(d) *n., v.* sound. *cf.* **soun**

sooperaniwat *ppl.* superannuated

soople *adj.* supple. *cf.* **souple**

soor *adj.* sour

soord *n.* sword. *cf.* **soward**

soorness *n.* sullenness; surliness

soorocks *n.* sorrel

soosh *v.* beat severely, flog

sooter *n.* cobbler. *cf.* **souter**

sooth *adj., n.* south

sooth-kwintra *adj.* southern; English

sorn *v.* sponge upon; loaf

sorra *n.* sorrow; the Devil, used in impatient questions, *e.g.* **fat sorra idder** what other?; **she hisna her sorras tae seek** she has plenty trouble on her hands

sorrafu *adj.* sorrowful

sort *v.* mend; see to, attend to, deal with (sometimes harshly)

sortin *n.* scolding

soss *n.* mess

sotter *n.* disgusting mess

souch *n.* sigh, whistling or rushing sound; *v.* sigh, make rushing sound. *cf.* **sough**

souder *n.* solder

souff, sowf(f) *v.* whistle in a low tone; *n.* fool, simpleton

sough *n.* sigh, low whistling sound; *v.* sigh etc. *cf.* **souch**

soun *adj., n.* sound; *adv.* soundly

souple *adj.* supple

souter *n.* shoemaker; **souter's deevil** shoemaker's last. *cf.* **sooter**

southron *adj.* southern

sowans, sowens *n.* dish made by steeping and fermenting the husks or siftings of oats in water, then boiling

soward *n.* sword. *cf.* **soord**

sowd *n.* a large sum; a quantity

sowff *See* **souff**

sowl *n.* soul

spaad, spad *n.* spade. *cf.* **spaud**

spae *v.* to tell fortunes
spae-wife *n.* female fortune-teller
spaingie, spainyie *n.* W. Indian
  cane, sometimes smoked by boys;
  osiers for basket-making among
  fishermen (B)
spairge *v.* bespatter
spak *v. pt.* spoke
span *n.* span of life
spang *n., v.* spring, stride; span,
  outstretched width of hand
spark *v.* splash, mark with drops of
  water. *cf.* **sperk, spirk**
sparry *n.* sparrow (J)
sparty tow *n.* coir yarn
spate *n.* flood
spaud *See* **spaad**
spaul *n.* shoulder or forequarter of
  an animal
spaver *n.* trouser fly
spawcious *adj.* spacious
spean *v.* wean
speecial *adj.* special
speel *v.* climb
speen *n., v.* spoon; **speen aboot**
  spoon about as farmworkers
  shared the same broth bowl
speer, speir, spier *v.* ask
speerit *n.* spirit
speeshal(ly) *adj., adv.* special(ly)
speet, speeth *n.* spate, flood (B1)
speldin *n.* fresh haddock, split
  open, salted and dried in the sun
spell *n.* wood shaving
spell-beuk *n.* spelling-book
spen *v.* spend; wean (F); spawn. *cf.*
  spean
spence *n.* spare room
sperk *v.* splash
spew *v.* vomit

spiel *v.* climb. *cf.* **speel**
spik *n.* speech; conversation;
  subject of talk or gossip; *v.* speak
spile *v.* spoil
spinner, at a *phr.* at a smart rate of
  speed, at a dash
spinnle *n., v.* spindle; **spinnle-**
  shanks spindly legs
spiritool *adj.* spiritual
spirk *n.* spark; drop of rain; splash
  or spot; *v.* splash; rain slightly. *cf.*
  sperk, spark
spit *v.* to rain slightly
splatch *n.* splash
splay *v.* to mend a tear in cloth by
  sewing edges together without
  patching
spleet-new *adj.* quite new
spleeter o weet *n.* heavy shower of
  rain
spleeters *n. pl.* spillings, splashings
spleuchan *n.* tobacco-pouch. *cf.*
  splochan
splew *v.* spit out, spue
splewin *n.* vomit; term of abuse,
  e.g. **ye lazy splewin**
split *n.* quarrel; *v.* separate
split-the-win *adj., n.* Y-junction
splochan *n.* tobacco pouch. *cf.*
  spleuchan
sploiter *v.* splash, spill
splore *n.* frolic; revel
splouter *v.* splutter
spluen (B1) *See* **splewin**
splutrich *n.* a scattered mess (B1)
splyter *See* **sploiter**
spoot *n.* spout; rone pipe
sprachle *v.* sprawl. *cf.* **sprauchle**
sprag *n.* piece of wood or iron used
  to block a wheel; medium-size cod

spraikle *v.* speckle

spraing *n.* streak, usually glittering

sprauchle *See* **sprachle**

spreeth *n.* a large number (B1)

sprent *n.* spring or elastic force of anything (B1)

spring *n.* lively tune

spring-cairt *n.* cart mounted on springs

sprod *n.* an implement for dislodging limpets from a rock

sproot *n.* Brussels sprout; *v.* grow, sprout

sprot *n.* reed, rush; a coarse grass

spull *v.* spill; **spullins** spillings. *cf.* **skale**

spunk *n.* a match; mettle, energy; courage

spur-bauk *n.* cross-beam in the roof of a building (B1)

spurdie *n.* house-sparrow

spurgie *n.* house-sparrow (O)

spurk (J) *See* **spirk** *etc.*

spurkle, spurtle *n.* wooden rod for stirring porridge etc. *cf.* **theevil**

spurtle-shanks *n. pl.* thin legs

spyauck *n.* example, guide; **a gryte spyauck** a good example

squaar, squarr *adj., n., v.* square

squallach *v.* squeal

squeeb *n.* firework

squeel *n.* school. *cf.* **skweel**

squile *v.* squeal. *cf.* **skwyle**

sta(a) *n.* stall

staamer *v.* stagger

stacher *v.* stagger

stack *n.* a pile of peats; *v. pt., ppl.* stuck

stackit *ppl.* (*e.g.* of hay) built into a stack

stackyaird *n.* rick-yard

staffy-nevel *adj.* staff-in-hand; **staffy-nevel job** a fight with cudgels

stag-moss *n.* alpine club moss

staig *n.* stallion

stail *v.* steal (S)

stainch *adj.* staunch. *cf.* **stanch**

stairch *n., v.* starch

stairt *n., v.* start, begin

stairvation *n.* starvation. *See* **sterve**

stairve *v.* to starve. *cf.* **sterve**

staito *n.* statue (A2)

stale *v.* steal

stamach, stam(m)ack *n.* stomach; *v.* stomach; endure

stame *n.* steam

stame-mull *n.* steam-driven threshing-machine. *cf.* **stem-mull**; **stame-mull breid** thick, poorly-made oatcakes (F)

stammack *See* **stamach**

stammygaster *n.* shock; *v.* flabbergast

stan *v.* stand; **stannin** *ppl.* standing

stance *n.* site; station

stanch *adj., v.* staunch. *cf.* **stainch**

stane *n.* stone. *cf.* **steen**

stane-cast *n.* stone's throw

stang *n.* sting; pole; steering-rod; tongue of a Jew's harp; **stang o the trump** the best of all, best of a family

stank *n.* pond; ditch; marshy ground; (*fig.*) **help a chiel ower a stank**

stap *n.* step; *v.* stop; block up; stuff

starkly *adv.* strongly, bravely

starn, starnie *n.* star; small quantity

sta(r)shie *n.* row, uproar. *cf.* **stushie**

staucher *v.* to stagger

steadin *n.* steading, farmstead

stech *v.* cram; satiate, gorge; create a stifling atmosphere; **stecht** *ppl.* overheated (G)

steed *v. pt.* stood. *See* **stan**

steek *v.* shut; clench; stitch; *n.* stitch

steel *n.* stool; fellow (B1)

steelbow *n.* system under which farm stock, implements etc. could be held by the tenant under contract to the landlord

steen *n., v.* stone. *cf.* **stane**

steen-chackert *n.* stone-chat (M)

Steenhive *pr. n.* nickname for Stonehaven, Kincardineshire

steeny *adj.* stony

steepin *n.* a wetting, drenching; stipend, minister's salary

steepit loaf *phr.* bread poultice (B)

steer *n., v.* stir, bustle

steigh *v.* fill with bad air or fumes

steil *See* **steel**

steilert *n.* steelyard, weighing machine (F)

stem *v.* (nautical) keep a certain course

stem-mull *n.* steam-driven threshing-machine. *cf.* **stame-mull**

stench *v.* staunch

sten(d) *v.* stride (A2)

stent *n.* extent of task, stint; *v.* stint

sterve *v.* starve. *cf.* **stairve**; **sterve o, wi the caul** feel chilled; **stervation** bitter cold

stey *adj.* steep; *n.* stay, support; *in pl.* corsets; *v.* stay

stibble *n.* stubble; **stibble ruckie** mini-cornstack built by cottar loons from stubble roots (T)

stick *v.* stick; come to a premature halt in a job etc.; **stickit minister** student of the ministry who has failed to be licensed as a preacher

stick in *v.* to persevere

stickly *adj.* (of peat) fibrous, woody

stiffen *n.* stiffening, starch

still an on *adv.* nevertheless

stilp *v.* stalk

stilpert *n.* stilt; long-legged, lanky person or animal

stilt *n.* handle of plough (F)

stime, styme *n.* a tiny amount

stinch *adj.* staunch; strict

stirk *n.* young bullock; a stupid fellow

stirkie's sta *n.* the place in the cow-shed reserved for the stirk; the place of a child, *(e.g.* father's lap) when the mother has a younger baby

stirlin *n.* starling

stite *n.* nonsense; stumble. *cf.* **stoit, styte**

stiter *v.* stumble. *cf.* **stoiter**

stob *n.* thorn; stake; **stobbit** thatched by means of a stake; *v.* stub (the toe etc.)

stock *n.* chap, fellow

stockit *adj.* obstinate

stodge *v.* walk slowly, stomp

stoit, stoiter *v.* stagger, totter. *cf.* **stite, styter, stotter**

stoker *n.* odd job-lot of fish, sold by a ship's crew for cash (B)

stoo *v.* cut (off) (animal's tail, shoots of tree, a fishing net)

stook *n.* a shock of sheaves; *v.* to put into shocks

stookie *n.* stucco, plaster of Paris

stookin *n.* the arrangement of corn in shocks, usually ten/twelve sheaves per shock

stoon(d) *n., v.* ache; throb. *cf.* **stound**

stoor *n.* flying dust. *cf.* **stour**; *v.* pour (can be used of rain); gush

stoorie *adj.* dusty

stoorum *n.* gruel

stoot *adj.* stout; strong (A, A2)

stop *v.* live or stay at an address

store the kin *phr.* to keep the human race in existence by living on. *fig.* to survive, to keep going, last out in general (M)

stot *n.* castrated bullock older than a stirk; **stot** *n., v.* bounce; walk with a spring; stagger

stots-and-bangs *adj., adv.* intermittent(ly); *n.* occasional work

stotter *v.* stumble. *cf.* **stoiter**

stound *See* **stoond**

stoup *n.* deep, narrow vessel for holding liquids: flagon; jug; *in pl.* props, supports; the two pieces of a cart which project beyond the body

stoupie *n.* small liquid measure; cream pot (B1)

stour *n.* dust; a downpour. *cf.* **stoor**

stourie *adj.* dusty

stovies *n.* stoved potatoes cooked in stew-pan with onion, fat and meat scraps

stow *v.* steal; **stowen** stolen; **stown-wyes** by stealth, secretly

stowff *n.* slow, measured gait; *v.* stump; plod

stra *v.* straw; *in phr.* **stra his beets** put straw (as soles) into his boots (formerly a custom of farm servants) (R). *cf.* **strae**

straaberry *n.* strawberry

strab *n.* stalk of loose straw lying on the field after harvesting or sticking out from a sheaf or stack; anything adhering loosely to one's clothes

strachen *v.* straighten. *cf.* **straichen**

stracht *adj., adv.* straight; **stracht-edge** strip of iron used to align the **couter** and **sock** with the body of the horse plough (T). *cf.* **straucht**

stracht-oot-the-gate *adj.* straightforward

strack *v. pt.* struck

strade *v. pt.* strode

strae *n.* straw; *v.* to give straw to animals; **strae his beets** put straw into his boots for warmth (T). *cf.* **stra**

strae-soo *n.* long stack of straw

straichen *v.* straighten. *cf.* **strachen**

straik *n., v.* stroke. *See* **strake**

straik *n.* sharpening board or stone for scythe; wooden cylinder for levelling a bushel measure (F)

strainer, strainin post *n.* post taking the strain of the wire in fencing (F)

strait *adj.* rigid

strak *v. pt.* stroked. *See* **strake**

strake *v.* stroke. *cf.* **straik**

stramash *n.* uproar, commotion

strang *adj.* strong; *n.* urine

strapper *n.* young farm servant looking after the **shalt** (F). *cf.* **shalt-loon**

strappin *adj.* tall, handsome and agile

strathspey *n.* Highland dance

strauchen *v.* to straighten

straucht *adj.* straight. *cf.* **stracht** *v.* straighten (A1). *cf.* **strauchen**

strauchtwye *adv.* straightaway

stravaig *v.* wander

streck *adj.* strict. *cf.* **strick**

streek *v.* stretch. *cf.* **streetch, rax**

streen, the *n., adv.* yesterday evening; last night; yesterday. *cf.* **yestreen**

streetch *v.* stretch (A2). *cf.* **streek, rax**

streeve *v. pt.* strove; struggled; fell out, quarrelled

strenth *n.* strength

strick *adj.* strict; *v.* strike

stridelins *prep.* astride

strik *See* **strick**

strin *n.* jet of milk from a cow's teat

stripe *n.* small open drain

strive *v.* quarrel; **striven** *ppl.* having quarrelled, fallen out

stroop(ie) *n.* spout (of teapot etc); spout; water tap; outlet at spring

stroud *n.* silly song

strucken *ppl.* struck

strunge *adj.* surly, gruff, morose

strush, strushie *n.* quarrel; disturbance

strushel *adj.* untidy, slovenly

strushlach *n.* untidy woman

struve *v. pt.* strove

strype *n.* small stream

stucken *ppl.* stuck

studdy *n.* anvil

stue *n.* dust. *cf.* **styoo, stoor**

stumpart, stumper *v.* walk clumsily in a stumping way

stur *n., v.* stir. *cf.* **steer**

sturken *adj.* sulky, sour

sturt *n.* strife (C)

styoo *n.* dust. *cf.* **styoo, stoor**

styoomer *n.* foolish person

styter *v.* stumble, totter; **styterin fou** incapably drunk. *cf.* **stoiter**

sub *n., v.* advance wages

subjeck *n.* subject

succar *n.* sugar

sucken *n.* the district thirled to a mill; generally, the district in which anyone carries on business (A2)

suddent *adj.* sudden (C)

suddenty *n.* suddenness; **in (on) a suddenty** suddenly

sudderinwid *n.* southernwood

sug *n.* easy-going individual

sumph *n.* fool, simpleton

sung *ppl., adj.* singed

sunnel *n.* sand-eel (B)

sunsheen *n.* sunshine

sup *v.* take food or liquid, esp. with a spoon

sup(pie) *n.* sip, small quantity

superannuat *ppl.* superannuated

suppersteetion *n.* superstition

supplicant *n.* a beggar

surtoo, surtout *n.* old-fashioned coat

suspeck *v.* suspect

swack, swak *adj.* supple, nimble

swacken *v.* make supple, pliant

swad *n.* swede, Swedish turnip

Swaddish neep *n.* swede
swaleheidit (S) *See* **swall-heidit**
swall *v.* swell
swall-heidit *adj.* swollen-headed
swally *v.* swallow
swap *v.* to rope thatch with a **cloo**
swarf *n., v.* faint, swoon
swarrach *n.* crowd, swarm. *cf.*
  smarrach
swashy *adj.* grand, dashing
swat *n., v.* sweat, *pt.* **swat; swattit**
  sweated (M). *cf.* **swate, swyte**
swatch *n.* sample
swate *v.* sweat (A2). *cf.* **swat,**
  swyte
sweel *v.* swill, rinse; swirl
sweem *v.* swim
sweemer *n.* swimmer; **twinty-**
  minute sweemer doughball (B)
sweeng *n., v.* swing
sweengletree *See* **swingle-tree**
sweer, sweir *adj.* lazy; unwilling; *v.*
  swear
sweer-tree, puin the *phr.* a game in
  which two people sitting on the
  ground, hold a stick between
  them and try to pull each other up
sweer(-wird) *n.* swear(-word)
sweesh *v.* swish, brush
sweety-wife *n.* female sweet-seller
sweir *See* **sweer**
sweirty *n.* laziness
sweetie-boolie *n.* round sweet
sweeties, readin *n. pl.* conversation
  lozenges
sweevle *v.* swivel

swey *v.* sway, swing
swick *n.* cheat; blame; *v.* swindle
swidder *See* **swither**
swig *v.* sway, move from side to
  side (J)
swine's hoose *n.* pigsty
swingletree *n.* as in Eng., bar in a
  plough-draught to which the
  theats are attached
swipe *v.* sweep. *cf.* **swype**
swippert *adj.* nimble. *cf.* **swyppirt**
swite *n., v.* sweat. *cf.* **swyte**
swith *adv.* swiftly
swithe *v.* hasten, get away
swither *n.* quandary; *v.* to be
  undecided; hesitate. *cf.* **swidder**
swourd *n.* sword. *cf.* **soord,**
  soward
swult *v.* sob deeply (B)
swuppert, swyppirt *adj.* nimble,
  agile; swift
swye *n.* pivoted rod in chimney for
  hanging pots over the fire-place;
  sway, influence; *v.* sway
swype *v.* sweep. *cf.* **swipe**
swyte *n., v.* sweat. *cf.* **swat, swate**
sye *v.* strain liquid; pour milk
  through a sieve. *cf.* **sey**
syer *n.* milk strainer. *cf.* **syre**
syne *adv.* since, ago; then
sype *v.* seep, drip; **sypit** *ppl.*
  soaked
syre *n.* drain in street gutter,
  including the covering grating. *cf.*
  syer

— **T** —

tablin *n.* top stones on a gable

tack *n.* lease of a farm; leased farm; **tack o life** lease of life

tacket *n.* stud, hobnail; **tackety beets** hobnailed boots

tackie, takie *n.* the game of tag

tae *n.* toe; *prep.* to; for; by; **tae masel** by myself. *cf.* **tay**

tae, the *adj.* the one, contrasted with the other. *cf.* **the taen**

tae-ee *n.* a pet

taen *ppl.* taken (S). *cf.* **tane, teen**

tag *n.* leather strap, tawse; **i the tag** hard at work

taik *n.* stroll; **tak taik** take stock (T)

taikle *n.* harness; tackle

tailer *n.* tool for taking roots off turnips (F)

tail-eyn *n.* the tail end

taings *n. pl.* tongs, hinged wire-tightener in fencing

tait *n.* lock of hair, wool etc.; small portion

tak *v.* take; **tak aboot** take care of, look after, see to; **tak aff** copy down; **tak in han** undertake; **tak throwe-han** discuss; **tak sheet** take flight (*orig. naut.* B, T)

Tam *pr. n.* deriv. of Thomas

Tamintoul *pr. n.* Tomintoul village

tamteen *n.* a tontine

tane *adj.* the one. *cf.* **taen**

tangles *n. pl.* kind of seaweed

tansy *n.* ragwort; tansy

tantaleeze *v.* tantalise

tap *n., v.* top

tapdress *n.* manure on the surface

tapner *n.* tool for removing turnip-tops (F)

tappit *adj.* crested

tappit-hen *n.* crested hen; Scottish quart measure of ale or claret, with a knob on its lid

tapsalteerie *adv.* topsy-turvy

tapster *n.* the person at the top

tare *n., v.* tear

tares *n. pl.* beans and peas grown among oats for cattle feed (T)

tarick *n.* Arctic tern (B)

tarlich *n.* any puny, worthless creature

tarraneese *n., v. (lit.* **tyrannise**) tease, torment

tarry-fingert *adj.* light-fingered

tase oot *v.* tease out (S)

tashed, tasht *adj.* fatigued; well worn

tasment, tastement *n.* will, testament. *cf.* **tesment**

tassie *n.* drinking cup; glass; goblet

tatterwallop *n.* ragged person

tatterwallops *n. pl.* rags and tatters

tattie, tatie *n.* potato

tattie-boodie *n.* scarecrow (A)

tattie-bootie *n.* scarecrow (C)

tattie-chapper *n.* potato masher

tattie-clamp *n.* earth pit for storing potatoes

tattie-doodle *n.* scarecrow (S)

tattie-dulie *n.* scarecrow (J)

tattie-howker *n.* potato-digger

tattie-howkin *n.* potato harvest
tattie-liftin *n.* potato harvest (J)
tattie-shaws *n.* potato foliage
taucht *ppl.* taught
taul *v. pt.* told. *cf.* **telt**
tawpie *n.* stupid fellow, blockhead
tawse *n.* leather strap for punishment
tay *n.* tea
tayspeen *n.* teaspoon; **tayspenfae** teaspoonful
tchach *excl. of disgust, contempt, impatience etc.*
tchoot *int.* tush!
ted *n.* toad, applied to men as term of contempt, to children or young women as term of endearment
tee *adv.* too; also
tee, keep her *naut. phr.* alter course to windward (B)
teel *n.* tool
teem *adj., v.* empty; **teem yer crap** get it off your chest
teen *n.* tune; humour, temper; **ill teen** bad mood; *ppl.* taken; **teen wi** charmed by, pleased with; **the teen** the one, *(in contrast with* **the tither** the other). *cf.* **tak, taen**
teep *n.* type
teer *n.* tare; tear
teet *v.* peep
teeth *in phr.* **a teeth in the sky** a broken rainbow (T)
teethache *n.* toothache
teetle *n.* title
teind *n., v.* tithe. *cf.* **tiend**
telt *v. pt., ppl.* told
tent *n.* care; **tak tent** give heed to
tentily *adv.* carefully, attentively

tenty *adj.* careful, attentive
term-time *n.* end of working contract: Whitsunday; Martinmas
terrible *adv.* exceedingly
terrifee *v.* terrify; **terrifeet** *ppl.* terrified
tesment *n.* will, testament. *cf.* **tasment**
teuch *adj.* tough. *cf.* **tyeuch**
teuchat, teuchit *n.* lapwing; **teuchat's storm** wintry weather in March, when the lapwings arrive
teuchter *n.* (sometimes disparaging) *ref.* to anyone from the North, to a Highlander or Gaelic-speaker
teuk *v. pt.* took
thack *n., v.* thatch; **thackit** *ppl.* thatched
thae *adj.* those (S, J, C)
thaese *See* **thase**
than *adv.* then; **than-an-awaa** long ago
thase *adj.* these
that *adv.* so, *e.g.* **it wis that caul**
theat *n.* trace by which horses draw plough etc.; **kick owre the theats** kick over the traces, become reckless; **lat the theats slack** take it easy; **oot o theat** unreasonable
theek *v.* thatch (J). *cf.* **thack**
theet *See* **theat**
theevil *n.* wooden rod for stirring porridge. *cf.* **spurtle**
thegidder, thegither *adv.* together
theirsels *pron.* themselves; *pred. adj., adv.* by themselves, alone; **theirsels twa** just the two of them

thenk *v.* thank (S)

thereoot *adv.* outside; in the open air

thewless *adj.* feeble

thiefie *adj.* thief-like, sneaky

thig *v.* beg, borrow, be a genteel beggar; generally applied to the practice of begging seed oats to sow first crop on entering a farm

thigger *n.* genteel beggar

thingumboob, thingumenderry *n.* thingummybob

thin-skint *adj.* sensitive, easily upset

thirl *v.* to thrill; tingle; to bring under legal obligation; **thirlt** *ppl.* bound, enthralled

thirlage *n.* bondage

thocht *n., v. pt., ppl.* thought

thocht-been *n.* wish-bone

thochtie *n.* a little bit

thole *v.* bear; endure; tolerate

thon *pron.* that; *adj.* that, yonder; those. *cf.* **yon**

thoom, thoomb *n., v.* thumb; **thoom-piece** *n.* oatcakes buttered with thumb; **thoom-raip** *n.* thumb rope

thoosan(d) *n.* thousand

thorther, thorter *v.* cross harrow (F)

thow *n.* thaw

thowless *adj.* lacking energy or mettle

thraan *adj.* stubborn. *cf.* **thrawn**

thrammle *n.* chain on cattle-binding, for attaching **sell** to a stake

thrang *n.* throng; *adj.* crowded; thick, intimate; busy

thrapple *v.* throttle; *n.* throat

thrash *n.* threshed grain

thrashin-mull *n.* threshing-mill

thraten *v.* threaten

thrave *n.* two **stooks** or 20/24 **shaifs**; *v. pt.* thrived

thraw *v.* throw, twist

thrawcruik, thrawheuk *n.* implement for twisting straw ropes

thrawn *adj.* stubborn; twisted

thraws, in the *phr.* in the grip of *(fig.)*

threep *n.* a vehemently held opinion; *v.* argue, quarrel; insist

threeple *adj.* triple, threefold; *v.* treble

threeplet *n.* triplet

threet *n., v.* threat; **threet'nin** *ppl.* threatening

three-threids-an-a-thrum *phr.* cat's purr (G)

threeve *v. pt.* thrived

threip *See* **threep**

thrissle, thristle *n.* thistle

thrist *n.* thirst

thristy *adj.* thirsty

thro(u) *prep.* through. *cf.* **throw**

throu-beerin *n.* livelihood, means of sustenance (A1)

throu-han *adv.* under consideration; **tak throu-han** discuss

throu-idder, -ither *See* **throwder**

throu-the-muir *n.* quarrel

throw(e) *prep.* through; **throwe the bows (of behaviour)** beyond all bounds; *adj.* finished. *cf.* **throu**

throw-come *n.* ordeal

throwder *adj.* untidy; muddled; in

a confused state

throw-gang *n.* passage

thrums *n.* ends of yarn; purring of a cat; **span her thrums** purred

thummle *n.* thimble

thunner *n.* thunder

tice (wi) *v.* coax

tichen *v.* tighten

ticht *adj.* tight

tick an tack *n.* the game of tag. *cf.* **tackie**

ticket *n.* someone of untidy appearance

tidder *adj., n.* the other. *cf.* **tither**

tiend *n., v.* tithe. *cf.* **teind**

Tiesday *n.* Tuesday. *cf.* **Tyesday**

tig *n.* fit of ill-humour; a sudden whim; **tae tak a tig** (R) to take a notion; *v.* touch lightly, tap; **tig wi** dally; have to do with; **tig-tire** a state of suspense

tike *n.* dog; unpleasant man

till *prep.* to; compared to

tillie-pan *n.* metal pan used as a scoop (F)

tillygraph *n., v.* telegraph

tillyphone *n., v.* telephone

tilter *n.* used for tilting loose sheaves off an old-fashioned mower or reaper

time-sairin *adj.* time-serving

timmer *n.* timber; **wun-timmer** seasoned timber (T); **Timmer-mairket** ancient fair held in Aberdeen in August; *adj.* wooden

timmer on, up *v.* work vigorously

tin *n.* money (A)

tin-can *n.* corrugated iron

tine *v.* lose; **tint** *pt., ppl.* lost

tink *n.* (term of contempt) foul-mouthed, quarrelsome, vulgar person

tinkie *n.* tinker, one of the travelling people; **tinkie's maskin** tea made in the cup

tinkler *n.* tinker; **tinkler's curse** something of no value

tint *ppl., adj.* lost; *n.* tent

tippen *n.* the hair that binds a hook to a fishing line

tipperteen *n.* bit of card with pin passed through it resembling a teetotum, a top

tire *n.* tiredness

tirl *n.* vibration; short bout of anything; *v.* vibrate

tirl the sneck *phr.* twirl the handle of the latch

tirr *v.* strip off; uncover, undress; unroof, tear off slates/thatch

tirran *n.* tyrant; awkward or exasperating person

tirravee *n.* commotion

tit *n.* teat; *v.* jerk, twitch, pull

tither, the *adj.* the other. *cf.* **tidder**

tittersome *adj.* (of weather) unsettled; (of a horse) restless

titty *n.* (child's word) sister

tobacca *n.* tobacco

tocher *n.* dowry

tod *n.* fox

toit *v.* trot; totter from age

tolerat *v.* tolerate

tongue *v.* scold, abuse

tongue-betroosht *adj.* outspoken

tongue-tackit *ppl., adj.* tongue-tied

tool *n.* towel

toom *adj.* empty (G1, M, J). *cf.* **teem**

toon *n.* a town; farmstead. *cf.* **toun**

toondie, toondy *See* **toonkeeper**

toonkeeper *n.* the person left in charge of a farmstead on Sunday. *cf.* **catcher, toondie**

toonser *n.* town-dweller

toopachin, toopican *n.* pinnacle, summit; steeple, turret

toor *n., v.* tower; **toorin** *ppl.* towering. *cf.* **tour**

toorie *n.* topknot (on bonnet)

toosht *v.* handle carelessly

tooshtie *n.* small quantity

toosle, toozle *v.* dishevel; tussle

toosy *adj.* tousled. *cf.* **tousy**

tooter *v.* work ineffectually

tooteroo *n.* wind instrument

tootie *n.* dram

toot-moot *n.* low muttered conversation; whispering (B1)

topper *n.* first class person or thing

toppers *n. pl.* rubber knee boots worn by fishworkers (B)

tory *n.* grub of cranefly, which consumes germinating grain

tossel, toshil *n.* tassle

tossle *v.* tousle. *cf.* **toosle, touzle**

tottum, totum *n.* a teetotum, four-sided top spun in games of chance; the game itself

toun *n.* farm. *cf.* **toon**

tour *n.* tower; **tourin** *ppl.* towering

tousy *adj.* tousled, dishevelled. *cf.* **toosy**

touzle *v.* ruffle, dishevel. *cf.* **toosle, tossle**

tow *n.* rope; strong twine; **claes tow** washing line

tow-heidit *adj.* fair-haired (G)

towmond, towmon *n.* twelve-months

trachel, trachle *n.* burden, hindrance, struggle; *v.* draggle; trudge; overwork. *cf.* **trauchle**

trachelt *adj.* overburdened, draggled. *cf.* **trauchlet**

track *n.* an oddity (used of untidy person); *v.* to train an animal to go in traces or harness

trackie *n.* earthenware teapot

traecle *n.* treacle

traet *v.* treat

trag *n.* trash

traik *n.* long, tiring walk, trudge; *v.* trudge

trail *n.* dirty, untidy woman; part, portion; *v.* tramp, trudge

trail the rape old Hallowe'en spell consisting in dragging a straw rope round the house (M)

traivel *n.* journey; walk (S); *v. tr., intr.* travel; walk

traleel *n.* something long and trailing; a tall person (B1)

tram *n.* shaft of barrow or cart

trammle *n.* chain on cattle-binding. *cf.* **thrammle**

tramp-cole *n.* large haycock, made up of smaller ones (F)

trampit *v. pt.* tramped

trams *n.* shafts as of a cart

trance *n.* passage in a house; entrance-hall

transack *n.* transaction; deal; dealings

trauchle *See* **trachle**

trauchelt *See* **trachelt**

travise, trevis *n.* division between stalls in cowshed

trebble *n.* trouble (B1). *cf.* **tribble**

treesh *v.* curry favour; treat in a

friendly, flattering way; call to
cattle
treetle *v.* trickle; trot (G)
treid *v.* tread (J)
tribble *n., v.* trouble. *cf.* **trebble**
tribbler *n.* a troublesome thing (A)
trickit *adj.* tricky; wicked; delighted (S); **fair trickit wi masel**
trickit (up) *ppl.* dressed (up)
triffle, trifflie *n.* trifle; small sum
trig *adj.* tidy; *v.* to tidy up, dress
smartly; *ppl.* **triggit (oot)**
trink, trinkie *n.* narrow channel;
rut
trinkle *n., v.* trickle
trippin *in phr.* **his face wis trippin
im** he looked glum, displeased
troch *n.* watering trough for cattle
and horses
trock *n.* goods of no value; trash; *v.*
exchange, barter. *cf.* **troke**
trogs *excl.* troth! (as an oath)
troke *See* **trock**
troo *v.* trust; believe
trool *n.* trowel
troonk *n.* lobster pot (term used in
St Combs)
troosers *n. pl.* trousers
troot *n.* trout
trowth *n., int.* truth
trowthfu *adj.* truthful
true, true the squeel *v.* play truant
truff *n.* turf
trump(e) *n.* Jew's harp
truncher *n.* trencher, wooden
platter
trykle *n.* treacle
trypal *n.* tall, lanky, ill-shaped
person
tryst *v.* appoint a meeting; entice; *n.*

an appointed meeting
trytle *v.* lag (A1)
tull *prep.* to; till
tulzie *n.* quarrel
tummle *n., v.* tumble
tummle-doon *adj.* tumbledown
tummler *n.* glass tumbler
tummle the cat *phr.* do a
somersault (O)
tummlin-tam *n.* hay-gatherer (F)
turk *adj.* angry, annoyed (A1)
turkis *n.* a pair of pincers
turned gyang *ppl., n.* row of
sheaves on a stack, with the shear
underneath (F)
turnkwite *n.* turncoat; backslider
turn-oot *n.* attendance
turn ower *v.* fare moderately well
Turra *pr. n.* nickname for Turriff
Turra Coo *pr. n.* dairy cow confis-
cated from a Turriff farmer who
refused to stamp the insurance
cards of his workers, when the
Health Insurance Act was intro-
duced in 1913. A riot ensued
when the cow was put up for sale
turse *v.* dress; adjust one's clothes
twa *adj.* two
twa-han *adj.* two-handed
twal *adj.* twelve
twalmont(h) *n.* a twelve-month
period
twa-three *adj., n.* two or three, a
few, several
tweetle *v.* tootle on a wind
instrument
tweezlock, tweezlick *See*
thawcruick
twig *n.* glance; *v.* glance; catch
sight of; see through a dodge

twine *n.* string; *v.* turn, twist
twiner *n.* rope-twister
twinty *adj.* twenty
twise *adv.* twice (A1)
tyangs *n. pl.* tongs
tyaave, tyauve *v.* work strenuously, struggle; *n.* struggle
tyce *v.* entice
tye *excl.* giving assent. *cf.* **ay**
Tyesday *n.* Tuesday (A). *cf.* **Tiesday**

tyeuch *See* **teuch**
tyeuk *v. pt.* took
tyke *n.* dog; ticking for beds. *cf.* **tike**
tyler *n.* tailor
tylie *n.* tailor
tyne *See* **tine**
type *v.* labour hard; **a typin job** physically exhausting job (A1)
typit *adj., ppl.* worn out by hard work

—— U ——

ug *v.* to feel disgust; **uggit** disgusted
ugsome *adj.* disgusting, ghastly, horrible
ulkie *adj.* each, every. *cf.* **ilka**
ull, ull- *See* **ill, ill-**
ulless-guidless *adj.* harmless
ull-wull *n.* ill will
umberella *n.* umbrella
umman *n.* woman. *cf.* **'oman**
umrage *n.* umbrage
un- *for most words beginning with* **un,** *see* **oon**
unbehauden *adj.* not obliged
unca, unco *adj.* strange; unknown; odd; peculiar; extraordinary; **unca man** stranger; *adv.* extremely; very
uncanny *adj.* dangerous, threatening (supernaturally); unearthly, ghostly; weird
unce *n.* ounce
unceevil *adj.* uncivil
unco *See* **unca**
unco-gweed *n.* self-righteous

uncolies *adv.* strangely; very much, extremely
unctioneer *n.* auctioneer. *cf.* **ungshineer**
unedicat *adj.* uneducated
ungshin *n.* auction
ungshineer *n.* auctioneer
unlade *v.* unload
unnersteed *v. pt.* understood
unsocht *ppl., adj.* unsought
unvrocht *adj.* unworked (land)
up-castin *n.* rising of clouds above horizon threatening rain
upcome *n.* quick-witted remark
upfessin, upfeshin *n.* upbringing
uphaud *v.* uphold
upo *prep.* upon
upple *v.* (of weather) clear
upsettin *adj.* pretentious
upsides wi *adv.* even with
up-tail *v.* depart in a hurry; run off
uptak *n.* apprehension
up-through *n.* upper part of the country
upwuth *adv.* up the way, upwards

— V —

vailyable *adj.* valuable
vailye *n., v.* value
vainish *v.* vanish
valinteen *n.* valentine
vauntie *adj.* vain; exultant; ostentatious
vawcant *adj.* vacant
vawpour *n.* vapour
veelent *adj.* violent
veeperate *adj.* venomous, vicious; bitterly abusive
veesion *n.* vision
veeshus *adj.* vicious
veesit *n.* visit
veesitor *n.* visitor
vennel *n.* alley, narrow lane
vera, verra *adj., adv.* very
verlies *adv.* actually
veshel *n.* vessel
vex *v.* distress, upset; **vexed** *ppl.* distressed; sorry
viackle *n.* vehicle
vice *n.* voice. *cf.* **vyce**
virr *n.* force, vigour, 'go'
vizzy *n.* look; view; **vizzy backart** backward look
vokie *adj.* jocular (A2). *cf.* **vyokie**

voo *v.* vow
vooch *v.* vouch
vrack *n.* wreck, ruin
vran *n.* wren
vrang *adj., n.* wrong. *cf.* **wrang**
vrap *v.* wrap
vrapper *n.* working smock, overall; woman's loose jacket, blouse
vrastle *v.* wrestle (B1). *cf.* **warsle**
vrat *v. pt.* wrote
vratch *n.* wretch
vreath *n.* a wreath of snow
vreet *v.* write; *n.* handwriting
vreeter *n.* writer
vreetin *n.* handwriting
vreetin-dask *n.* writing-desk
vreetin-paper *n.* writing paper
vricht *n.* wright, joiner, carpenter
vring *v.* wring
vrocht *v. pt.* wrought, worked
vrote *v. pt.* wrote
vrung *ppl.* wrung
vrutten *ppl.* written. *See* **vreet**
vyaig *n.* loose woman
vyce *n.* voice. *cf.* **vice**
vyokie *adj.* jocular. *cf.* **vokie**

— W —

wa *adv.* away; *n.* wall; way; **come yer was ben** come away in or through. *cf.* **awa**
waal *n.* well
waal-tams *n. pl.* Buchan name for **nicky-tams**

waan *n.* wand
waar *adj.* worse; **waar o the weer** the worse for wear. *cf.* **waur**
waares *n.* wares
waav *n.* wave
wab *n.* web, woven fabric

wabbit *adj.* exhausted
wabster *n.* weaver
wa-cast *adj., n.* (anything) worthless
wacht *See* **weicht**
wachy *adj.* stale (B)
wad *v.* wed, marry; would. *cf.* **wid**
waddin *n.* wedding
waddit *v. pt.* wedded, married
wadge *v.* brandish threateningly
wadna *v. neg.* would not
wadset *v.* mortgage
wae *n.* woe; *adj.* sad, sorrowful; sorry; **wae for** sorry for; **wae's me** woe is me!
waefu *adj.* woeful
waesome *adj.* sorrowful, sad
waff *n.* puff of wind; whiff, odour
waffle *adj.* limp from weakness; shaky
wag *v.* wave, shake
wag-at-the-wa *n.* wall clock with pendulum
wa-gawn *adj.* departing; *n.* departure
waik *adj.* weak. *cf.* **wyke**
waikness *n.* weakness. *cf.* **wykeness**
wainished-like *adj.* (vanished-like), thin, pinched
wair *v.* spend. *cf.* **ware**
waister *n.* something, someone of no further use, due to infirmity, disease etc.
waistry *n.* waste. *cf.* **wastrie**
wale *v.* choose; *n.* choice, selection
wale *int.* well (S). *cf.* **weel**
walgin *n.* something large and roomy (incl. an article of dress)
wall *n.* well. *cf.* **waal**

wallant *adj.* (of flowers) withered
wallet *n.* bag for carrying personal necessaries on journey
walloch *n.* Highland dance; *v.* cry, shriek, wail
wally-draggle,-draigle *n.* sloven; good-for-nothing; insignificant, untidy person. *cf.* **warridrag**
walthy *adj.* wealthy
wame *n.* belly; stomach. *cf.* **wime**
wamfle *adj.* flexible
wammle *v.* roll, undulate, writhe
wan *adv.* way; **Kintore wan** in the direction of Kintore; *n.* wand, fishing-rod; *v. pt.* won; **wan aff** got off
wan'er, wanner *v.* wander
wanworth, wanwurth *n.* a mere nothing, something of little value (A1)
wap *n.* sharp stroke; *v.* strike sharply; flap
war *v.* were; **warna** were not
wardle *n.* world. *cf.* **warl**
wardly *adj.* worldly
ware *n.* cash (S); wire (S). *cf.* **weer** *v.* spend. *cf.* **wair**
wark *n.* work; **a wark** a job; fuss; **sic a wark** what a fuss
warl, warld *n.* world. *cf.* **wardle**
warly-wise *adj.* worldly-wise
warn *v.* warrant
warna *v. neg.* were not
warridrag *n.* good-for-nothing; undersized person or animal; slow-coach; **warriedrags, towrags an swypins o the pier** riff-raff (B)
warsh *adj.* insipid. *cf.* **wersh**
warsle, warstle *v.* wrestle, struggle

warst *adj., n.* worst

was *in phr.* **was-a-year** a year ago

washen *ppl.* washed

waskit *n.* waistcoat. *cf.* **weskit**

wast *adj.* west; **waster** western; **wastward** *adv.* westward

wastrie *n.* waste. *cf.* **waistry**

wat *adj.* wet

watna *v. neg.* wot not, did not know

watrence *n.* an entry cut through hedge or bank to give stock access to drinking water

watter *n.* water; **wattery** water closet, lavatory

watter-brash *n.* heartburn (with watery acid eructations)

watter-gless *n.* water-glass, a solution used for preserving eggs

wauble *adj.* of a weak watery flavour; wobbly; *v.* wobble

wauch *n.* swig

wauchle *v.* struggle; waddle; wade

waucht *n.* large draught; weight. *cf.* **wecht**

wauchty *adj.* weighty, heavy

wauger *n., v.* wager

wauges *n. pl.* wages

wauk *n., v.* walk

wauken *v.* waken

wauker *n.* walker; **by wauker's bus** on Shanks' pony, on foot

waukie *n.* walk; walkway, path

waukrife *adj.* wakeful

waur *adj.* worse; **waurst** worst; *v.* spend (money); **waur i the weer** the worse for wear

wean *n.* child (A, M)

wear awa *v.* to take one's leave; to fade away; die

weariet *adj.* wearied

wecht *n.* weight. *cf.* **wacht, waucht** sieve with solid base

wedder *n.* wether, castrated ram

wee *adj.* small; *n.* a little bit; a little while; **bide-a-wee** stay a while

weeda *n.* widow

weel *adj., excl.* well

weel-a-wat *excl.* assuredly

weel-a-wins *See* **weel-a-wuns**

weel-a-wite *excl.* assuredly

weel-a-wuns *excl.* of soothing and endearment

weel-faured, -faurt *adj.* well-favoured, handsome

weel-geddert *adj.* well off

weelins *v., n.* full use of one's limbs or faculties, *e.g.* **tae hae the weelins o yer airms** (B1)

weel-kent *adj.* well-known

Weelum *pr. n.* William

weemen, weemin *n.* women

weemple an wample *phr.* turn and twist

weeng *n.* wing

weepies *n.* ragweed (J)

weer *n.* wear; wire; knitting-needle; *v.* wear; **weerin geylies throu** nearly finished; **weer on** (of time) approach; **weer tee** come to, recover

weers o, on the just about (to), on the point of. *cf.* **aweers**

weesh(t) *v. pt.* washed

weesht *imp.* hush

weet *adj., v.* wet; **weety** rainy

weffle *adj.* pliable

weichen (doon) *ppl.* weighed down

weird *n.* fate, destiny

weirdless *adj.* ill-fated; worthless

weit *See* **weet**
welkin *n.* sky (M1)
went *n.* glance; glimpse; blink
wersh *adj.* tasteless. *cf.* **warsh**
we's *pr. with v.* we'll; we're
weskit *n.* waistcoat. *cf.* **waskit**
wha *pron.* who (G1). *cf.* **fa**
whaal *n.* whale
wham *pron.* whom
whang *n.* blow; lash
whapper *n.* lie
whaup *n.* curlew; empty peapod (T)
whaur *adv.* where (G1). *cf.* **far**
whause *pron.* whose
whazzle, wheezle *v.* wheeze
wheel *n.* spinning wheel
wheeber *n.* whistling sound
wheeble *See* **wheeple**
wheech, wheek *v.* move through the air with a whizzing sound; whisk away; flick
wheelie-birr *n.* child's imaginary toy car (T)
wheen *n.* number; quantity
wheep *n.* whip. *cf.* **whup, fup**
wheeper-in *n.* school attendance officer
wheep-han *n.* whip-hand, upper-hand
wheeple *n.* shrill, intermittent note with little variation of tone; *v.* whistle; call (of birds)
wheeriorums *n. pl.* intricate pieces of machinery
wheetie *adj.* mean, shabby
whigmaleerie *n.* a fantastic, useless ornament; foolish fancy; contraption
whilie *n.* a little while

whilk *rel. pron.* which
whip-the-cat *n.* tailor with no fixed place of business, who goes from house to house (M)
whirligig *n.* any rapidly revolving object
whitet-, whitie-broons *n. pl.* unbleached thread
whittle *n.* long knife
whummle *v. tr., intr.* overturn (J)
whundyke *n.* fence consisting of furze bushes
whup *n., v.* whip. *cf.* **wheep, fup**
whusky *n.* whisky
whylock *n.* little while
wi *prep.* with
wice *adj.* wise. *cf.* **wyce**
wice-like *n.* seemly, respectable
wicht *n.* wight; person
wick *n.* corner; corner of the eye or mouth
wicket *adj.* wicked
wid *adj.* mad (A1); *n.* wood. *v.* would; *cf.* **wud**
widda *n.* widow. *cf.* **widdie**
widden *adj.* wooden
widder *n.* weather. *cf.* **wither**
widder-gaw trick (**gaw**) of the weather (T); *v.* wither
widdie *n.* small wood; gallows; widow (J). *cf.* **weeda; as dry as a widdie** haddock dried without being split
widdiefu *n.* rogue; scamp
widdie-waan *n.* willow wand
wide *n.* weed; *v.* wade. *cf.* **wyde**
widna *v. neg.* would not
wife, wifie *n.* woman, married or not
wik *n.* week

wik-en *n.* week-end

wil *adj., adv.* wild, wildly

wile *v.* choose, select; **wile warst** the worst of the selection. *cf.* **wale, wyle**

wilipen *v.* (vilipend), vilify, defame

willieway *v.* (wellaway! alas!) bewail, lament

wime *n.* belly; stomach

wimple *v.* wind; meander

win *n.* wind; *v.* dry (the stooks); harvest; go, reach a place; get; **win awa** go away; **win oot** get out, escape; **win tee wi** get even with; catch up with; **win up wi** catch up with

win-casten *adj.* cast aside by the wind

winceys *n.* petticoats made of wincey

windae *n.* window. *cf.* **winnock**

windae-sneck *n.* window catch

windlestrae *n.* tall, thin, withered stalk of grass of various kinds; crested dogstail grass

windlin *See* **winlin**

windy *n.* window (J)

wink *v.* brim

winker *n.* eyelash

winlin *n.* bundle (of straw)

winna *v. neg.* will not

winner *n., v.* wonder

winnerfu *adj.* wonderful

winnister *n.* fan for winnowing corn

winnock *n.* window (A1)

winny *adj.* windy; boastful; *v.* winnow (S)

winraa *n.* gathered row of hay (F)

winrin *ppl.* wondering

wint *v.* want, be without; desire

winter, to get *phr.* to clear the fields of harvested grain

wi'oot *prep.* without. *cf.* **withoot, athoot**

wip *v.* wrap, bind tightly. *cf.* **wup**

wir *pron.* our

wird *n.* word

wire intae *v.* set to work on

wirker *n.* worker

wirm *n.* worm

wirsels *pron.* ourselves. *cf.* **oorsels**

wirsit *adj., n.* worsted

wirth *n.* worth

wis *v. pt.* was

wise *v. tr.* advise

wish! *imper.* turn right! (command to Buchan plough-horse) (T)

wisna *v. neg.* was not

wiss *n., v.* wish. *cf.* **wuss**

wissen *v.* wither, shrivel

wistna *v.* did not know (M)

wite *n., v.* blame. *cf.* **wyte**

wither *n.* weather. *cf.* **widder**

withoot *prep.* without. *cf.* **athoot**

witril, wittrel, witterel *n.* peevish, waspish person

witter *n.* barb of a dart or hook; *in pl.* the throat

wivven *ppl.* woven

wizzen *n.* gullet; *v.* wither, shrivel

wob *n.* web

wobby *adj.* covered with cobwebs

womble-brees *n.* soup made with offal

womle *v.* be squeamish; (of the stomach) rumble queasily

won *v. pt. See* **win**

wonner *n.* wonder

woo *n.* wool

woorlich (B1) *See* **oorlich**
woorthy *n.* worthy
wordle *n.* world. *cf.* **wardle**
wordy *adj.* worthy, deserving
wormit *n.* wormwood
worn awa *ppl.* deceased
worry *v.* choke; strangle
worsit *n.* worsted; woollen yarn, knitting wool; **worsit-bag** *n.* wool-bag
worth *in phr.* **gaed worth** went to pot
wrack *n.* wreck; destruction
wraith *n.* drift; wrath
wrang *adj., n.* wrong; **wrang spy** mistaken identity
wrapper *n.* working apron, overall. *cf.* **vrapper**
wreth (B1) *See* **raith**
wreith *n.* wraith, ghost
wricht *n.* carpenter. *cf.* **vricht**
wrocht *v. pt.* worked (S). *cf.* **vrocht**
wrocht-up *adj.* overwrought
wrunkelt *adj.* wrinkled
wud *adj.* mad; *n.* wood; *v.* would; **wudna** would not. *cf.* **wid**
wudden *adj.* wild; mad
wudden-dream *n.* sudden frantic motion or effort
wuddie, wuddy *n.* gallows. *cf.* **widdie**
wulk *n.* whelk; periwinkle
Wull, Wullie *pr. n.* William
wull *adj.* wild; bewildered; *adv.* astray; *n., v.* will; **o wull** of one's own accord
wull-like *adj.* wild-like

wullin *adj.* willing
wully-goo *n.* grotesque person
wumman *n.* woman
wummle *v.* turn over and over. *cf.* **whummle**
wumple *n.* tangle of objects; *v.* (of a river) twist, turn
wun *v. pt.* wound; harvested; *see* **win**
wunna *v. neg.* will not
wunt *v.* want
wup *v.* bind, bandage, wrap. *cf.* **wip**
wur *v. pt.* were
wusp *n.* wisp
wuss *n., v.* wish. *cf.* **wiss**
wut *n.* wit; *in pl.* wits
wutness *n.* witness
Wutsunday *n.* Whitsunday
wutter *n.* barb on a fish hook
wyce *adj.* wise. *cf.* **wice**
wyde *n.* weed; *v.* wade. *cf.* **wide**
wye *n.* way; **there's nae twa wyes aboot it** there's only one possibility
wye *v.* weigh; **wyed, wyet** *ppl.* weighed
wyke *adj.* weak
wykeness *n.* weakness
wylin *n.* selection
wyme *n.* belly; womb
wynd *n.* narrow lane or street
wynin *n.* division of a field (F)
wyte *n.* blame; *v.* wait
wyve *v.* weave; knit
wyver *n.* spider
wyvin *n.* weaving; knitting

— **Y** —

(yab-)yabber *v.* talk excitedly
yab-yabble *n.* gabble
yacht *v. pr., pt.* own, owned; owe
yafa *adj.* awful (M). *cf.* **aafa**
yaird *n.* yard (unit of measurement)
Yakkie *pr. n.* Peterhead name for the Eskimo, deriv. from Yaqui (B)
yaldie *n.* yellow-hammer (C)
yalla *adj.* yellow; *n.* yellow turnip
yammer *v.* chatter, whine
yamph *adj.* hungry, ravenous (A1)
yap *adj.* hungry; **yappy** hungry-looking
yard *n.* farm garden
yark *v.* jerk, tug; work hard; **yark in** drive in
yarlins *n.* device for winding yarn into skeins
yarp *v.* carp, complain
yarr *n.* corn spurrey
yaucht *See* **yacht**
yaum *n.* foolish talk (R)
yaummer *v.* cry out. *cf.* **yammer**
yauws *n. pl.* arms *e.g.* of a windmill
yavil *n.* second year crop
yavil-broth *n.* second day's broth
yavin *n.* awn, the beard of oats or barley
yawfu *adj.* awful. *cf.* **yafa**
ye *pron.* you
yea *adv.* yes
yearock *n.* hen not exceeding a year old, pullet. *cf.* **earock**
Yeel *n.* Christmas. *cf.* **Yule, Eel**
yeld *adj.* (of an animal) barren; not yielding milk for any reason. *cf.* **eel**
yeldrin *n.* yellow-hammer
yer *pron.* your
yerd *n.* yard (unit of measurement)
yerl *n.* earl
yersel *pron.* yourself; *pred. adj., adv. phr.* by yourself, alone
ye's *pron. with v.* you'll
yestreen *adv., n.* yesterday evening. *cf.* **the streen**
yett *n.* gate
yill *n.* ale
yim *n.* thin film or coating on a surface
yird *n.* earth, soil; the earth
yird (doon) *v.* bury; **yirdit** *ppl.* buried; covered in earth, dirty
yirlin *n.* yellow-hammer
yirn *v. tr., intr.* curdle; **yirnt milk** curds and whey
yirnin *n.* rennet; the stomach of a calf; the human stomach (A2)
yist *v.* hiccup
yivvery *adj.* eager, hungry for
yoam *v.* to blow with warm air; belch
yock *n., v.* itch
yockie *adj.* itchy
yoke *n.* yoke, wooden spar for pulling a plough; *v.* to attach horse to plough, harness, etc; to start work; begin; **yoke intae** begin
yokin *n.* working period during which horses are in harness

yokin-time *n.* the time to begin or resume farm-work

yole *n.* yawl, small two-masted sailing-boat

yon *adj.* that, those

yonner *adv.* yonder

yont *adv.* yonder, farther away or along

you eens *pron. pl.* you

youkie *adj.* itchy. *cf.* **yockie**

youthheid *n.* youth

yowden-drift *n.* wind-driven snow

yowder *n.* bad smell of fumes from burning

yowe, yowie *n.* ewe; fir cone

Yule *pr. n.* Christmas; Christmas Day; the Christmas season till after New Year, now mainly lit. *cf.* **Yeel, Eel**

PART TWO

English~Doric

— A —

Aberchirder *pr. n.* (nicknamed) Foggieloan
Aberdeen *pr. n.* Aiberdeen
Aberdeen football team the Dons
Aberdour *pr. n.* Aiberdour
ability *n.* can; capawcity
ablaze *adv.* alow(e); alunt
about *prep.* aboot
above *adv., prep.* abeen; atheen
abreast *adv.* abreist
abundance *n.* rowth; (to have) to be biggit oot; **in abundance** galore
abundant *adj.* rowth, routh
abuse *v.* ill-eese; (verbally) tongue; ill-tongue; kyaard; misca
abusive language ill-win (A2)
abusive *adj.* (bitterly) veeperate
accept *v.* accep; *ppl.* acceppit
accident *n.* amshach; mishanter
accommodate *v.* accommodat
accomplish *v.* (by means) moyen
accord, of one's own *phr.* o wull
account *n., v.* accoont; **on no account** naewye (S)
accountable *adj.* accoontable
accoutrements *n. pl.* graith
accumulate wealth *v.* fog
ache *n., v.* stoond, stound
acquaint *v.* (intimate) forquant
acquaintance *n.* acquantance
acquainted *ppl.* acquant (G); acquaint (B); acquint (S)
acre *n.* aacre; awcre
across *prep.* athort
act *v.* ack

action *n.* ack
active *adj.* forcie; kibble
actor *n.* ackir
actually *adv.* verlies
acute *adj.* (in understanding) lang-nebbit, -nibbit
adapt *v.* adap; **adapted** adappit
add (on or to) *v.* eek, eik, eke
addition *n.* eek, eik
addition to, in *prep. phr.* forbye
admit *v.* own
adorn *v.* busk
adornment *n.* (vain or fanciful) flumgummery
adroit *adj.* nacky
advance *n., v.* (wages) sub
advancement *n.* fordal, fordle
advantage *n.* nip
advantage of, take *phr.* tak the gweed o; tak a len o
advertise *v.* scry
advise *v.* rede (J); wise
adze *n.* each
aerated drink *n.* ale
affable *adj.* humoursome
affair *n.* rickmatick; **the whole affair** the hail rickmatick
afflicted *adj.* afflickit
afford *v.* affoord
afraid *adj.* feart; **don't be afraid** fearna
after *prep., conj.* aifter, efter; **after all** efter-an-aa
afternoon *n.* aifterneen (A); aifter-nin (S)
afterwards *adv.* aifter, efter;

108

efterhin, aifterhin
against *prep.* agin
aged *adj.* eildit
agent *n.* aagent; deester
agile *adj.* keeble; kibble; swuppert
agitate *v.* flucht; **agitated** fluchtit
ago *adv.* syne; seen; **a year ago** a
   year syne; was-a-year
agree *v.* gree
ahead *adv., prep.* aheid; **get ahead
   with** get fordalt wi
ailment *n.* *(in pl.)* sairs; (of
   unknown cause) income
aim *n.* mint; *v.* ettle; mint
ajar *adv.* ajee, agee
akin *adj.* sib
alarm *n.* alairm
alas *excl.* alis(s)
alder *n.* arn-tree (J)
ale *n.* ale; yill. *cf.* **aerated drink**
alehouse *n.* chynge-hoose
Alexander *pr. n.* Ackie; Ake; Akie;
   Saaners, Sauners; Saaney,
   Sawney; Sandy
alight *v.* licht
all *adj.* aa; **all over** *adv.* athort; **not
   at all** deil the bit
alley *n.* vennel
allure *v.* goy
alms *n.* awmous
alone *pred. adj., adv.* aleen, alane;
   masel etc.; (ma leen, yer leen, oor
   leen, him leen, her leen; their,
   them leen); **all alone** aa ma leen
   etc.; **quite alone** bird-aleen;
   leeful-leen, -lane
along *prep.* alang
aloud *adv.* heich
allow *v.* alloo; *v. pt.* alloot
Almighty *adj.* Almichty

alms *n.* amous
aloof *adj.* abeech, abeich
already *adv.* aready
also *adv.* an aa; tee; tae (S)
always *adv.* aye
amazement *n.* (state of) maze
ammunition *n.* ammuneetion
am not *v. neg.* amnin; **am I not**
   amnin aw?
among *prep.* amang; amo; amon;
   amin (S); 'mon
amount *n.* amunt; (small) inchie
amusement *n.* ameesement
amusing *adj.* shortsome
ancient *adj.* aancient, auncient
and *conj.* an
Andrew *pr. n.* Andra; Andro
Andrewmas *pr. n.* Anersmas
anger *v.* kittle
angry *adj.* mad; raist; turk
animal *n.* (old, outworn) runk
ankle *n.* queet
announce *v.* lat licht that
announcement board *n.* (at
   church) scries-boord
annoy *v.* kittle
annoyance *n.* bucker
annoyed *adj.* turk
annoying *adj.* angersome
annual *adj.* annwal; onwal
another *adj., pron.* anidder;
   anither; anodder (A2)
ant *n.* emmerteen
anvil *n.* studdy
anxious *adj.* airch (A2); arch (**ch**
   gutteral)
any *adj., adv., pron.* ony
anybody *n., pron.* onybody
anyhow *adv.* onywye
anyone *n., pron.* onyeen

anything *n.* aacht, ocht; onything
anyway *adv.* onyroad; onywye; onygate
anywhere *adv.* onywye
apart *adv.* apairt
apparatus *n.* leems
apparently *adv.* appearandly
appeal *n., v.* appale
apple *n.* aipple
appoint *v.* appynt; (a meeting) tryst
appointed meeting *n.* tryst
apprehension *n.* uptak
approach *v.* come in aboot; (of time) weer on
approve *v.* appruv
April *n.* Awprile; Prile
apron *n.* aapron; naapron; (working) wrapper; (of sackcloth) seck-aapron
apt to *adj.* liken tae
arch *n.* airch; (also arched passage-way) pend, pen(n)
Archie *pr. n.* Airchie
Arctic tern *n.* tarick
argue *v.* argie; argie-bargie; argle-bargle; threep, threip; **argue the matter** delve the bank (B1)
argument *n.* argie-bargie; argle-bargle; argiement
arithmetic *n.* coontin
arm *n.* airm; gaidy (A)
armchair *n.* airm-cheer; bow-cheer
armful *n.* oxterfu; oxterlift
armpit *n.* oxter
arms *n. pl.* (e.g. of a windmill) yaaws, yauws
army *n.* airmy
around *adv.* aroon; roond an aboot; *prep.* aroon
arrange *v.* arreenge

arrest *v.* nab; reest
arrow *n.* barbet
arse *n.* erse; doke
art *n.* airt
articulate *v.* moo-ban
ash, ashes *n.* aiss; ess; (on top of a pipe) dirry
ash-can *n.* aiss-backet
ash-heap *n.* aiss-midden
ask *v.* (request) bid; (for) sik, seek; (a question) speer, speir
askance *adv.* asklent
askew *adv.* skew
asp *n.* aisp
aspen *n.* quaikin-aish
assail *v.* lat at
assistant *n.* (minister's) helpender
associate *v.* (with) colleague (wi)
assure *v.* asseer; asser
assuredly *adv.* awyte; *excl.* weel-a-wat; weel-a-wite
astir *adv.* asteer
astonish *v.* dammer (R)
astray *adv.* wull
astride *adv.* stridelins
as well *adv.* an aa
at all *adv.* ava; neen (nae neen pleast); ony (gin it's ony weet)
atom *n.* (particle) hait
attach *v.* (horse to plough) yoke
attempt *v.* mint
attendance *n.* turn-oot
attendance officer *n.* (school) wheeper-in
attend to *v.* sort
attentive *adj.* tenty
attentively *adv.* tentily
attracted to, to be *v.* tae hae a lang ee at
attractive *adj.* bonnie, bonny

auction *n.* rowp, roup; ungshin; **sell up by auction** rowp oot
auctioneer *n.* ungshineer
audience *n.* owdience
aught *n.* ocht
August *n.* Aagist
aurora borealis *pr. n.* the Merry Dancers
austere *adj.* door, dour
Australia *pr. n.* Australya

authorise *v.* owthereese
aware *adj.* awaar
away *adv.* awa; wa; furth; **away abroad** awa foreign; **far away** hine awa
awful *adj.* aafa, affa, aafu; yafa
awl *n.* (shoemaker's) ellieson; elshin
awry *adj.* agee; ajee
axle *n.* aixle

— B —

babbler *n.* gab
baby *n.* bairn; bairnikie; babbity
baby's flannel coat *n.* barrie
back band *n.* (of harness) backbin
back-bone *n.* back-been
back-garden *n.* backie
backslider *n.* turnkwite
backwards *adv.* backlins
bad *adj.* coorse; ill; ull; *adv.* ill; ull; **in a bad state** sair awa wi't
badly *adv.* ill; sairly
badly off *adj.* ull-aff; sair-aff
badly behaved *adv., adj.* ill-gatit, ill-gettit
bade *v.* bad
bad-mannered *adj.* ill-farrant
bad-tempered *adj.* crabbit; cankert
bag *n.* pock, poke; powk; pyock; (farmworker's) chackie; (for personal necessities on journey) wallet
baggage *n.* (loose woman) limmer
baker *n.* baxter
baking *n.* byaakin
bald *adj.* beld; baaldie-heidit
ball *n.* (bouncing) ba; ballie; (of rope, cord, wool) clew, cloo; (of butter) pat
ball *n.* (dance) baal
ballad *n.* ballant
bamboozled *ppl., adj.* boggit; bumbazed
bandage *v.* wup
bang about *v.* breenge
bankrupt, became *v. pt.* broke
bank up *v.* (a fire) reest, reist
banns *n. pl.* (giving notice of impending marriage) cries
bantam *n.* bantin
banter *n.* hyze
baptise *v.* bapteese
baptism *n.* bapteesement
barb *n.* (of a hook) witter; wutter
Barbara *pr. n.* Baabie, Baubie
barbed-wire *n.* barbit-weer; pykit-weer
bare *n.* nakit; nyakit; **bare patch in field** blain
barefooted *adj.* barfit
bargain *v.* cowp; niffer
bark *v.* (of a dog) bowff; bouch
barley *n.* (when four or six-rowed)

bear, bere

barnacle *n.* scaa, scaw

barrel *n.* bowie; (for oatmeal) meal-bowie

barren *n.* (of an animal) eel; yeld

barrow *n.* barra; hurlie; seck-lifter

barter *v.* hooie; niffer

base *n.* (in children's games) dell

bashful *adj.* blate; bauch

basin *n.* (wooden for brose) bicker

basket *n.* (for fish) creel; (fitted into top of fish-wife's creel) murlin; (shallow, wicker) scull, skull; (esp. for sowing seed) happer

bass *n.* bess; **to sing bass** bess

bat *n.* baakie; baukie

bathe *v.* baathe; dook

bather *n.* dooker

bayonet *n.* baignet

be *v.* be; **be not** *v. neg.* (don't be) binna; **be without** *v.* wint

beak *n.* neb, nib

beam *n.* (of sun) blink; (across chimney from which the crook is suspended) rantletree

bear *v.* thole

beard *n.* baird; birse; (of oats or barley) aan, awn

beat *v.* (surpass) baet; bleck; cow; ding; (strike) clowt; dird; (severely) soosh; **beaten** *ppl.* baet; **that beats everything** yon cows aa

beaten track, off the *prep. phr.* at the back o beyond; oot o kent boons

beautiful *adj.* byowtifu; bewotifie

beauty *n.* byowty

because *conj.* cause; **because of** *prep.* ower the heids o

bed *n.* (small) beddie; (wooden, shut in with doors) bun-bed; (~ doors) bed-lids; (~ in semi-parlour end of but-an-ben) but-bed; (low, on castors) hurlie-bed; (makeshift) shakky-doon; **in bed, put to bed** beddit

bedaub *v.* skaik

bed-clothes *n. pl.* bed-claes

bedraggle *v.* bedraigle

bedridden person *n.* beddal

beehive *n.* (simple type) bee-ruskie; skep

beetle *n.* gollach, goloch; horny-gollach

befall *v.* befa; come ower; fa

before *adv., prep.* afore; ere, or; *conj.* ere, or; **before long** belyve

beforehand *adv.* aforehan

beg *v.* thig

began *v. pt.* begood

beggar *n.* gaberlunzie; supplicant; (threatening) sorner; (genteel) thigger

begin *v.* fa tee; set tee; stairt, stert; yoke

beginning *n.* aff-go

behaved, badly *adj.* ill-gatit, -gettit

beheld *v. pt.* beheeld

behind *adv., prep.* ahin(t)

beholden *adj.* behudden, behauden

behoof *n.* beheef

behove *v.* beheeve

belabour *v.* belaabour

belch *n., v.* rift; (of vapour etc.) yoam

believe *v.* troo

belittle *v.* lichtlify

bell *n.* (sound of) jow

bellow *v.* (of cattle) rowst; rowt (G1)

bellows *n. pl.* bellas
belly *n.* wame; wime, wyme
belly-band *n.* (of harness) belly-ban
belong *v.* belang; **he belongs to Buckie** he belangs Buckie
below *prep.* aneth; ablo(w), alow (S); in alow
bench *n.* binch
bend *n.* bennin
bend *v.* boo; loot; (with age) creep doon; *ppl.* boo't; **bend double** boo't twa-faal
beneath *See* **below**
benighted *ppl., adj.* nicht-boon, -boun
benumb *v.* daver; dozen
beside *prep.* aside
besides *adv.* forby(e); forbyes; *prep.* (apart from) byes
besmear *v.* drabble
bespatter *v.* spairge
best *n.* (of the lot) stang o the trump; (~ room) the room; (~ room in two-roomed cottage) horn-en, -eyn
bet *v.* beet
between *prep.* atween; atweesh; **between times** atween hans
bewail *v.* willieway
bewildered *adj.* wull
beyond *adv.* ayon; ayont
bid *n.* (at sale) bode
big *adj.* muckle; meikle
bilberry *n.* blaeberry
bill *n.* bull; lawin
bin *n.* (for corn, turnips) bing
bind *v.* bin'; bin (rhyme with tin); (tightly) wip; wup
binding *n.* (for cattle) binnin

birch *n.* birk; birken (C)
bird *n.* (unfledged) gorbel; gorblin; gog (S); (state of egg with young bird partially formed) gorbellt
birth, give *v.* (of rabbits) cleck
bit *n.* (small) bittock; thochtie; wee
bitch *n.* bick
bite *n.* gnap; rive; (a mere) knap-at-the-win
black *adj.* bleck; blaik
blackberry *n.* bramble; brammle
blackbird *n.* blackie; ouzel (M)
blacken *v.* blaik; blaiken, blecken
blackguard *v.* blackguaird; *joc.* bleck
blacking *n.* bleck; bleckin
blacksmith *n.* smith; brookie
blacksmith's shop *n.* smiddy
bladder *n.* bledder
blame *n.* wyte
blanket *n.* (fisher term) plaid
blast *n.* (of wind) blaffert; bluffert; bloiter; blouter
blaze *n.* bleeze; lowe
bleak *adj.* (of weather) oorlich
bleary-eyed *adj.* bleart; bleery
bleed *v.* blood (S)
blessed *adj.* seely
blight *n.* blicht
blind *adj.* blin
blink *n.* went; *v.* (weakly) blinter
blockhead *n.* gomeril; tawpie
block up *v.* stap
blonde *n.* blon
blood *n.* bleed
blood-curdling *adj.* bleed-jeelin
blood-red *adj.* bleed-reid
blossom *n.* floorish
blow *n.* clowt, cloot; daad; lick; plowt; whang; (of a sounding

kind) binner; (resounding) clink;
v. blaa; blaave; blyaav; (the nose
with finger and thumb) snyte;
(with warm air) yoam
blown out *ppl.* (of cattle, having
over-eaten) hoven
blubber *v.* bubble; snotter
blue *adj.* blae; **black and blue** blae
bluebell *n.* blewart
bluish *adj.* blae
blunt *adj.* (of speech) aff-han
blushing *ppl., adj.* kindlin (J)
bluster *v.* howder
board *n.* brod; boord; (moveable on
front of boxcart) front shelvin; (at
rear) hin shelvin; (for sharpening
scythe) scythe-brod; straik
boarding-school *n.* buirdin-squeel
boast *v.* blaw; braig; blyaav; craa,
craw
boastful *adj.* winny
boat *n.* (built with planks edge to
edge) carvel-biggit; (built with
planks overlapping) clinker-
biggit; **in the same boat** i the
same box (A1)
Boddam *pr. n.* (nickname) Dowp
bogie-roll *n.* (tobacco) bogie-rowe
boil *n.* beil; beilin; blin lump; *v.*
bile, byle
boiling *n.* (e.g. of rhubarb) bilin,
bylin
boistrous *adj.* bowsterous;
hallyrackit
bold *adj.* baul; bauld; croose; deft
boll *n.* (old Sc. measure) bow
bollard *n.* paal
bolster *n.* bowster
bolt *v.* tak sheet
bondage *n.* thirlage

bone *adj.* been; **a bone to pick** a
craa to pluck
boney *adj.* beeny
bonfire *n.* bale-fire; bondy (O)
book *n.* beuk, byeuk
boot *n.* beet; buit (S); (rubber knee
boot worn by fish-workers)
topper
bored (with) *ppl., adj.* scunnert (o,
wi)
borrow *v.* borra; thig
bosom *n.* bosie; oxter. *cf.* **armpit**
botch *v.* bucker
both *adj., pron.* baith
bother *v.* badder; bather
bottle *n.* (earthenware) pig; (hot
water) pig; (with handle(s) for
holding liquor) grey-beard
bottom *n.* boddom; (buttocks) doke
bought *v. pt.* bocht; coft (G1)
bounce *v.* stot; daad, daud (aboot);
(up and down) dyst
bound *v. pt., ppl.* bun; bunt; thirlt
boundary *n.* boon, boun; mairch;
boundary wall mairch-dyke
bow *n.* (tied) doss; *v.* boo; loot
bow and arrow *phr.* bow an barbet
bowl *n.* (for bowling) bool; (large
wooden for baking) bossie;
(wooden dish for oatmeal) brose
caup
bow-legged *adj.* bow-hoched
boy *n.* loon; laddie; (small)
laddikie; (fisher term) bokie;
(coddled) Grunnie's John; (term
of endearment) mannikie
boyfriend *n.* laad
braces *n. pl.* (for trousers) galluses
brag *v.* blaa, blaw; blyaav; braig
brain(s) *n.* harns

brainless *adj.* glaikit
bran *n.* pron
branch *n.* brench, brinch
brandish *v.* (threateningly) wadge
brass *n.* bress
bravely *adv.* starkly
brawl *n.* brulzie
bread *n.* loaf; breed, breid
breadth *n.* breid
break *v.* brak
breakfast *n.* brakfast
break down *v.* (from drink, exhaustion, illness) fooner
break wind *v., n.* pump; let off
breast *n.* breest, breist
breath *n.* braith (G); breith (J); in-draacht; (of wind) funk; **out of breath** birsin
breeching *n.* (part of harness round hind-part of shaft horse to allow backward movement) britchin
breeze *n.* pirr-winnie
brew *n.* browst
bridegroom *n.* bridegreem
bridge *n.* brig
bridle *n.* (with blinkers) blin bridle
bright *adj.* bright; croose; (gaudy) galliart (B1)
brighten *v.* brichen; (of person) *intr.* cantle up
brim *v.* (be full to the brim, brim over) lip; ream; wink; **brimming** *ppl., adj.* reamin fu
bring *v.* fesh; fess; **bring out** rank oot; **bring to mind** fess back; **bring up** fess up
bristle *n.* birse
brittle *adj.* bruckle; freuch
broad *adj.* braid
broke *v. pt.* brook, bruik; brak;

bruk
bronchitis *n.* broncaidis
brood *n.* cleckin; brodmell
brooding, broody *adj.* (of hen) *adj.* clockin
broom *n.* (brush) beesom; besom; (shrub) breem
broom-bush *n.* breem-buss
broom-handle *n.* besom-shaft
brother *n.* brither; breeder; bridder; broder (A2)
brother-in-law *n.* gweed-brither, -breeder, -bridder
brought *v. pt.* brocht; foosh. *cf.* **fesh**
brow *n.* broo
brow-band *n.* (in harness) broobin
brown *adj.* broon
bruise *n.* birse; malagruze
brush *n.* beesom; besom; *v.* sweesh
brushwood *n.* hag
brute *n.* breet
Buchanhaven native *pr. n.* Buchaner
Buchan Observer, the *pr. n.* the Buchanie
bucket *n.* backet
Buckie native *pr. n.* Bucker
build *n.* book, bouk; **of small build** sma-bookit, -boukit; **of lean build** nairra-bookit; *v.* big(g); **built** biggit
builder *n.* bigger
building *n.* biggin
building-ground *n.* seet
bulk *n.* book, bouk
bulky *adj.* (muckle-)bookit, -boukit
bull *n.* bul
bullock *n.* (young) stirk; (older, castrated) stot

bully *v.* bullyrag
bumble-bee *n.* bumbee; in Buchan, (Auchmacoy) bummer
bump *n.* doosht; *v.* (up and down) dyst
bumpkin *n.* gillieperous; gileepris (hard g)
bun *n.* (floury) bap; (glazed, with sugar on top) heater; (plain) soft biscuit, softie
bundle *n.* (loose, untidy) fushach
bungle *v.* bucker
bungler *n.* footer
buoy *n.* bowe
burden *n.* birn; (of a discourse) owercome
bureau *n.* buroo
burgh *n.* broch
burgler *n.* hoosebrakker
burial *n.* beerial
burial place *n.* (reserved in grave-yard) lair
buried *ppl.* beeriet; yirdit
burly *adj.* buirdly; muckle-bookit, -boukit
burn *v.* burn; *pt., ppl.* brunt; brent

(G1); plot; **burning brightly** (of fire) reevin
burst *v.* birst; (asunder) rive; **bursting** *ppl.* burssen
bury *v.* beery; yird (doon)
bush *n.* buss; (stunted) scrog
bushel *n.* bushle; bussle
business *n.* buzness
bustle *n., v.* steer; feerich; hash
busy *adj.* thrang
but *conj.* bit
butter churn *n.* kirn
butterfly *n.* butterflee (R); buttery (M1)
butterhand *n.* clapper
buttocks *n. pl.* dowp, doup; (vulg.) dock, doke; hurdies
buy *v.* buy; coff (G1)
buzz *v.* bizz; (of thoughts) ream
buzzing *n.* bizzin
by *prep.* by, b'; (used of time) gin; **by seven o'clock** gin seyven o'clock; **by the time that** gin
by-and-by *adv.* belyve
byway *n.* bywye

— **C** —

cackle *v.* keckle
cairn *n.* carn; cyarn
calf *n.* caaf, caafie; **calves** *n. pl.* car
calk *v.* (fix guard on horse's hoof) caak, cauk
call *v.* ca, caa
call on *v.* cry on; cry in by; cry tee
callous *adj.* scorie-hornt
calm *adj.* (of the weather) lown
calve *v.* caav

came *v. pt.* cam
candle *n.* cannle, cunnle
Candlemas *pr. n.* Cannlemas
candy *n.* gundy
cane *n.* (West Indian) spaingie; spainyie
can not *v. neg.* canna
canvas *n.* cannas
cap *n.* (man's) bonnet; caip, kep; (woman's) mutch

capable *adj.* cawpable

capacious *adj.* capawshus

capering *adj.* (of children) royd, royt

caprice *n.* maggot

card *n.* (playing) cairt; **to play cards** cairt; *v.* (wool) caird

care *n.* tent; (anxiety) cark; **not a care in the world** nae cark nor care; **take care** tak tent; *v.* car; raik; **don't care at all** carna doit; **take care** ca canny

careful *adj.* carefu; tenty

carefully *adj.* tentily

care of, take *v.* notice

caress *v.* daat, dawt

cargo *n.* cargie

carouse *n.* ran-dan; **on the carouse** oot on the ran-dan

carp *v.* yarp

carpenter *n.* jyner; vricht, wricht

carriage *n.* kerridge

carrier *n.* cadger

carrion crow *n.* hoodie(-craw)

carry *v.* cairry; cairt; (loads) cadge; (something heavy) humph; **carry-on** cairry-on; on-cairry

cart *n.* cairt; (mounted on springs) spring-cairt; *v.* (corn in from field) lead

carter *n.* cairter

carting *n.* (corn, hay) leading

cartload *n.* cartil

case, in *conj.* case be; (in neg. context) for fear

cast *v.* cast; *pt.* ceest, keest

castle *n.* castell

cast-off *adj., n.* aff-cast

castrate *v.* cut; lib

casual dress *adj., n.* go-ashores

catch *n.* (of fish) shot; **a good catch** a cran-the-net; *v.* cleek; (with the hand) kep; (fish with the hands) guddle; **catch sight of** twig; **catch up with** win up wi

catechise *v.* catecheese

catechism *n.* carritch(es); catechis

cattle *n. pl.* beas' (C); bestial (A2); kine (A); kye; nowt; (disease; in the hindlegs) crochle; (to call to cattle) treesh

cattle binding *n.* (iron) bowsell; (retaining rod for binding) slider; (rope or chain on binding to attach sell to a stake) thrammle

cattle fold *n.* bucht

cattleman *n.* bail(l)ie; bylie; cattlie (S)

caul *n.* kell; seelyhoo

cause to *v.* gar

causeway *n.* causey; cassie

cautious *adj.* canny; cowshus

cease *v.* devall; jeho(y)

centipede *n.* meggie-monyfeet

certain *adj.* siccar

chafe *v.* chaff

chaff *n.* caff; **chaff mattress** caff-bed; caff-seck

chain *n.* chine; (by which pot hung over fire from crook) links; (to bind cattle) sell

chair *n.* cheer

chairman *n.* cheerman

chalk *n.* chack; *v.* caak, cauk

challenge *v.* dip; (for repayment of a debt) caak, cauk

chamber *n.* chaamer, chaumer (esp. for sleeping place for farm servants in Banff and Buchan); **to live in a chamber** to chaamer, chaumer

chamber-pot *n.* chantie, chanty, chuntie; dirler
change *v.* cheenge; chynge
changeable *adj.* changefu
changeless *adj.* cheengeless
channel *n.* (narrow) trink(ie)
chap *n.* billie; chiel; stock; (effect of cold) hack
characterless *adj.* eedle-oddle
charge *n., v.* chairge
charity *n.* chairity
Charles *pr. n.* Chae; Chairlie
charlock *n.* skellach
charmed with *phr.* teen wi
chat *n., v.* blether; crack; newse; *v.* ca the crack
chatter *n.* jaa, jaw; *v.* bledder; blether; gab; jaa, jaw; yammer
chatter-box *n.* gab
chattering *n.* gabbing
chatting *n.* chirr-wirrin (S)
chatty *adj.* crackie; newsy
cheap *adj.* chaip, chape
cheapjack *n.* chaip-john
cheat *v.* chait, chate; jink; snype, swick; (in marble-playing) foodge; *ppl.* snypit; swickit
cheating *n.* chaitry
checked *adj.* (of a pattern) chackit
cheek *n.* chik
cheek-by-jowl *adv.* cheekie-for-chowlie
cheeks *n. pl.* chafts
cheep *n.* chowp; peek; **not a cheep** nae a chowp
cheerful *adj.* blithe(some), blyth
cheery *adj.* canty
cheese *n.* chyse; (a round) kebbuck (soft) hangie
cheese press *n.* chessel; chesset

chemise *n.* sark
chequered linen *n.* chack
cherry *n.* chirry
cherry tree *v.* (wild) gean
chest *n.* kist; **get it off your chest** redd yer crap; teem yer crap
chew *v.* chaw
chewing-gum *n.* chuddy
chicken *n.* chucken; chucknie; **chicken soup with leek** cock-a-leekie
chickweed *n.* chuckenwort
chiefly *adv.* feckly
child *n.* bairn; geet; (small) eeshan (M2); (young) etsleel (B1); littlin; little een; wean
childhood *n.* bairnheid
chilled *adj.* chilpit; stervin o caal, stervin wi the caal
chilly *adj.* airish; caaldrife
chimney *n.* chimley; lum
chimney-corner *n.* ingle-neuk
china *adj., n.* cheena
chink *n.* bore
chinless *adj.* soo-moo't
chinwagging *n.* chirr-wirrin (S)
chipping *n.* (granite) chuckie-steen
chives *n.* size
choice *n.* wale
choir *n.* kyre; kire
choke *v.* smucht; (on food) worry
cholic *n.* belly-thraw
choose *v.* chyse; wale; wyle
chop *v.* chap
christen *v.* kirsen
christening *n.* kirsenin
Christmas *n.* Eel; Yeel
Christmas pudding *n.* dumplin
chuckle *v.* keckle
chummy *adj.* chuff

chunk *n.* skelp
church *n.* kirk; **at church** *prep.*
phr. kirkit; **church-gallery** laft
Church of Scotland *pr. n.* the Aul
Kirk
churchyard *n.* kirk-yaird
churl *n.* carl; nabble, nabal
churlish *adj.* nabble, nabal;
churlish man tike
churn *v.* (butter) kirn
chute *n.* (conveying corn to
elevator) shakkin-spoot
cinder *n.* shunner
circumspect *adj.* douce
cirrus clouds *n. pl.* (high)
mackerels' backs an meers' tails
city *n.* ceety
civil *adj.* ceevil
clad *adj.* cled
clairvoyant *adj.* fey
clamber *v.* rink
clatter *n.* reemis(h)
claw *n.* claa; clook; faach, fauch
(B1); **seize with the claws** cleek
clawed *v. pt.* clew
clean *v.* dicht; (a byre) muck
clear *adj.* clair; *v.* (out) redd (oot);
(your throat) pyocher, redd yer
throat; (up) redd up; (of weather)
upple
clench *v.* steek; **clenched fists**
steekit nieves
clever *adj.* clivver; fell; heidie;
lang-heidit
cliff *n.* scaar, scaur
climb *v.* clim; *pt.* clam(b), clum;
sclim; speel, speil
clinch *v.* (settle) clench
clod *n.* (of earth) knibloch
close *v.* dit

close by *adv.* aside
close together *adv.* curduddoch (J)
cloth *n.* claith; cloot; (very thin)
flinrikin; (made of hards) harden;
(sackcloth) harn
clothe *v.* claithe; clead
clothes *n. pl.* claes; clyes; cleadin;
duds; graith; (second best)
scuddlin claes
clothes peg *n.* pin
cloud *n.* clood; (small clouds flying
before the wind) pack-merchants
cloudberry *n.* aiv(e)rin
clover *n.* clivver. *cf.* **clever**
club-foot *n.* clog-fit
clumsy *adj.* gaakit, gawkit; **clumsy
person** hoffin; howfin; hurb
cluster *n.* dossie
clutch *n.* (of eggs); settin; *v.*
claught; clootch
coal *n.* (live) eyzle; kwile
coal-dust *n.* coal-coom
coarse *adj.* coorse; grofe
coat *n.* kwite, kwyte; (dreadnought)
fer-nothing; (old-fashioned)
surtoo, surtout
coating *n.* (thin) yim
coax *v.* tice wi
coaxing *ppl., adj.* fraiky
cobbler *n.* sooter, souter
cobbler's wax *n.* rosit
cobblestone *n.* causey; cassie
cobweb *n.* moosewob; wob;
covered in cobwebs wobby
cod *n.* (of medium size) sprag
coffin *n.* kist; **to put in a coffin** *v.*
kist
cohabitee *n.* bidie-in
coin *n.* (of little value) doit; bodle
(J); plack

coir yarn *n.* sparty tow

cold *adj.* caal(d); caaldrife; (as ice) jeel; (of weather only) fresh; (bitter) stervation; (of the wind) snell

colewort *n.* kail, kale

collapse *v.* (with drink, exhaustion, illness) fooner

collar *n.* (of iron, as instrument of punishment) jougs

collecting-box *n.* (offertory plate at church door) brod; (with long handle, passed round church) ladle

collection *n.* rickmatick; (of small objects) smyteral

colourful *adj.* (highly) kennelt

colt *n.* cowt

comb *n.* kaim, kame

come away *imp.* c'wa

comely *adj.* gatefarrin

come to *v.* (recover) weer tee

comfort *n.* easedom

comfortable *adj.* bien

comfortless *adj.* bienless

common *n.* (small) loan; (village green) loaning (S)

common-sense *n.* gumption; mense, minse; rum(mil)-gumption; rumigumshun

commotion *n.* stramash; tirravee

communicant *n.* commeenicant

company *n.* (musical or convivial) core

compared with *prep.* byes; forbye; till

compel *v.* gar

complain *v.* compleen; crowp; peek (peevishly) girn; peenge; yarp; **complaining feebly** goranichy (B1)

complaint *n.* compleent

completely *adv.* fair

comrade *n.* billie

conceited *adj.* bigsie; concaited; full

concern *n.* concairn; *in phr.* **the whole concern** the hail rickmatick

condescending *adj.* skichent

condition *n.* condeeshun; precunnance; (in good ~) clear

conduct *v.* conduck

confident *adj.* croose, crouse; **brisk and confident** croose i the craw

confound *v.* confoon; dag; deg; **confound it** dag it; dozen't

confuse *v.* dammer

confused *adj.* (of things) throwder; (of people) daivert; doilt, dylt; (mentally) dottelt; raivelt

confusion *n.* (state of) kirn; mixter-maxter

congeal *v.* jeel

congregated *v. pt.* congregat

connect *v.* conneck; *ppl.* conneckit

consciousness *n.* (recover) come alist

considerable *adj.* gey

consideration, under *phr.* throw-han

consort (with) *v.* colleague (wi)

constipated *adj.* corkit

constipation *n.* dry-darn

constitution *n.* constiteetion

constrained *adj.* hudden doon; hudden in aboot

constrict *v.* hank

contempt *excls.* of footers; tchach, tchoot; terms of (used of a person) scadden; scoot; skate;

splewin; (for someone of dirty
habits) sklype; (for fellow of low
character) slung; (for worthless
type) slype; (puny, worthless
type) tarlich; (foul-mouthed,
vulgar type) tink
contemptible *adj.* dirten
contend *v.* conten
contest *n.* (esp. curling) bonspiel
continual *adj.* conteenwal
continue *v.* conteena (B1), *pt.*
conteenit; hud
contradict *v.* conter; cwanter
contradictory *adj.* contermin't
contraption *n.* whigmaleerie
contrary *adj.* contermashious;
contermin't; cwanter-kine
contribute *v.* contreebit
control, beyond *phr.* oot o han; nae
tae hud nor bin'
controversial *adj.* kittle; kittlesome
convenience *n.* convainience
conversation *n.* a blether; news(e);
spik; (low, muttered) toot-moot
conversation lozenges *n. pl.* readin
sweeties
converse *v.* collogue; **conversing
intimately** corrieneuchin
convey *v.* convoy
convince *v.* goy (B1)
convolvulus *n.* creepin-eevie. *cf.*
slow
cook *v.* keuk, kyeuk
cool *adj.* cweel, kweel
copse *n.* shaw (J)
copy down *v.* tak aff
coracle *n.* currack
cord *n.* (used to pull cleaning-rag
through a rifle) pul-throwe
corker *n.* beezer; binder; bummer

cormorant *n.* scrath
corn *n.* corn; oats; **corn chest**
cornkist; bruise-box; **corn husk**
sheelock
cornbin *n.* bing
corner *n.* neuk; (esp. of the eye and
mouth) wick; **having corners**
neukit
corn spurrey *n.* yarr
corps *n.* core
corpse *n.* corp
correct *v.* correck
corresponding to *ppl.* confeerin tae
corrugated iron *n.* sheet iron; tin-
can
corsets *n. pl.* steys
cost *in phr.* **cost them a lot** pyke
their pooch
cottage *n.* (for farmservants) bothy;
(two-roomed) but-an-ben
cottager *n.* (in tied farm cottage)
cottage; **farm cottage** cotter-
hoose
cotton-wool *n.* caddis. *cf.* **fluff**
cough *n.* hoast; (deep-seated) kirk-
yaird hoast; (catarrhal) pyocher;
blocher; (whooping) kink-hoast;
v. (bark) bouch; clocher; pyooch;
(huskily) craighle
could *v. pt.* cud; cwid; *neg.* cudna;
cwidna
coulter *n.* (iron cutter at front of
plough) couter
count *v.* coont
countenance *n.* coontenance
counter *n.* (shop) coonter
country *n.* kwintra; kwintry
courage *n.* spunk
course *n.* coorse; **of course** of
coorse; an coorse (A2)

court *n., v.* coort
courteous *adj.* mensefu
cover *n.* hap; (thin) scriffon;
striffin; *v.* hap; *ppl.* happit; (over)
hap up
cow *n.* coo; *pl.* kye; (suckling
calves) sooker; (name for a cow)
Crummie
coward *n.* coord(ie); coof
coward's blow *n.* coordie-lick
cow-dung *n.* sharn; (liquid) sharn-
bree
cower *v.* coor; coorie, coory; corrie;
crulge (doon)
cowrie shell *n.* (small) kysie;
calfie's mooie; Johnny Groatie
cowshed *n.* byre; (division between
stalls) traivis, trevis
crab *n.* partan; (small, greenish,
found in shore pools) (B) grindie;
grindie tocher
cracked *ppl.* crackit
crafty *adj.* sneck-drawin (A2)
crag *n.* heuch
cram *v.* pang; stech
crash *n.* reemis(h)
cravat *n.* graavit, grauvit
crazed *adj.* dylt, doilt
crazy *adj.* gyte; **drive him crazy**
raise him wull
cream *n.* ream; crame (S)
cream pot *n.* stoopie (B1)
crease *n.* lirk, lurk; *v.* crunkle; *ppl.*
crunkelt; gruggelt
creature *n.* craitur, cratur
credit *v.* crydit
creditor *n.* craver
crept *v. pt.* crap
crested *adj.* tappit
crevice *n.* bore

criminal *n.* ranegill
cringe *v.* creenge
crinkle *v.* crunkle
cripple *n.* laimiter
crippled *ppl.* crochle; crochly;
hypal (B1)
crisis *n.* creesis; bit; **in a crisis** at
the bit
critic *n.* creetick
critical *adj.* lang-nebbit
criticise *v.* creeticise; misca; redd
up (somebody)
criticism *n.* (severe) kail throwe the
reek
croak *n., v.* crowp; craik
crockery *n.* lame
croft *n.* craft
crop *n., v.* (of land) crap; *n.* (of
bird) crap
cross *adj.* crabbit; cankert
cross-beam *n.* (in rafters) baak,
bauk; spur-baak, -bauk
crouch *v.* coorie, coory; corrie;
crulge (doon)
crow *n.* craw; corbie; (hooded)
hoodie(-craa)
crowberry *n.* knowpert
crowd *n.* (small) boorach(ie),
bourach, bing; (noisy) clamjamfrey, clanjamfry; crood;
(confused, noisy) currieboram;
mardle, merdle; mengyie;
(confused) smarrach; swarrach; *v.*
crood
crowded *adj.* thrang
crown *n.* croon; (of a woman's cap)
cockernony, *v.* croon
cruel *adj.* ill; ull
crumble *v.* murle
crumbly *adj.* bruckle

crush *v.* pran
crusty *adj.* nibawa
crutch *n.* oxter-staff, oxter-stav
crutches *n. pl.* dooble-legs
cry *v.* (weep) greet, *pt.* grat; **cried
his head off** roared an grat; (call
out) scrie, scry; (esp. when
dancing) hooch; (scream)
walloch; (cry out) yammer,
yaummer
cry-baby *n.* bubbly-bairn
cuckoo *n.* gowk. *cf.* **fool**
cud *n.* kweed
cuddle *v.* delt
cup *n.* (of tea) shallie (o tay) (old
term)
cupboard *n.* aamrie; (wall-) press
curb *v.* pit the haims on

curdle *v.* yirn
curds *n. pl.* curds; **curds and whey**
croods an fy; yirnt milk
curiosity *n.* keeriosity; (inquisitiveness) ill-, ull-fashence
curious *adj.* keerious
curlew *n.* whaap, whaup
curl papers *n. pl.* (hair in) curlie
wurlies
currant *n.* curran
currant bun *n.* curran bap
curry favour *phr.* hud in wi;
treesh; *ppl.* in-huddin
curse *v.* (swear) ban
curt *adj.* nippit
curtsey *n.* beck; *v.* bob
cut *v.* cut; *pt.* cuttit; clip; sned; (nip
off) stoo

— **D** —

daffodil *n.* daffie
dagger *n.* dirk
dainty *adj.* denty; *n.* (delicacy)
flagarie
dairy *n.* dyrie, diry
daisy *n.* gowan
dally (wi) *v.* tig (wi)
dam *n.* dem
damage *n.* scaith; *v.* (suffer) get the
flacht
damn *n.* (euphemism) dang
damp *adj.* (of the weather) mochie
dance *n.* duncie; dince (S); hooch
(S); *v.* duncie; caper; (slow
Highland dance) strathspey;
(Highland) walloch
dandle *v.* (a child) diddle (B)
dangerous *adj.* fell; (from

supernatural causes) uncanny
dangle *v.* dauchle
dare *v.* daar, daur; **dare not**
daarna; dursna; *pt. used as pr.*
durstna
darling *n.* dawtie
dark *adj.* murky; dairk (J); (very)
pitch-dark; pick-mark
darkness *n.* mirk; markness;
(extreme) pitch-dark; pick-mirk
dart *n.* dert
dash *v.* (hurry) skelp; (noisily)
blatter; (down) ding, *pt.* dang,
dung; (about) flee aboot; **at a
dash** at a spinner
dashing *adj.* swashy
daub *v.* clart; skaik; sclarry (J)
daughter *n.* daachter (A2); dochter

(A1); dother
daughter-in-law *n.* gweed-dother etc.
David *pr. n.* Daavit
dawdle *v.* dachle; dackle
dawn *n.* skreek o day
day *in phr.* **day's work** darg; **day labourer** darger; **every day** daily-day
daze *v.* dozen
deacon *n.* deykon, dykon
dead *adj.* deed, deid
deadly *adj.* deidly; fell
deaf *adj.* deef, deif
deafen *v.* deeve, deave
deal *n.* dale; transack; *v.* dale; **deal with** sort; tak throw han
dealer *n.* (itinerant) cadger
dealt (wi) *v. pt.* deelt (wi)
dear *adj.* (expensive) daar
death *n.* daith; deeth (A2), deith (J); the hinner-en
death-throw *n.* deid-thraw
death-watch beetle *n.* chackie-mull
deceased *ppl.* worn awa
deceitful *adj.* forty-faal
deceive *v.* mislippen; fugle (B1)
decent *adj.* dacent, daicent; dassint; douce
defame *v.* ca for aathing; misca; (vilipend) wilipen
defeat *n.* defait; *v.* bleck; bauchle (B1); defait, *ppl.* defait
defecate *v.* cack; kich; drate *(pr., pt., ppl.* dritten)
defer *v.* defar
deformed *ppl., adj.* mishachlt
defraud *v.* snype
degrade *v.* degraad; **degrading** *ppls.* degraadin, degraadit

dehorn *v.* dodd
dehydrated *ppl.* druchtit
dejected *adj.* doon i the moo; disjaskit; blue
deliberate *adj.* deleebrate; *adv.* deleebrately; designtly
delicacy *n.* flagerie
delighted *adj.* trickit (S)
delve *v.* dell
demented *ppl.* demintit
demon *n.* deevilock
denial *n.* na-say
dent *v.* cloor, clour
deny *v.* na-say
departing *adj.* wa-gaan, wa-gaun
departure *n.* wa-gaan, wa-gaun
depend (on) lippen (tae) (B1)
dependable *adj.* siccar
depressed *adj.* doon
deprived (of) *ppl.* runtit (o)
describe *v.* descrive, descryve
deserving *adj.* wordy
desire *n.* (slight) inklin; *v.* sik, seek
desirous *adj.* keerious
desk *n.* dask
destitute *adj.* nace; but hoose an haa
destroy *v.* connach; misaacre, missaucre
destruction *n.* crockaneetion; gowf(f); wrack
detain *v.* deteen
Devil, the *pr. n.* Aul Nick; Clootie; Cloots; the Earl o Hell; Hornie; Nicky Cloots
devil *n.* deevil; deil; fient; sorra
devious *adj.* forty-faal
devour *v.* (greedily) gluff
dew *n.* dyow
dexterous *adj.* nacky

dialect *n.* leid
diarrhoea *n.* skitter(s); (suffering from) lowss
didn't *interrog.* didnin?
die *v.* dee, *pt.* deet; slip the timmers. *cf.* **do**
difference *n.* odds
difficult *adj.* ill; ull; (of a task) kittle, kittlesome; (of words) lang-nebbit, -nibbit
difficulty *n.* diffeekwalty (accent second syllable); fyke; snorl
dig *v.* cast; dell; howk; **dug** *ppl.* cas(s)en; howkit
digest *v.* disjeest
dignity *n.* deegnity
diligent *adj.* eident
din *n.* remis(h)
dinner *n.* dainner, denner; **provide dinner** *v.* denner
diphtheria *n.* diphthairy
direction *n.* airt; **in all directions** aa the airts
dirtied *ppl.* dirten
dirty *adj.* barkit; clorty; fool; muckit; yirdit; *v.* fyle; daidle (S)
disagreeable *adj.* (of weather) drabbly
disappoint *v.* disappynt; begeck; miscomfit (B1)
disappointed *ppl., adj.* nicket; hingin-luggit
disappointment *n.* begeck; hertscaad (B1)
disbelieve *v.* misdoot
discharge *v.* (any missile) fire
discomfit *v.* pit oot
disconsolate *adj.* doon i the moo; disjaskit
discord *n.* dispeace

discount *n.* discoont; (returned to the buyer) luckpenny
discourage *v.* dachle; dackle (C)
discourse *n.* discoorse; say-awa
discuss *v.* tak throw-han; dip
disdainful *adj.* sanshach
disembowel *v.* (deer carcase) gralloch
disfurnish *v.* displenish
disgust *n.* scunner; *v.* backset; scunner; (nauseate) skaichen, skaiken; (feel disgust) ug; (excl. of) feech, feich; **disgusted with** scunnert o/wi; skaikent; uggit
disgusting *adj.* fusome; ugsome; scunnerfu; scunnersome
dish *n.* (for serving) ashet
dish-cloth *n.* dish-cloot
dishevel *v.* toosle, toozle, tousle
dishevelled *adj.* hudd(e)ry
dishonesty *n.* oonhonesty
dismal *adj.* darksome; oorie
dismiss *v.* skail, skale
disordered *ppl.* agee; ill-shooken up; (in the mind) fey
disorderly *adj.* ramshackle; **in a disorderly way** over the bows
disperse *v. tr., intr.* skail, skale
display *n.* (fine) brevity, braivity; *v.* kythe
displease *v.* miscomfit
displeased, looked *phr.* his face wis trippin him
disputatious *adj.* din-raisin
dissatisfied, to be (with) *v.* ail (at)
distaff *n.* rock
distant *adj.* oot-by
distinct *adj.* clair
distorted *adj.* bogjavelt; bogshaivelt

distress *(excl.* of) feech; *v.* vex
district *n.* districk; (thirled to a mill or in which anyone carries on business) sucken
distrust *v.* mislippen
disturbance *n.* strush(ie); stramash
ditch *n.* dutch (G, M1); sheuch; stank
diversion *n.* (entertainment) divert
divested (of) *ppl.* runtit (o)
divide *v.* pairt; (in two) haaver
do *v. inf.* tae dee; adee; dae (S, J); *(pr. tense* I, you, we, they div; he, she, it dis; *imp.* dee/dae); **do not so badly** dee awa; **much to do** muckle adee
dock plant *n.* docken
doctor *n.* physeeshun
document *n.* dockiment
dodge *n.* ginkum; ginkmen (B1); *v.* jink; jook, jouk
doer *n.* deester (often contempt.)
doesn't *v. neg.* disna; *interrog.* disna, disnin
dog *n.* fulp; tike, tyke; doag (J); (bitch) bick, bik
doll *n.* dall
domicile *n.* doomsil
done *ppl.* deen, dune; daen (S). *See* **fatigued**
donkey *n.* cuddy
don't *v. neg.* dinna; *interrog.* divnin
doormat *n.* bass
dotage *n.* (in one's) dytit, doitit; donnert
double *adj.* dooble
double-jointed *adj.* dooble-jyntit
doubt *n.* doot; *v.* doot, misdoot
doubtful *adj.* dootfu
doughball *n.* twenty-minute-sweemer (B)
dovecot *n.* doocot
down *adv.* doon
downcast *adj.* disjaskit; blue (A1)
down-draught *n.* (in chimney) flan
downfall *n.* dooncome; doonfa
downpour *n.* doorpoor
downright *adv.* doonricht; evendoon
down with *phr.* hoot awa wi
down yonder *adv.* doonby
dowry *n.* tocher
doze (off) *v.* dover (ower)
dozen *n.* dizzen
draggle *v.* trachel, trachle, trauchle
drain *n.* (small open) stripe; (in cowshed) greep; (in street gutter) syre; *v.* (boiled solids) bree; (to last drop) dreep
drain-cover *n.* brander
dram *n.* skite; (in the morning) mornin; tootie
draught *n.* dracht; (of air) drucht
draught-board *n.* dambrod
draughts *n. pl.* (the game) draachts
draw *v.* draa; *ppl.* draan; (on a pipe) lunt
dread *n., v.* dreed, dreid
drench *v.* drook; *ppl., adj.* drookit
drenching *n.* steepin
dress *n.* (loose) slip; *v.* busk; rig; (for a journey) buckle; turse; (to go out) rank; (smartly) trig
dressed up *ppl.* trickit up; triggit oot; (showily) cockit up
dressing-down *n.* dixie; hanlin; sedarin
dribble *v.* dreeble
dribblet *n.* (small quantity of liquid) jibble (contempt. term)

drift *n.* (snow) wraith
drill *n.* (furrow with ridge on top) dreel
drink *n.* dracht; (of spirits) donal(ie); (small quantity) lab(b)ach
drip *n.* dreep; *v.* dreep; sype
dripping *n.* dreepin; **dripping enclosure (for sheep)** dreepin-penn
drive *n.* gurr; *v.* ca, caa; (animals, esp. poultry) hish; (~ in) yark in
drizzle *n.* sma weet; smirr
drizzly *adj.* dribbly; (with fog) muggly
drone *v.* bum
drop *n.* (sometimes of alcohol) drap; *v.* drap
drought *n.* drooth, drouth; drucht
drove *v. pt.* dreeve
drown *v.* droon; *ppl.* droont
drowsy, become *adj., v.* drow
drubbing *n.* nizzin
drug *n.* drog
druggist *n.* droggist
Drumlithie *pr. n.* (nicknamed) Skite
drummer *n.* (town) drumster
drunk, drunken *adj.* foo, fou; drucken; (very) bleezin; as foo's a buckie; greetin foo; (incapably) styterin foo; (wildly) fleein

drunkenness *n.* druckenness
dry *adj.* (sapless) foggy; (used of cows which have stopped giving milk) eel; yeld; *v.* (stooks) win
dryer *n.* (of grain) dryster
dry out *v.* skurken
dry up *v.* gizzen
duck *n.* deuk, dyeuk; *v.* jook, jouk
dull *adj.* dreich; ducksie (A)
dulse *n.* (edible seaweed) dilse
dumbfounded *ppl.* dumfoonert
dumbstruck *ppl.* dusht
dun *n.* craver
dung *n.* muck; sharn; (liquid) sharn-bree; (on the hind-quarters of cattle or sheep) knapdarloch
dungarees *n. pl.* dungers
dunghill *n.* midden; **moisture from dunghill** midden-bree; **top of the midden** midden-tap
duplicitous *adj.* dooble
dust *n.* dist; stue, styoo; (flying) stoor, stour
duster *n.* dister
dusty *adj.* stoorie, stourie
dwarf *n.* ablach
dwell *v.* dwaal, dwall
dwelling-house *n.* dwallin-hoose; firehoose
dyer *n.* dyester
dying (for) *ppl.* mangin (for)

— **E** —

each *adj.* ilk; ilka; ilky; ulkie
eager *adj.* ettlin; fain; gleg; yivvery
eager, to be *adj., v.* ettle; fidge (B1)
ear *n.* lug

earl *n.* yarl
earlier *adj.* earer
early *adj., adv.* airly; air; ear
earn *v.* airn

earnest *n.* (given on striking a
bargain) arles; **in dead earnest**
in gnappin earnest (B1)
earrings *n. pl.* lug-babs
earth *n.* airth; (also the earth) yird;
covered in earth yirdit
earthenware *n.* lame
earwig *n.* forkie-(tail); horny-
goloch
ease *n.* easedom
Easter *n.* Pase, Pess; Pesch
easy *adj., adv.* aisy (S); **no easy job**
nae mowse job; **take it easy** hud
doon the deece; lat the theats
slack
easy-going *adj.* easy-osy; **easy-
going person** sug
eat *v.* aet; **eaten** *ppl.* aeten, etten;
(voraciously) gaap; (noisily and
greedily) hamsh, humsh
eaves *n. pl.* easin, eezen(s)
edict *n.* edick
edify *v.* edifee; **edifying** *ppl.*
edifeein
educate *v.* eddicat
education *n.* eddicashun
eerie *adj.* oorie
effect *n.* effeck
egg *n.* aig; (state of egg with young
bird partially formed) gorbelt; *v.*
(someone on) eik him up (A2)
egg shells *n. pl.* egg shallies
eight *adj.* acht, aucht; aicht, echt
eighteen *adj.* achteen; aichteen,
echteen
eighty *adj.* achty; aichty, echty
either *adj., conj., pron.* edder;
edderan (can be used at end of
sentence as in Eng.)
elbow *n.* elbick, elbock, elbuck

elder *n.* (of the Church) eller; elyer
elder-tree *n.* boortree, bourtree;
elyer
elevated *ppl., adj.* liftit
eleven *adj.* aleyven; eleeven,
eleiven
else *adv.* anse
elude *v.* jink
embarrassed *ppl., adj.* affrontit;
deeply embarrassed black
affrontit
ember *n.* emmer; eyzle
embrace *v.* oxter
emotional *adj.* (showing emotion)
great-hertit
empty *adj., v.* teem; toom (G1, J,
M)
enamel *adj.* nammle
enclosure *n.* close, closs; (for
poultry) crive; ree
encouragement *n.* hertnin; cuttins
(usually in the neg., *e.g.* nae/sma
cuttins)
end *n.* en; eyn; hinner-en; hint; (of
yarn) thrum; *v.* en, eyn; *ppl.* eynt;
end of harvest, of the year the
back eyn; **make ends meet** get
eyns tae rug the gidder
endearment (term of) *n.* (for
children) chowter; smowt
endeavour *v.* mint
endless *adj.* eynless
end-ridge *n.* en-, eynrig
endure *v.* dree; thole
energetic *adj.* fersell
energy *n.* birr; spunk; virr; (great)
rake; *adj.* (lacking) fen(d)less;
thowless
engage *v.* (a farmhand) fee
engine *n.* engeen; ingine

English *adj.* suddron, sooth-kwintra
enlist *v.* list
enough *adj.* aneuch; aneu; enew
entangle *v.* insnorl; raivel; *ppl.* insnorlt; raivelt
entertainment *n.* a divert; enterteen-ment
enthralled *adj.* thirlt
enthusiasm *n.* (fit of) feerich
entice *v.* goy; tryst; tyce
entitle *v.* enteetle
entrails *n. pl.* (animal) harigals; monyfaalds, monyfaulds
entrance *n.* (at ground-floor level) low door
entrance-hall *n.* trance
entrap *v.* insnorl
equal *adj., adv.* (shares) eeksy-peeksy; -picksy; *n.* marra, marrow; *v.* peer wi
equipped *ppl., adj.* riggit oot
errand *n.* eeran
escape *v.* win oot
escapade *n.* ploy
escort *v.* convoy
Eskimo *n.* Yakki (deriv. from Yaqui) (B)
especially *adv.* espeeshully
estate manager *n.* grun offisher
evasive behaviour *n.* hunker-slidin
even *adv.* aiven, ayven; eyven; **even with** upsides wi
evening *n.* even; een; (from twilight to bedtime) forenicht; **in the evening** at even, at een
ever *adv.* iver, ivver
everlasting *adj.* iverlaistin
every *adj.* ilk; ilka; ilky; ulkie
everybody *pron.* aabody
everyone *pron.* aabody; **everyone**

else aa ither body
everything *n.* aathin(g)
everywhere *adv.* aawye; aa gate
evil *adj.* coorse
eviscerate *v.* (of deer) gralloch
ewe *n.* yowe; (from one to two years old) gimmer
exaggeration *n.* hose an sheen
exalt *v.* heeze
example *n.* spyack, spyauck; **for example** likein
exceedingly *adv.* byous; feerious; fell; terrible
excel *v.* ding
excellent *adj.* braw; capital; rare
except *prep.* 'cep; 'cepin; excep; **except for** hud awa fae
exchange *v.* cowp; hooie; niffer; trock, troke
exciseman *n.* gaager, gauger, gager
excite *v.* flocht; raise; **in a state of excitement** flochtit; raist
excited *ppl., adj.* kittelt up
excitement *n.* (nervous) picher
exclamations (of surprise) goshie; heth; jings; loshins; loshtie (be here); loshtie-goshtie guide's; meggins alive; megstie me; michty me; (blood) sang; saal, saul; (troth) trogs; (of doubt, contempt) hoots; (of soothing and endearment) weel-a-wins, -wuns
excrement *n.* kich
excusable *adj.* exkeesable
exercise *n.* exerceese
exercise-book *n.* exerceese-beuk
exhaust *v.* jabb
exhausted *ppl.* deen; foonert; for-fochen; forjeskit; jabbit; wabbit
exhibition *n.* exhibeetion

expanse *n.* (of ground) sklyter
expect *v.* expeck; **expected**
expeckit
expenditure *n.* (costly) hairrial,
herrial
expensive *adj.* daar
experience *n.* expairience; *v.* pree
expound *v.* expoond
expression *n.* (e.g. of emotion)
ootlat

extraordinary *adj.* byordnar;
byous; exterordnar; ondeemas;
unco
extremely *adv.* unco
extremity *n.* hinner-en
exult *v.* craa, craw
exultant *adj.* vantie, vauntie
eye(s) *n.* ee(n); **eyes like burning
coals** eyzly ee't
eyelash *n.* brier; winker

— **F** —

face *n.* face; phizog; **facial
expression** mudgeon
fact *n.* fack
fad *n.* aivis
fade away *v.* weer awa
faded *ppl.* cassen
failed *adj.* stickit
faint *n.* dwaam, dwam; fant; swarf;
v. fant; swarf; tak a dwam
faint-hearted *adj.* chucken-hertit;
henny-hertit
fair-haired *adj.* tow-heidit
fair play *phr.* fair hornie
faith *excl.* fegs; heth
faithful *adj.* faithfu
fall *n.* (sudden and heavy) clyte;
(heavy) doosht; (with a bump)
dird; (downfall) doon-come;
(heavy) sklyte; sklyter; (light, of
rain, snow) skiffin; *v.* fa; (with a
thud) dyst; (with a bounce) dird;
(heavily) sklyte, sklyter; (of
heavy rain, snow) ding; (of light
rain, snow) skiff; (sound of fall
into water) plype; (of rain) onding
fall asleep *v.* (fisher term) to catch

her
fall out *n.* cast-oot; strive, *pt.*
streeve
fall over *v. intr.* cowp
fallow land *n.* faugh
fall to *v.* fa tee
false *adj.* faase, fause
family *n.* faimly
famished *adj.* faimished
famous *adj.* faamous
fan *n.* (for winnowing corn)
winnister
fancy *n.* maggot; (romantic) noshun
(o); (foolish) whigmaleerie
fancy cake *n.* fancy
fancy work *n.* fineerin
far *adv.* hine; **far off** hine awa; **far
gone** sair come at
fare *v.* faar, faur; (quite well) turn
ower; **fare badly** misthrive
farewell *int.* faar-ye-weel
farm *n.* fairm, ferm; toon, toun
farm cottage *n.* cottar hoose
farmer *n.* fairmer
farmhouse *n.* fairmhoose; firehoose
farmhand *n.* fairm-servan

farming *n.* fairmin
farmservant *n.* fairm servan; (very experienced) docknell
farmstead *n.* steadin; toon, toun
farm tools (implement for clearing ground of roots etc) (Eng.) grubber; (for pulling turnips) neep-click; (for slicing turnips for fodder) neep-hasher; (for pulling turnips) neep-pluck; (for hoeing turnips) neep-rinner; (horse-hoe for weeding) shim; (skimmer for surface soil and weeds) skreefer; (small rake) smiler; (for removing turnip roots) tailer; (for removing turnip tops) tapner; (for twisting straw ropes) thrawcrook, thrawheuk; (for tilting loose sheaves off old-style reaper) tilter
farmworker's bag *n.* chackie
farmyard *n.* closs
farrier *n.* fairrier
farther *adv.* farder; (away, along) yont
farthing *n.* fardin
fast *adj., adv.* faist; *n., v.* fas(t)
fasten *v.* faisten; cleek; hank
fastidious *adj.* dorty; **over-fastidious** pernickety
fat *adj.* stoot; *n.* creesh; **fat person** fatty-bannocks
fatal *adj.* fattal
fate *n.* weird
father *n.* fadder; faither (C1, F)
father-in-law *n.* gweed-fadder, -faither
fathom *n.* faddom
fatigue *n.* harassment (A2); *v.* jabb; jaap, jaup
fatigued *ppl., adj.* deen; dylt;

daivert; jaapit; jabbit; tasht; typit; wabbit
fault *n.* faat, faut
fault-finding *n.* fittie-fies; (fretful) girn; *adj.* grumlie
favour *n.* faavour; **in favour with** (esp. with God) far-ben wi
favoured *adj.* faavourt; faart; **well-favoured (good-looking)** weel-faart; **ill-favoured (ugly)** ill-faart
favourite *adj.* faavrit, fauvrit
fear *n.* fear; ferr (S)
feast *n.* (of farewell or completion) foy
feather *n., v.* fedder
fed up (of) *adj.* doon; scunnert (o/wi)
feeble *adj.* dwebble; dweeble; dweebly; dweemly-dwamly; shilpit; thewless; *v.* (grow feeble in mind) doit
feed *n.* aet; **a good feed** a gweed aet; rim-rax; *v.* mait, *ppl.* maitit; (from a pail) cog; (with oats) to corn
feeding-bag *n.* (for horses) moo-bag; mou-bag
feel *v.* fin, *pt.* fan
feign *v.* feingie
felloes *n. pl.* (of wheel) fillies
fell out *v. pt.* streeve
fellow *n.* chiel; billie; folla; steel (B1); stock; (of low character) slung; (worthless) slype
felt *v. pt.* fan
fence *n.* palin; (of furze bushes) fundyke
ferment *n.* barm
fern *n.* fairn; bracken; breckan
fetch *v.* fesh; fess, *pt.* feese, feish,

foosh

Fetterangus *pr. n.* (nicknamed) Fishie

fettle *in phr.* **in fine fettle** in richt bone

fever *n.* fivver

few *adj.* fyow, fyou; *n.* fyow; a twa-three

fewer *adj.* fyower

fibrous *adj.* stickly

fiddle (with or about) *v.* ficher; footer; **fiddly job** ficher; footer

fidget *v.* fyke; fidge (B); fyaach

field *n.* feedle (A, A2), fiedle; park (A); (for sowing turnip seed) patcher; (division of a field) wynin

fifty *adj.* fifety

fifteen *adj.* fifeteen, foifteen (A2)

fifteenth *adj.* fifeteent

fight *n., v.* fecht; pilget; shangie; sharrie; (with cudgels) a staffy-nevel job

fill *n.* sairin; **get your fill of** get yer sairin o; *v.* ful, full (rhymes with gull); *ppl.* fullt; bowden

film *n.* (membrane) scriffan; (thin) yim

final(ly) *adj., adv.* feenal(ly)

find *v.* fin

Findochty *pr. n.* (locally) Finechty

fine *adj.* braw

fine-looking *adj.* buirdly

finely *adv.* brawlies

finery *n.* braivity; (esp. of dress) braws; flagerie

finger *n.* finger (rhymes with singer); **the little finger** crannie; **finger tips** finger-eyns

finicky *adj.* jinipperous

finish *n., v.* feenish

finished *ppl., adj.* throw

fir-cone *n.* (fir-)yowe; yowie

fire *n.* ingle; (blazing) ingle-lowe; (small, blazing, coal or peat) cutchack; (big) bevie; (flame-less, of red-hot embers) greeshach (A1)

fireside *n.* ingle; ingle-cheek

firewood *n.* firewid; kinlin

firework *n.* squeeb; (primitive, home-made) poother-deevil

first rate *adj. phr.* bencape

fish *n.* (ungutted) rounder; (useless small species found in harbours) buddick; (take-home parcel of fish in the fishing industry) fry; *v.* (catch with hands in stream) guddle

fisher-boy *n.* fisher-loon

fisher-girl *n.* fisher-quine

fishing-line *n.* (hand) hanlin

fishing-rod *n.* waan

fish roe *n.* raan

fist *n.* nieve, niv; **fistful** nievefu

flabbergast *v.* stammygaster

flagged *ppl.* (of floor) flaggit

flagon *n.* stoop

flame *n.* lowe

flannel *n.* flannen

flap *v.* flaff; flaffer; wap

flash *n.* (of lightning) flacht

flattened *ppl.* (of crop) laid

flatter *v.* fraise; fleetch; **given to flattery** fraisie

flea *n.* flech

fleam *n.* (for bleeding of horses) fleem

flexible *adj.* wamfle

flick *v.* wheech

flicker *v.* flicher
flight *n.* (of birds) flacht; flicht;
  take flight tak sheet
flighty *adj.* flichty
flinch *v.* flench
flint and steel *phr.* flint an fleerish
flirt *v.* daff
float *n.* (for fishing) bowe
flock *n.* (of sheep) hirsel; (of birds)
  flacht
flog *v.* soosh
flood *n.* (of river, stream) spate;
  speet; speeth
floor *n.* fleer
flop *v.* flap
flour *n.* (wheaten etc.) floor
flourish *v.* fleerish
flower *n.* flooer, floor; (artificial)
  gumfleer, -floor
flowering currant *n.* (blossom
  appearing before the leaves) son-
  afore-the-father. (A name applied
  to other plants.)
fluff *n.* caddis
flukeworm *n.* (on the lung of
  sheep) the hooze
flung *v. pt.* flang
flurry *n.* flocht
flutter *v.* flaff; flaffer
fly *n., v.* flee
flywheel *n.* (of a spindle) whorl
foal *n.* foalie
foam *n.* faem, faim; *v.* ream
fodder *n.* fodd(e)rin
foe *n.* fae
fog *n.* lichen
foggy *adj.* (fog with drizzle)
  muggly
fold *n.* lirk, lurk; (of sheep) faal(d),
  faul(d); *v.* faald

folk *n.* fowk *(gen.);* folk (G, M)
folly *n.* madden-dreem
fondle *v.* daat, dawt; delt
food *n.* mait; meat (J); **off his food**
  aff o's mait; **able to take food**
  mait-haill
fool *n.* feel, fule; gapus; gaak,
  gawk; gaakie; gillieperous,
  gileepris (hard **g**); gock; gowk;
  gomeril; gype; haveral; neip-heid;
  styoomer; sumph; tawpie;
  (outstanding) dunderheid; *v.*
  begowk; **fool's errand** feel's
  eeran; Prile eeran
foolish *adj.* feel; daft; fulage (B1);
  gockit; gowkit; gypit
foolishness *n.* feelness; gypery
foot *n.* fit; *v.* **to foot it** fit it; **footed**
  fittit
foot-and-mouth *n.* (disease) fit-an-
  moo
football *n.* fitba
Footdee *pr. n.* (old fisher district of
  Aberdeen) Fittie; Futtie
footing *n.* precunnance
footpath *n.* roddie
footstep *n.* fitstep
for *prep.* tae
force *n.* birr; virr
forceful *adj.* fersell
foreign *adj.* fremd; fremmit
forequarter *n.* (of an animal) spaal,
  spaul
foreshadow *v.* foreshaida
Forfar *pr. n.* Farfar
forget *v.* foryet; *v. pt.* foryat
fork *n.* (of a tree, in the road etc)
  glack; (used in farming) graip; *v.*
  graip
form *v.* fack (B1); *n.* (bench) furm

forsake *v.* forhooie, furhooie
forth *adv.* furth
fortune *n.* fortin
fortunate *adj.* chancy
fortune-teller *n.* (female) spay-wife; **tell fortunes** *v.* spay
forward *imper.* (instruction to a horse) gee up!
foul *adj.* foosome, fousome
found *v. pt.* fan; *ppl.* fun(d). *cf.* **fin**
foundations *n. pl.* foons, founs
fountain *n.* funtain
fountainhead *n.* funtainheid
four *adj.* fower
fowl *n.* (of the the first year) earock
fox *n.* tod
fragile *adj.* (feeling) aa egg shallies
fragment *n.* skirp
Fraserburgh *pr. n.* nicknamed The Broch; Faithlie
Fraserburgh native *n.* Brocher
fraud *n.* snype
freckled *adj.* ferny-ticklt
freckles *n. pl.* fern-tickles
freeze *v.* jeel
freight *n.* fraacht
fresh *adj.* caller
fret *v.* chirm
fretful *adj.* cankert; capernicious
Friday *n.* Freday
friend *n.* freen
friendly (with) *adj.* chief (wi)
fright *n.* fleg; gast; (Abdn. city and coastal) fear
frighten *v.* fleg; fley; frichten; (Abdn. city and coastal) fear; *ppl.* fleggit; fleyt; feart
frivolity *n.* (piece of) flagerie
frivolous *adj.* freevolous

frog *n.* poddick; puddock
frolic *n.* hyze; ploy; splore
frolicsome *adj.* daft
from *prep.* fae; (much less common) frae
front in (of) *adv.* afore; *prep.* afore; anent
frost *n.* freest; (hoar) rime; *v.* freest
frost-nail *n.* pike, pyke; sharp
frown *v.* froon
frugal *adj.* canny
fruit slice *n.* curran daad
fugitive *n.* (from the gallows) rin-the-wuddie
full *adj.* fou, fu; ful, full (rhymes with gull)
full up *ppl.* (after eating) bowdent
fulmar *n.* mallie
fumble *v.* fummle
fume *v.* feem
funeral *n.* beerial; (refreshment) dregie
furious *adj.* feerious
furnish *v.* plenish
furniture *n.* furnitur; plenishin
furrow *n.* fur, furr; sheugh; (open furrow between two ridges) mids; (shallow) scart; *v.* (set up the first furrow when ploughing a field) feer. *cf.* **feerin**
further *adj.* farrer
furthest *adj.* farrest; **furthest out** farrest ootbye
fury *n.* rampaage
fuss *n.* fyke; adee; (great) mineerum; a wark; (outcry) scronach
fussy *adj.* fashious; perjink

— **G** —

gabble *v.* yab-yabble

gable *n.* gaivel (G); gale (M); (top stones on gable) tablin

gadfly *n.* cleg; gleg

gaiters *n. pl.* cweetikins; queetikins

gallery *n.* (in church) laft

gallows *n.* wuddie, wuddy

game (ball-) sappy sodgers; (catching) leavie-oh; (selection) pye; (marbles played against a door) doorie; (playground) jyne-on; (seashore) rocky-on; (team game for boys) hucky-ducky (S); (for two with a stick) pooin the sweer-tree; (tag) tackie, takie; tik-an-tak

gamekeeper *n.* gamie; (the work) keeperin

gander *n.* ganner

gang *n.* gyang

gaol *n.* jivvle

gap *n.* (in wall or fence) slap

gape *v.* gaap, gawp

garden *n.* gairden; (on farm) yard

Gardenstown *pr. n.* (local) Gaimrie

Garioch *pr. n.* (pro. Geery; Gerry)

garments *n. pl.* (outer, usually untidy) bullaments

garter *n.* garten

Gartly *pr. n.* (local) Gairtly

gas *v.* (talk idly) lyaag; laig

gasbag *n.* blether; bleeter; gab

gate *n.* yett

gather *v.* gaither; gedder; gether; gidder

gatherer *n.* (of grain to make sheaves, usually female) gaitherer; gedderer; lifter

gaudy *adj.* skiry, skyrie; galliart (B1)

gave *v. pt.* gae (M, A2); gya; gied, gid

Gavin *pr. n.* Ga'in

gawp *v.* gowp, goup; gype

generation *n.* ashun

generous *adj.* fraachty; gweedwillie, gweedwullie

genial *adj.* humoursome

gentility *n.* genteelity

gentle *adj.* douce

George *pr. n.* Dod; Geordie

get *v.* get; win; **get off** win aff; **get out** win oot; **get even with** win tee wi; **get away** swithe; **get on with something** hing in; **get over** (recover from) cower; **get ready** (esp. dress to go out) rank; **get up** rise, *pt.* raise, rase

gewgaw *n.* flagerie

ghastly *adj.* gash; ugsome

g(h)illie *n.* gheelie

ghost *n.* ghaist(ie); boodie; wreith

ginger-beer *n.* ginch-breid

girl *n.* (young) deemie; lassickie, lassockie; quine

girlfriend *n.* blon; laas

give *v.* gie

give me *phr.* (when someone chooses a particular thing) chaps me

glad *adj.* gled; gledsome; blythe

glance *n.* glent; skance; went; twig;

135

v. twig
Glasgow *pr. n.* Glaisga
glass *adj., n.* gless
gleam *n.* flacht; leam; glaik
glen *n.* cleuch
glide *v.* snoove
glimpse *n.* glint (M); went
glitter *v.* (gaudily) skire
gloomy *adj.* dowf; drumly
glossy *adj.* sleekit
glove *n.* glive (A2); (without
    separate division for the four
    fingers) doddy-mitten
glow *n., v.* glowe; lowe
gluttonous *adj.* gutsy
gnaw *v.* gnaave, gnauve
go *v.* gae; gang; ging; gyang (A,
    A1); gaan, gaun (coastal); (reach
    a place) win; **go away** *excl.*
    g'wa; *v.* win awa; **go off**
    something tak a scunner till; **go**
    on hud awa; **go over** owergae;
    go your way gang yer gait; **go**
    up and down dyst; **as you go by**
    i the byg(y)aan
goad *n.* (for driving horses or cattle
    or directing corn to the scythe or
    binder) gaad, gad; **one who uses**
    a gaad gaadsman
goal *n.* (in children's games) dell
God *pr. n.* Gweed; *(euph.)* dyod;
    nyod; od; frequently *good* in
    expletives, *e.g.* good be here;
    good al meggins (prob. *euph.* for
    God Almighty); **God grant**
    Gweed sen; **God knows** Gweed
    kens; **God preserve us** Gweed
    keep's aa, Gweed preserve's
godly *adj.* gweedlie
going *ppl.* gaan, gaun; gyaan,

gyaun; **going about** *ppl.* agyaan;
    going on *ppl.* agyaan
goings-on *n. pl.* ongaans, ongauns
gold *n.* gowd
golden *adj.* gowden
golf *n.* gowf
golfer *n.* gowfer
gone *ppl.* geen, gane
good *adj., n.* gweed, guid; geed (F);
    (very) capital
good-for-nothing *n.* ranagant;
    hurb; wally-draigle; warridrag
good-hearted *adj.* gweedwully
good-humoured *adj.* canty
goodies *n. pl.* chit-chow; galshachs,
    galshochs; perlyaag
good-looking *adj.* weel-faart, -faurt
goodness *excl.* gwestie, gweeshtie,
    gweeshtens
goodness knows *excl.* Gweed kens
goodness sake, for *excl.* for ony
    faavour!
goodnight *int.* gweednicht
goodwill *n.* gweed-wull
gooseberry *n.* grozart
gorge *v.* stech
gosh *excl.* goshie; jings
gossamer *n.* slammach
gossip *n.* claik; clash; (chat) crack;
    (person) kimmer; claik; sclave; *v.*
    claik, clash; crack; sclave; sclaver
got *v. pt.* gat; gowt
Gourdon *pr. n.* Gurdon
gown *n.* goon
grab *v.* glammach, glammoch;
    mitten
grain *n.* (freed from husks) shillans;
    (threshed) thrash; (particle)
    sinacle (B1)
grain-loft *n.* corn-laft

grain prices *n. pl.* (fixed for the year) fiars
grand *adj.* gran; (very smart) fantoosh
grandchild(ren) *n. (pl.)* oe(s)
grandfather *n.* granda; deydie (B); lucky daddy (A2)
grandmother *n.* grunny; lucky minnie
grasp *v.* glammach, glammoch; lat glammoch at; fist (B1)
grasping *adj.* nabble, nabal
grass *n.* girse, girss; (coarse) sprot; (near the sea) bent; (long, left standing in winter) fog; (long, thin) ling (J); (any tall, thin, withered stalk) windle-strae; (crested dogstail) windlestrae
grassland *n.* green
grassy *adj.* girssy
grave *n.* greff; (earth) mools
gravel *n.* graivel; (compacted) chad
gravelly *adj.* chaddy
gravestone *n.* lair-steen, -stane
grease *n.* creesh
great *adj.* gryte; muckle; meikle; (considerable) gey
greedy *adj.* gutsy; **greedy person** guts; (mean) hungry
green *n.* (village) loaning (S)
greenish *adj.* greenichtie
grey *adj.* hyaave; (turning) grizzelt; (streaked with) lyart
griddle *n.* (circular iron plate with bow handle for baking) girdle
gridiron *n.* brander
grief *n.* dool
grievances, expressed their *phr.* shook their craps

grim *adj.* door, dour
grimace *n.* murjin, murgeon; mudgeon
grindstone *n.* grinsteen
grip *n.* grip; purchase; *v.* grup; **in the grip of** i the thraws o
groan *n., v.* grain
groom *n.* (in charge of horse) strapper; shalt-loon
grope *v.* grape
ground *n.* grun; (large piece of wasteland) gleebrie; gliberal (B1)
group *n.* boorach(ie)
grow *v.* growe; sproot
growl *n., v.* gurl; gurr
grub *n.* (of cranefly, eating germinating grain) tory; *v.* (of birds) dorb
gruel *n.* stoorum
gruesome *adj.* gash
gruff *adj.* strunge
grumble *v.* grummle; girn; mump
grumbling *adj.* grumlie; nyattery
grunt *v.* gruntle
guano *n.* (fertiliser) gwana
guard *n., v.* guaird, gaird
guernsey *n.* (seaman's jersey) gansey; ganjie
guess *v.* jaloose, jalouse
guffaw *n.* gaff, gauff; guffa
guide *n.* (example) spyaack
gull *v.* gow
gullet *n.* wizzen
gumboil *n.* gumbyle, gumbile
gunpowder *n.* gunpoother
gusset *n.* gushet
gust *n.* (of wind) flan; (sudden) howder

—— H ——

habit *n.* haibit

had *v. pt.* hid; hed (A2); **had not** hidna

haddock *n.* haddie; (split open, salted, dried in the sun) speldin; (dried without being split) widdie

haft *n.* (of knife) heft

hag *n.* (withered) runt

hair *n.* (haircut) snod-in-aboot; (cut with a bowl) bowel-crappit

hairpins *n. pl.* oots-an-ins

hairy *adj.* nep

half *adj., n.* haaf

half-holiday *n.* haafie

halfpenny *n.* maik

halfpennyworth *n.* maikst

half share *n.* haaver

halfway *adv.* mids; half-roads; **a halfway point** the mids

halfwit *n.* haveral

hall *n.* ha

halt *v.* hult

halter *n.* helter

halve *v.* haaver

hammer *n., v.* haimmer, hemmer; *n.* (heavy) mell

hand *n.* han; *v.* rax

hand's breadth *n.* han-breed; spang

handcart *n.* hurlie

handful *n.* hanfae; (what two cupped hands can hold) gobbinfae; gowpenfu; (of unthreshed corn/hay) ripp

handkerchief *n.* hankie; naipkin

handle *n.* hannle; lug; *v.* hannle

(carelessly) toosht

handless *adj.* smeerless (B1)

handline *n.* (for catching cod) ripper

handloom *n.* han-leem

handsel *n., v.* hansel

handsome *adj.* weel-faart, -faurt

handwriting *n.* vreet; vreetin

hang *v. tr., intr.* hing

hanging *n.* hingin

hangman *n.* hangie

happy *adj.* seely

harangue *n.* lay-aff

harbour *n.* hairbour, herbour

hard *adj.* (difficult) ill; ull; **hard-pressed** sair dung, sair made; **hard struggle** sair fecht; **hard at work** i the tag; **hard-working** hard-vrocht; **hard to please** dorty; fashious; **hard up** *adj.* deft; grippit (R)

hare *n.* bawd; maakin, mawkin; myaakin

harelip *n.* hare-shard

harm *n.* hairm; skaith; *v.* hairm

harmless *adj.* hairmless; ulless-gweedless

harness *n.* graith; taikle; (for attaching harness at front of cart shaft) foreslings; (part of britchin, for attachment to rear of cart) hin-slings; (fitment on cartshaft) slider

harnessed *ppl.* (of a horse) drachtit

harp *n.* herp

harrow *n.* harra

Harry *pr. n.* Hairry
harsh *adj.* maroonjus
harvest *n.* hairst; (opening of) moo
o hairst; *v.* win, *pt.* wun
harvest home *n.* meal-an-ale
has *v.* his; **has not** hisna
hash *n.* (of potatoes and salted fish)
hairy-tatties
hasp *n.* hesp
haste, hasten *v.* hist; swithe
hasty *adj.* ramsh
hat *n.* (deerstalker type worn by
gillies and grieves) pickiesay; **top
hat** lum-hat
haughty *adj.* heich-heidit
haunch *n.* hinch
haunt *n.* howff
have *v.* hae; hiv; **have not** hinna,
pt. hid, *ppl.* haen, hin
hawk *v.* (clear throat) haach
hay *n.* hey; (built into a stack) *ppl.*
stackit; (gathered row of hay)
winraa
haycock *n.* cole; (large) tramp-cole
hay-gatherer *n.* tummlin-tam
haymaker *n.* hey-makker
hay-shed *n.* hey-hoose (S)
haystack *n.* hey-ruck; hey-soo
haze *n.* gull
head *n.* heid; knowe; napper; pow;
riggin; **head-first** heelster-heid;
head over heels heels ower
gowdie; heelster-gowdie; hystergowdie
head for *v.* ca for
headmaster *n.* heid(maister)
head-stall *n.* heid-stall
headstrong *adj.* heidie; ramshackle
heal *v.* haill
healthy *adj.* hale; hale an fere; (and

active) kneef
heap *n.* dossie; hullock; hape (S);
(large) kyarn; (loose heap or
stack) rickle
heard *v. pt.* hard
heart *n.* hairt, hert
heartburn *n.* hertscaad; watter-
brash
hearth *n.* ingle; chimbly-chik;
hairth (J)
heat *v.* het, *pt.* het
heathen *n.* haythen
heather *n.* hedder
heave *v.* haive; heeze
heaven *n.* hivven; heeven (C)
heavy *adj.* wachty
heed of, take *v.* reck; tak tent
heifer *n.* quake, quaik
height *n.* heicht, hicht
heighten *v.* heichen
held *v. pt.* heeld, *ppl.* hudden
hell *n.* the ill pairt
hello *int.* ay, ay
helping *n.* sairin
hempen *adj.* himpen
hen *n.* hen; chucken, chuckney;
(free-range) gaan-aboot hen; (not
exceeding a year old) yearock
hen-pecked *adj.* hudden-doon
hen-run *n.* ree
herdsman *n.* herd
heretic *n.* heretick
herring *n.* herrin; heerin; **herring
fever** herrin fivver
herself *pron. (also* **by herself**)
hersel
hesitate *v.* dachle; dackle; swither
hiccup *n.* esk; *v.* esk; yist; **get
hiccups** tak the esk
hide *v.* hod, *pt.* hid, *ppl.* hodden

hiding *n.* sack ful o sair beens
high *adj.* heich, hich; (of wind) reevin
highland *adj.* hielan(t)
Highlander *n.* Hielander; (sometimes disparaging) teuchter
hill *n.* ben; hull
hillock *n.* hullock; (small) knablich (A2); **top of a hillock** knowe-heid
himself *pron.* (also by himself) himsel
hinder *v.* hinner
hint *n.* sleumin
hip-joint(s), aching *adj., n.* hippit; hip-grippit
hired-hand *n.* fee't man
hiring fair *n.* feein-fair; feein-mairket
his *adj.* his; 's
hit *v.* hit, *pt.* hat
hoard *v.* hain
hoar-frost *n.* rime
hoarse *adj.* hairse; roopy, roupy
hobble *v.* fuffle; hirple
hobnail *n.* tacket; **hobnailed boots** tackety beets
hoe *n., v.* hyow(e); *v.* (turnips) single
hoist *v.* hyste
hold *n.* had; hud, haud; hid (S); purchase; *v.* hud; hid (S); **hold your tongue** hud yer tongue
hole *n.* bore
hollow *adj.* boss; halla; *n.* howe; sheuch; (small, scooped out of ground for use in game of marbles) kyp(i)e; **hollow-backed** *adj.* howe-backit
holm *n.* howm (J)

home *n.* hame; doonsit (B1); (belonging to) *adj.* hamel(t)
home farm *n.* hame-fairm
homely *adj.* hamel(t); haimal(t)
homesick *adj.* hamesick
homespun *adj., n.* hamespun; hodden; **grey homespun** hodden grey
homewards *adv.* hameward; hamewith
honest *adj., adv.* (fair-)furth-the-gate
honey *n.* hinny
hoof *n.* hiv
hook *n.* heuk, hyeuck; (used on fishmarket floor) lowrie
hoop *n.* (child's) gird
hop *v.* hap
hope *v.* howp
hornless *adj.* doddit; hummel, hummle; hummel-doddie
horrible *adj.* ugsome
horrify *v.* horrifee
horse *n.* (small) garron; (walking in furrow) furrer; fur-beast; (landside) lanner; (disease affecting legs) grease
horse-hoe *n.* (small plough for weeding) shim
horse-trough *n.* horse-troch
hot *adj.* het; (scalding ~; ~ and sweating) plottin; **hot foot** het fit
hotel *n.* hottle
hot water bottle *n.* pig
hour *n.* oor
hour-glass *n.* san-gless
hourly *adv.* oorly
house *n.* hoose; (the laird's) the Hoose, the Big Hoose, the Place; (temporary, for shepherds)

sheilin; (removal) flittin
houseful *n.* hoosefae, hoosefu
house-room *n.* hooseroom
housewife *n.* hizzie
housewifery *n.* hizzieskep; hoosewifeskip
how *adv.* fit wye; foo; hoo; **how
are you** fit like
however *adv.* fooivver; hooever;
hoosomever; hoosomediver
hubbub *n.* gilgal (hard **g**)
hullabaloo *n.* heelabalow
humble *adj.* hoomble
humble-bee *n.* foggie-bee
humbling *adj.* heemlin
humid *adj.* blobbie-like
humiliate *v.* mortifee; *ppl.*
mortifeet
humour *n.* eemur; teen; **fit of ill
humour** *n.* tig

hump *n.* humph
hunchbacked *adj.* humphie-backit
hundred *n.* hunner
hundredweight *n.* hunnerwecht
hunger *n.* hunger (**ng** as in singer)
hungry *adj.* hungert; (very) yamph;
yap; **hungry-looking** yappy;
hungry for *adj.* yivvery
hurdle *n.* (for penning sheep, used
as a gate) flake
hurricane *n.* heerican
hurry back *imp.* hist-ye-back
hurry off *v.* scoot; skirt
hurt *v.* (severely) missaacre,
missaucre; (severely, fatally) pran
husband *n.* man; goodman (A2);
gweedman; *v.* hain
husk *n.* (corn) sheelock
hussy *n.* hizzie
hypocrite *n.* heepocreet

— **I** —

I *pers. pron.* A; Aw; I
ice-cream *n.* (between two wafers)
slider
icicle *n.* ice-tangle
idea *n.* adaya; noshun
idiot *n.* eediot; gapus
idle *adj.* orra
idle frolics *n. pl.* idelties
idleness *n.* idlety; idleseat; idleset
if *conj.* gin; gif (B1); **if only** *conj.*
gin (M2)
I'll *pron. with v.* Aw'se; I'se
ill-fated *adj.* weirdless
ill-humour *n.* bung
ill-humoured *adj.* cankert
ill-natured *adj.* ill-gruntit; ill-

naturt; nabble
illness *n.* (a fit of) drow
ill-tempered *adj.* nyattery
ill-use *v.* ill-, ull-eese
ill-will *n.* ull-wull
imagination *n.* imaiginashun
imagine *v.* imaagine, imaigin;
jaloose, jalouse
immediately *adv.* immediantly
imp *n.* buckie; deevilock
implements *n. pl.* leems
improve *v.* impruv
improvement *n.* impreevement
impudent *adj.* impident; (of the
tongue) ill-hung; **impudent
person** smatchet

in *prep.* i
incapable *adj.* feckless
incidental *adj.* overly
incidentally *adv.* in the bygaan, bygaun; bygyaan
incline *n.* brae
inconsequential *adj.* sma drink
inconvenience *v.* pit aboot
indeed *adv.* awat; deed; fairly; faith
indigestion *n.* belly-rive
induce *v.* gow (ower)
induct *v.* induck
industrious *adj.* eident
infect *v.* smit
infectious *adj.* smittin
infested *adj.* hotchin
inflamed *ppl., adj.* (by cold) frostit
influence *n.* moyen; **through your influence** in the leethe o ye
influenza *n.* inflooensie
infuriate *v.* raise
infuse *v.* mask
ingenious *adj.* jinipp(e)rous
inhalation *n.* (of air) gluff
inherit *v.* heir; fa heir till
inheritance *n.* heirskip
inhibited *adj.* hudden-doon
injury *n.* scaith
injustice *n.* oonjustice
inlet *n.* (narrow and rocky) gwite
inn *n.* chynge-hoose
innermost *adj.* benmaist
inner workings *n. pl.* intimmers
innovatory *adj.* new-fanglelt
inquire *v.* inquar
inquiry *n.* inquary
inquisitive *adj.* ill-, ull-fashent
inquisitiveness *n.* ill-, ull-fashence
inside *adv.* ben; in-by(e); *prep.* ben
insipid *adj.* saarless, saurless;

warsh; wersh
insist *v.* threep
instinct *n.* enstinck
instrument *n.* enstrument
intelligence *n.* smeddum
intelligent *adj.* lang-heidit
intend *v.* ettle, *ppl.* ettlin; mint
intention *n.* mint
inter *v.* beery; yird
intercept *v.* kep
interdict *n.* enterdick
interesting *adj.* interaistin
interfere *v.* enterfere
interment *n.* beerial
intestines *n. pl.* intimmers; mony-faalds
intimate *v.* intimat; forquant
intimate (with) *adj.* chief (wi); thrang (wi); (esp. in favour with God) far ben (wi)
intimidate *v.* coonjer
into *prep.* intil
intoxicate *v.* deleer
intoxicated *ppl.* glorious
inventory *n.* inveetor
Inverurie *pr. n.* In'rurie
invitation *n.* inveet
invite *v.* bid; inveet; seek
irregular *adj.* (in appearance) shammelt
irresponsible *adj.* haaf-hung-tee
irritable *adj.* sanshach; short i the trot
irritation *n.* aggravation
Isabella *pr. n.* Beldie
island *n.* inch
it *pron.* it; 't; hit
itch *n., v.* yock
itchy *adj.* yockie
ivy *n.* eevie

— J —

jacket *n.* jaicket; (woman's loose) vrapper
jade *n.* (woman) jaad, jaud; bizzar (J)
jail *n., v.* jile
jalopy *n.* shan-dre-dan
jam *n.* jeely; **jam jars** jeely pigs
James *pr. n.* Jamie; Jeems(ie)
Janet *pr. n.* Jinse
janitor *n.* jannie
January *n.* Janwar; Janiwar
jar *n.* (earthenware) pig
jasmine *n.* jassamine
jaundice *n.* the jandies
jaunt *n., v.* jant
jaunty *adj.* jinkie
jaw *n.* jaa, jaw
jaws *n. pl.* chowks
jeer *n.* fleer (J); *v.* jamph; lant
jelly *n.* (table) shoggly-wullie
jellyfish *n.* (stinging) scalder; (harmless) slivvery-doctor (B)
jeopardy *n.* jipperty
jerk *v.* (gently) tit; (strongly) yark; (repeatedly) joggle
jersey *n.* maasie (G); (seaman's) gansey; ganjie
Jew's harp *n.* trump
job *n.* jot; a wark; (troublesome, fiddly) footer; (involving much detail) scutterie jobbie; **a job of work** a jot wark
jocular *adj.* vokie; vyokie
jog *n., v.* cadge

joggle *v.* joogle
John *pr. n.* Jock
join *v.* jyne; (together, esp. roughly in sewing) ranter
joiner *n.* jyner; vricht
joint *n.* jynt; (segment) lith
joist *n.* jyst
joke *n.* (funny story) bar; (at someone's expense) rise; **make fun of** tak the rise o; *v.* fun joking; *adj.* (normally used in the neg.) **no joking matter** nae jeesty; nae mowse; nae a mowse concairn
jolly *adj.* jelly
jolt *v.* daad, daud; (severe) junny
journey *n.* traivel
jovial *adj.* joco
judge *v.* jeedge
jug *n.* joog; stoop, stoup; stowp; (whisky) jorum
juice *n.* bree
juicy *adj.* sappy
jumble *n., v.* jummle
juniper *n.* etnach
junk *n.* rottacks
junk food *n.* galshachs, galshochs perlyaag
just *adv.* jist; joost (A2)
just after *prep.* (of time) the back o
justice *n.* joostice
just like *prep.* siclikes
just now *adv. phr.* enoo, eenoo; eynoo; eyvnoo; iv noo; iv now

— K —

kail stalk *n.* kail runt
keen *adj.* gleg, glegsome; keerious;
  keen on teen wi
keep *v.* kep; (away) hud oot ower;
  (clear of) hud redd o; (in with)
  hud in wi
keeper *n.* (of farm at weekends)
  catcher; toondie, toondy;
  toonkeeper
keep in with *phr.* hud in wi
keep up *v.* keep tee
kennel *n.* cooch
kennel-attendant *n.* dog-dirder
kept *v. pt.* keepit
kettle *n.* byler (R); **a different**
  kettle of fish a different Maggie
  Rennie (B)
kill *v.* fell
kilted *ppl.* kiltit
kind *adj.* douce; kine; *n.* (nature,
  sort) kine
kindle *v.* kennle
kindling *n.* kinlin; kennlin

kindly *adj.* couthie
king *n.* keeng
kingdom *n.* keengdom
kiss *n.* smeerich; smoorich
kitchen *n.* kitchie; but-the-hoose
kitchen-maid *n.* kitchie-deem
kite *n.* (plaything) draigon; (bird)
  gled; gleed
kitten *n.* kit(t)lin
knave *n.* (in cards) munsie
knife *n.* futtle; whittle; (large) gullie
knight *n.* knicht
knit *v.* shank; wyve
knitting *n.* wyvin
knitting-needle *n.* weer
knitting-wool *n.* worsit
knob *n.* knag
knock *v.* ca; chap; knack; knap;
  (about) cadge
knoll *n.* knap, knowe
knot-hole *n.* navus-bore
know *v.* ken; wat; **I know** awyte; I
  ken; *neg.* kenna; dinna ken; watna

— L —

labour *n.* laabour, lawbour
lack *v.* wint
lad *n.* callant; laad; loon
ladle out *v.* lave (B1)
lady's man *n.* a bit o a lad
lag *v.* trytle
lain *ppl.* lyen
lamb *n.* (little) lammie; (male with
  only one descended testicle) rig-
  lamb; (pet brought up on the

bottle and summmoned by the
  call 'sick') sick lamb
lament *v.* willieway
laminate *v.* skelve (B1)
lamp-lighter *n.* leerie
lancet *n.* fleem
land *n.* lan; (exchanged) excamb;
  (low-lying, beside river) haagh,
  haugh
landmark *n.* prop

land on *v.* licht (on)
landowner *n.* laird
landside *adj.* (side of plough next the unploughed land) lanside
lane *n.* (narrow) wynd
language *n.* leid
languor *n.* langer
languish *v.* dwine
lanky person *n.* stilpert
lantern *n.* (han-)booet; booit
lap *v.* lab; lapper; lerb
lapwing *n.* pee-weet (M, R); peesie (-weep) (S); teuchat, teuchit
larch *n.* larick
large *adj.* bookit, boukit; muckle; meikle
lark (about) *v.* hollach (aboot)
lash *n.* whang
last *adj., n., v.* laist, lest; hinmaist
last out *v.* (of people) store the kin
latch *n.* sneck
late *adv.* ahin
laudanum *n.* lodomy
laugh *n., v.* laach, lauch, *pt.* leuch; (loudly) gaff, gauff; (heartily) bicker; **to be laughed at** laachen at; **how I laughed** fit I leuch
laughter *n.* laachter, lauchter
launch *v.* lench
Laurencekirk *pr. n.* Lowrenkirk
lavatory *n.* wattery
law *n.* laa, law
lawful *adj.* laafu, lawfu
lawn *n.* green
Lawrence *pr. n.* Lowrin
lawyer *n.* laavyer, lawvyer
lay *v.* plank
lay hold of *v.* claaght, claught
laziness *n.* sweirty
lazy *adj.* latch; sweer, sweir

lea *n.* (unploughed land) ley; **lea-corn** ley-corn
leader *n.* heid-bummer
leaf *n.* (of potato, turnip etc.) shaw
lean-to *n.* lean-tee
leap *v.* lowp, *pt.* lowpit; lape, *pt.* lap
learn *v.* lairn; leern
learned *adj.* leernt
learning *n.* lairnin; leernin; lear
lease *n.* (of a farm) tack; **leased farm** tack; *v.* set
leather strap *n.* (formerly used by school teachers for punishment) tag; tawse
leave *n.* (of absence) afflat; *v.* lea, ley (A1); lave (S); (one home for another) flit; (in the lurch) lanter; **take one's leave** weer awa
lectern *n.* laiteran; lettrin
left, turn *imper.* (instruction to a plough horse in Buchan) hi
leftovers *n. pl.* orrals
leg *in phr.* **pull my leg** draa ma leg
legless *adj.* shankless
leisure *n.* leasure, leesure
lemonade *n.* ale (also used of other aerated waters)
lend *v.* len
length *n.* lenth; linth
let *v.* lat; lit; lut; *pt.* lat; leet; loot; *ppl.* latten, lutten; **let alone** latten be; **let it be known that** lat licht that
let *v.* (land, property) set
let-down *n.* snipe, snype
lethargic *adj.* oonfersell; smeerless; thowless
letter-be *n.* (the one who feeds in the straw in rope-twisting) latter-oot

liberal *adj.* fraachty, frauchty; leebral; (extravagantly) lordlifu; *n.* Leebral

library *n.* leeberary

licence *n.* leeshens, leeshins

lick *n.* (of fluid) lerb

lie *n.* lee; (big) whapper; *v.* lee, *ppl.*, *n.* leein; **without a word of a lie** onleet; *v.* (in bed etc) lig (lit.)

lift *n.* (in a vehicle) hurl; *v.* heeze; luft; (up) heft; (with effort) heist, hyste

light *adj., n., v.* licht; **indirect light** borrat licht; **make light of** lichtlifie

light-fingered *adj.* tarry-fingert

light-headed *adj.* litchie

lighthouse *n.* lichthoose

lightning *n.* lichtnin; (streak of) flacht o fire

liked *v. pt.* liket, likit

likely *adv.* lickly; belike

likened (to) *ppl.* lickent wi

liking (for) *n.* noshun o

limp *adj.* (from weakness) waffle; *v.* hirple; clench (A2); crochle;

line *n.* (fishing snood made of horse hair) tippen

lingo *n.* linga

linnet *n.* lintie

liquid *n.* bree

liquor *n.* (from Eng. *naphtha*) naftie, naphtie

listen *v.* hearken

listless *adj.* oonfersell; smeerless; heepochondreech (B1)

litany *n.* leetiny

literary *adj.* leeterary

litter *n.* (brood) cleckin

live *v.* (at an address) bide, *pt.* bade; bed(d); stop

livelihood *n.* liveliheid; throw-beerin

lively *adj.* croose

livestock *n.* beas'

living being *n.* leevin

load *n.* lade, laid; (two or more cartloads, barrowloads) fraacht, fraucht; draacht, draucht

loaf *v.* sorn

loathsome *adj.* scunnerfu; scunner-some

lobster *n.* (fisher term) labster

loch *n.* (small) lochan

lock *n.* (of hair) tait

loft *n.* laft

loiter *v.* lyter

long *adj.* lang; **the long and the short of it** the reet an the rise o't

long ago *phr.* lang syne; than an awa

long (for) *v.* green (efter); mang (for)

long-gone *adj.* lang-geen, -gane

long-legged *adj.* lang-leggit; **long-legged person** stilpert

look *n.* leuk; scance; (evil) scook, scouk; vizzy; **backward look** vizzy backart; *v.* leuk; scance

look after *v.* tak aboot

look for *v.* sik, seek

look out *v.* (search and find) rank oot; **on the look-out for** on the haik for

loosen *v.* lowssen

Lord *excl.* lod; losh; loshins; loshtie; **Good Lord guide us** loshtie-goshtie guide's

lordship *n.* lairdskip

lorry *n.* larry

lose *v.* loss; tyne, tine, *pt. ppl.* tint
loss *n.* (by cheating) snipe, snype
lost *in phr.* **get lost** flee up
lot *n.* (situation) billet; **the whole lot** the hale jing-bang
loud *adj.* lood
louse *n.* loose
lousy *adj.* loosie
lout *n.* fang; fleep; flype; (rough) gillieperous; gileepris (hard **g**)
love *n.* luve; *v.* loo, loe
lovely *adj.* bonnie, bonny
low *adj.* laich, laigh; lyaach; **low-lying ground** laigh

lowland *adj.* lallan
lowlands *n. pl.* laalands, lawlands
loyal *adj.* leal
lucky *adj.* chancy; licky
lug *v.* humph
lumbago *n.* lumbaga
lumber *n.* rottacks
lump *n.* (large, of cheese, beef etc) kneevlick; knyte; fang; (also used as mild insult) knibloch
lungs *n. pl.* (human or animal) lichts
lychnis floscuculi *n.* raggit robin (S)

— **M** —

Macduff native *pr. n.* Duffer
mad *adj.* gyte; wid; wud
madam *n.* muddim
madden *v.* raise
madness *n.* madden-drim, -dreem; (sudden) wudden-dream
magic *n.* glamour; glamourie
magnet *n.* lodesteen, lodestane
magpie *n.* pyot
manners *n. pl.* mainners
mainpin *n.* docknail
maintain *v.* (assert) hud, haud oot
majority, the *n.* the feck
make *v.* mak; fack (B1); (cause, compel) gar; **make known** lat licht; **make no difference** mak nae odds
maker *n.* makker
makings (of) *n. pl.* makkins o
malcontent *n.* (female) peekin-eevie
mallet *n.* mell

malt *n.* maat, maut
maltreat *v.* ill-eese; ill-guide
man *n.* maan; maanie; carl; chiel; (little) mannikie; (little, old) carlie; (form of address) min
manage *v.* tak aboot
manager *n.* (of farm) grieve; (of an estate) grun offisher
manger *n.* foresta
manly *adj.* byoordly; beerdly; buirdly
manner *n.* menner; *pl.* menners; **well-mannered** weel-mennert; **ill-mannered** ill-mennert
mantel-shelf *n.* chumla; chumlay
manure *n.* muck; (on the surface) tapdress; **manure-barrow** *n.* muck-barra; **manure distributor** *n.* (horse-drawn) bone davy
many *adj.* mony; **many a one** mony een
marble *n.* (glass) bool; (game of

147

marbles played against door)
doorie

March *n.* Mairch

march *n., v.* mairch, merch

mare *n.* mear, meer

Margaret *pr. n.* Marget; Muggie

market *n.* mairket, mercat; (agric.)
mart; mairt

marking substance *n.* (for sheep)
keel

marriage *n.* mairrage, mairritch;
(paraphernalia) bucklins (A2)
married woman *n.* kimmer

marrowbone *n.* marra-been

marry *v.* mairry; mairry on (to),
ppl. mairrit; wad, *pt.* waddit

marsh *n.* stank

Martinmas *n.* Martimas

marvel *n.* mervel

mash *v.* chap; **mashed potatoes**
chappit tatties

masquerade *v.* guise

mass *n.* (great crowd) mengyie;
(seething) hotter

master *n., v.* maister

match *n.* (stick) spunk; (equal)
marra, marrow; **not matching**
marless; *v.* peer wi

matter *n.* maitter; **doesn't matter**
maksna, disna mak; **no matter**
deil-ma-care

maximus *n.* (gravest error in Latin
prose composition) maxie

May *n.* Mey

me *pron.* ma

meadow *n.* ley

meal *n.* brose; **meal-chest** *n.*
girnal; (farm-servant's) meal-kist;
meal-bunk (S); mealer (S)

mealy-mouthed *adj.* mealy-moo't,
-mou't

mean *adj.* dirten; (shabby) wheetie;
(unsporting) skicy (children's
word); (tight-fisted) hungry;
meangie; near the been; nar (B1);
mean person *n.* hunger; a
hungry Angus

meander *v.* wimple

meanness *n.* near-beg(y)aanness;
near-begaunness

means *n.* moyen

meant *ppl.* meent

measles *n. pl.* the mirrles

measure *n., v.* mizzer;
measurement *n.* mizzerment

measures (grain, six bolls) chalder;
(fourth part of a boll) firlit;
(fourth part of a peck) lippie,
leepie; (liquid, equal to Eng. pint)
mutchkin

meat pie *n.* braddie; bridie

meddle *v.* mell; middle

medicine *n.* feesick

meet *v.* (by chance) kep

meeting *n.* (arranged) tryst

melancholy *adj.* darksome; dowf;
oorlich

mellow *adj.* maamie, maumie,
mawmie

membrane *n.* scriffan

memorial *n.* prop

men *n. pl.* mannies; mennies; men;
chiels

mend *v.* sort; (patch) cloot; (by
coarse darning or sewing) ranter

mention *v.* moo-ban (B1); *in phr.*
not to mention forbyes

mercy *n.* leenity; merciment

merry *adj.* blithe(some), blythe;
mirky

mess *n.* kirn; queeger; soss; (disgusting) sotter; (wet or dirty) slorach; (scattered) splutrich (B1)

mess about *v.* pleiter; (at domestic work) scuddle; scutter

messenger *n.* (sent ahead of bridegroom to summon bride) sen

mettle *n.* spunk

middle *n.* mids; (of the night) riggin o the nicht

midge *n.* midgie; midgeck

mid-ridge *n.* mid-rig

midst *n.* mids

midwife *n.* howdie

might *n.* micht; *v.* micht; mith; **might not** *v. neg.* minna; mithna; mithnin

mignonette *n.* meeninit

migraine *n.* megreem

mildew *n.* mildyow

milk *n.* (jet from a cow's teat) strin

milk-cow *n.* milker; **preparation of milk** milkness; **milk-strainer** *n.* search

mill *n.* mull; (stone hand-mill) quern

miller *n.* mullart, mullert

million *n.* meelyin

millionaire *n.* meelyinaire

mind *n.* myn

minister *n.* meenister; minaister (A2)

minnow *n.* minnon, bandie

minute *n.* meenit

mire *n.* (bog) lair; (mud) dubs; gutters

mirror *n.* gless

mischief *n.* ill-tricks; mischeef; (a bit of) protick; **mischief-maker** *n.* buckie

mischievous *adj.* ill-trickit; **mischievous boy** nickum

miser *n.* hunger (**ng** as in singer)

miserable *adj.* oorlich

miserly *adj.* nar (B1); near-beg(y)aan, near-begaun; grippy

mishap *n.* mishanter; scavie (B1)

mismanage *v.* mislippen

misshapen *ppl., adj.* mishachelt

missionary *n.* missioner

mist *n.* haar; (thin, cold) gull; (in a billow) folm

misty *adj.* mochie

mistake *n.* mistak

mistaken *ppl.* misteen, mistaen

mix *v.* kirn; mell

mixture *n.* mixter; mixter-maxter; queeger

mix-up *n.* quigger

moan *n., v.* main

mob *n.* kinallie

mock *v.* jamph; scowff

mockery *n.* jamphin

moderate *adj.* (in price) canny

moderately *adv.* middlin

modern *adj.* modren

moist *adj.* sappy

mole *n.* mowdie(warp), mowdiewart; **molecatcher** *n.* molie

Monday *n.* Monanday

money *n.* bawbees; siller; tin (A); (just enough to pay one's way) rin-watter

monkfish *n.* (Buchan) caithick; (Moray Firth) oof (B)

monologue *n.* say-awa

monument *n.* moniment

mood *n.* teen; bin; **bad mood** ill teen; **in the mood for** on for

moody *adj.* maggotive
moon *n.* meen, mune; **moonlight**
n. meenlicht, munelicht
moor *n.* meer, muir; (peat moor)
moss
moorcock *n.* muircock
mooring-pot *n.* paal
moorland *n.* muirlan
mope *v.* mump
more *adj.* mair; **more than** *prep.*
passin
morose *adj.* strunge
morsel *n.* glammach, glammoch
mortgage *n.* wadset
moss *n.* fog; (alpine club) stag-moss
moss-covered *adj.* foggit
mossy *adj.* foggy
most *adj., n.* most; the feck
mostly *adv.* maistly; feckly
moth *n.* moch
moth-balls *n. pl.* moch-baas
moth-eaten *adj.* moch-aeten;
mochie
mother *n.* midder; mither; mammy;
(pet name) minnie
mother-in-law *n.* gweed-mither
mould *n.* moold; (a mould for ball,
spoon etc.) caam, caum
mould-board *n.* cleathin
mouldy *adj.* foostie; fooshtie;
foostit
mount *v.* munt; **mounted (on)** *ppl.*
cockit (on)
mountain *n.* ben
mountain-ash *n.* rowan; rodden;
rantree; (berry) rodden
mourn *v.* murn
mourning clothes *n. pl.* murnins
mouse *n.* moose
moustache *n.* mowser

mouth *n.* gab; maa, maw; moo,
mou
mouthful *n.* moofae, moufu; gnap
(large) rive; (of food or drink)
howpie
move *n.* meeve; (jolting) hotter; *v.*
meeve; muv (B1); gee, jee;
(hurriedly) fudder; (quickly and
noisily) bicker; binner; (with
rocking motion) jow; (with
friction) hirstle, hurschle, hursle;
(awkwardly or jerkily) hodge,
hotch; (smoothly) snoove; **on the
move** on the ca; **move house** flit
moved *adj.* (emotionally) affeckit
movement *n.* (quick) binner;
(jolting) hotter
mow *v.* maw
mucus *n.* (nasal) snotter(s)
mud *n.* dubs; clort; glaar, glaur;
gutters; lair; slabber; (alluvial, left
in tidal rivers) sleek; slich
muddle *n.* queeger
muddled *adj.* throw-idder;
throwder; (mentally confused)
raivelt
muddy *adj.* dubby; dubbit; (of
water) drumly; plytery
mud-spattered person *n.* drablich
muggy *adj.* mochie
multitude *n.* multiteed
multure *n.* (miller's fee) moolter,
moulter; mooter, mouter
mumble *v.* mum; mummle
mummer *n.* guiser; guizard (J)
mumming, to go *v.* guise
murder *n., v.* muther
murmur *n.* chirm; myowte; *v.*
chirm; (plaintively) chunner
museum *n.* musaium

music *n.* meesic; **musical tones** airels
mussel *n.* (shelled) sheelter (B)
must *v.* maan, maun; *neg.* maana, mauna; beet, *pt.* beed
mute *n.* dummie

my *poss. pron.* ma
my goodness *excl.* my cert; my certie
myself *pron.* (also by myself) masel; masellie; ma nainsel

— N —

naked *adj.* nakit; nyaakit
napkin *n.* nepkin
nappy *n.* hippen
narrative *n.* say-awa
narrow *adj.* nairra, nerra
nasty *adj.* naisty
national *adj.* naitional
native wit *phr.* mother wit
natty *adj.* jinipperous
natural *adj.* naitral
natural herbage *phr.* natur-girss
nature *n.* natur, naitur
nauseated (by) *ppl.* ska(i)kent (wi)
near *adj.* nar
nearly *adv.* nearhan; naarhan; geylies
neat *adj.* nait; nacket; snod; **neat person** nackety
necessary *adj.* necessar
necessity *n.* needcessity
neck *n.* (to one side) gyke-neckit
need *n.* needcessity; *v.* need; *neg.* needsna, *pt.* nott, *pt. neg.* nottna
ne'er-do-well *n.* neer-dee-weel
neglect *v.* mislippen; negleat
neigh *n.* (of horses) nicher
neighbour *n.* neebour; neeper, neiper
neighbourly *adj.* neiper-like
neither *conj., pron., adj.* naither,

nether; nedder; nedderin
nephew *n.* neffy
nervous *adj.* nervish
nest *n.* (of wild bees) bike
nestling *n.* cheeper; gorbal; gorblin; gog (S)
never *adv.* niver, nivver; ne'er
nevertheless *adv.* natheless; still-an-on
next *adj.* neest, neist; neesht
new *adj.* (quite) spleet-new
Newburgh *pr. n.* (near Ellon) Neebra
newly *adv.* new; newlins
news-starved *adj.* news-gizzent
New Year's Eve *n.* Hogmanay
niggardliness *n.* near-beg(y)aan-ness; near-begaunness
niggardly *adj.* near-beg(y)aan; near-begaun; *adj., adv.* scuddy
night *n.* nicht; **last night** the streen; **overtaken by night** nicht-boon, nichtboun
nimble *adj.* swack, swak; swippert, swyppert; swuppert
nitwit *n.* gapus
no *adj.* nae, *e.g.* nae wark
no *adv.* na; **no thank you** na thenk ye
nobbly *adj.* knablick

noise *n.* (loud) dirdum, dundeerie, min(n)eer, mineerum
noisy *adj.* raachle, rauchle
nominated *v. pt., ppl.* nominat
none *pron.* neen, nane
nonsense *n.* blethers; blickers; buff; havers; stite, styte
noose *n.* mink
Norway *pr. n.* Noroway (A2)
Northern Lights, the *pr. n.* the Merry Dancers
northland *adj.* norlan
nose *n.* cooter, couter; neb, nib; niz; nob; snoot
nosebleed *n.* bleedy cooter
not *adv.* nae, *e.g.* she's nae gaan; no *e.g.* she's no gaen (C1, G1, S); the Deil., *e.g.* the Deil he did; fient a, *e.g.* **not one** fient een; **not likely** fient afears; **not a bit** fient hait; deil a nip **not at all**

excl. fie na
notch *n.* hack; nick
nothing *n.* naething; nocht; (absolutely) naither eechie nor ochie; **a mere nothing** *n.* wanwurth
notion *n.* noshun; (foolish) gee; **to take a notion** *phr.* tae tak a tig
nought *n.* nocht
now *adv.* noo; **just now** aenoo; eenoo, eynoo; eyvnoo; ivnoo; **now and then** fyles; noo an than; noo an aan; noos an aans
nowadays *adv.* nooadays
nowhere *adv.* naewye
nuisance *n.* bucker; scutter
number *n.* nummer; a wheen; a curn; a puckle; (large number) a gweed curn; dose; hantle; spreeth
numskull *n.* gapus

— **O** —

oak *n.* aik
oatcakes *n. pl.* (ait) kyaaks; cyacks; bannocks (S); (in a round) kyaak o breid; (taken as dessert in bowl of milk) breid; (crumbled into milk) murly-tuck, snap-an-rattle; (buttered by thumb) thoomb-piece
oaten *adj.* aiten
oat husks *n. pl.* (used for sowans) sids
oatmeal *n.* aitmeal, meal; (quantity received from the mill at one time) maillyer; (when boiled thicker than gruel, with butter and

honey) brochan; (~ or peasemeal mixed with boiling water or milk) brose; (mixed cold with water) crowdy; (with boiled milk) knotty tams; (pudding) mealie puddin; (pancakes) saatie-, sautie-bannocks; (cooked with onion, dripping and seasoning) skirlie; (~ ball given to children during baking) sooie
oath *n.* aith; charge
oats *n. pl.* ait(s); corn; (fermented husks of ~ boiled) sowans
obedient *adj.* obaidient
object *n., v.* objeck

oblige *v.* obleege
obliged *ppl.* behudden; obleeged;
    not obliged onbehudden
obstacle *n.* bunkert
obstinate *adj.* stockit; thraan,
    thrawn
occasional *adj.* antrin
occasionally *adv.* fyles
occupy *v.* occupee
October *n.* Jocktober
odd *adj.* orra; (peculiar) unco
oddity *n.* ferlie; (untidy person)
    track
odd-job man *n.* (on farm) orra man
odd-job boy *n.* (on farm) orra loon
odour *n.* waff
of *prep.* o
off *adv., prep.* aff
offence *in phr.* **take offence at**
    someone tak the gee wi
offend *v.* miscomfit; offen
officer *n.* offisher
officiate *v.* offeeshyat
often *adv.* afen; aft; aften
oh *excl.* och
oh yes *excl.* hoot ty
oil *n.* ile
oil-cake *n.* ile-cake
oil lamp *n.* ily(-lamp); (old-
    fashioned) cruisie, crusie
oil-skin *adj. n.* ile-skin
oily *adj.* eely
ointment *n.* saa, saw
old *adj.* aal(d), aul(d)
old age *n.* eild; eld (C1)
older *adj.* aaler, auler
oldest *adj.* aalest, aulest
old-fashioned *adj.* aal-farran(t)
on *prep.* on; o
once *adv.* eence; ance (G1); **once**

upon a time eence on a day
one *adj.* ae; *n.* (numeral) een; **the**
    one (contrasted with the other)
    the teen; the taen (S)
onion *n.* ingan
onslaught *n.* dirdin
ooze *n.* glaar, glaur
open *adj., v.* apen; **open air** the
    furth
open air, in the *phr.* thereoot
opening *n.* slap
opinion *n.* opeenion; opingan
opinionative *adj.* heidie; noshunate
opportunity, at every *phr.* at aa
    hans
opposite *prep.* anent; fornent
ordain *v.* ordeen
ordeal *n.* throw-come
order, out of *prep. phr.* agley
ordinary *adj.* ordinar
ornament *n.* (showy) furligorum;
    (fantastic and useless)
    whigmaleerie; (elaborate
    architectural ornamentation)
    furlimafaals
ostentatious *adj.* vantie, vauntie
other *adj., n., pron.* idder; ither;
    odder; **the other** (contrasted with
    the one) the tither
ought *v.* ocht
ounce *n.* unce
our *pron.* oor; wir
ours *pron.* oors
ourselves *pron.* (also **by ourselves**)
    oorsels; wirsels
out *adv.* oot
out of *prep.* oot o; (bed, a cart etc.)
    ootower; **out of favour with** oot
    wi; **out of things** oot amint (S);
    out of the way ootby

outbreak *n.* ootbrak
outcast *n.* ootlin
outcry *n.* (querulous) scronach
  (A2)
outdo *v.* cow(e)
outfield *n.* ootfeedle
outfit *n.* rig-oot
outgoing *n.* (departure at end of
  season) ootgang
outhouse *n.* oothoose
outlay *n.* ootlay, ootlie
outlet *n.* ootlat; (at spring) stroop
outlines *n. pl.* rinnins
outmost *adj.* ootmaist
outrageous *adj.* maroonjus (A)
outside *adv.* ootby; thereoot
outspoken *adj.* tongue-betroosht
outstanding thing of its kind *n.*
  beezer; binder
outward(ly) *adj., adv.* ootwith,
  -wuth
over *adv.* ower; (past) by; by wi't;
  over against *prep.* fornent
overall *n.* vrapper; wrapper
overboiled *ppl.* (of potatoes)
  throwe the bree
overburden *v.* (yourself) forfecht
  (yersel)
overcast *adj.* owercassen
overcome *adj.* (by emotion) great-
  hertit; *v.* ding

overdo *v.* forfecht yersel
overflow *v.* jibble ower; ream
overheated *ppl.* stecht
overjoyed *ppl., adj.* liftit
overlay *v.* owerlay
overlook *v.* owerleuk
overnight *adv.* owernicht
over-particular *adj.* jinipperous
overrun (with) *adj.* hotchin (wi)
overseer *n.* (of farm) grieve;
  owersman
overtake *v.* owertak
overturn *v. tr.* (turn upside down)
  folm; *tr., intr.* cowp; whummle
  (J); **overturned** *ppl.* (sheep)
  cowpit
overwrought *adj.* wrocht-up
owe *v.* acht, aucht; awe; **owing**
  awin
owl *n.* oolet (A); hoolet; howlet
  (G1)
own *adj.* ain; nain; nown; **hold
  your own** hud yer nain; **one's
  own self** yer nainsel; *v. pr. (in
  third pers. sing.)* acht; yacht; *ppl.*
  echt; yacht
ox *n. sing.* nowt; owse; (fattened for
  market) feeder; (killed at
  Martinmas for winter use) mart;
  mairt; **oxen** nowt; owsen

— **P** —

pacify *v.* peshifee
pail *n.* (wooden, for milking or
  herring guts) cog(gie), cogue
pain *n.* jip; pyne; (animal suffering
  pain) pyner; (*excl.* of) feech;

  seized with pain (in the hips)
  (hip-)grippit
paint *n., v.* pent, pint; **painting the
  town red** oot o yer box
palace *n.* pailace

pale *adj.* gowsty
paling *n.* palin
pampered *ppl., adj.* (of farm animals) fence-fed
pane *n.* peen
pant *v.* blyaav; pech; (with heat or exertion) fob
parapet *n.* (of a bridge) lanstell
parched *ppl.* gizzent
parent *n.* paarent
parish *n.* pairis
part *n.* pairt; trail; (small) tait; (very small) nimp; nippock(ie); *v.* pairt; sinder, sinner; (the hair, or sheep's wool) shed
particle *n.* hait; sinacle (B1)
particular *adj.* parteeclar; (very) pernickety
particularly *adv.* freely; **particularly fine** freely fine
partin *n.* pairtin
partner *n.* pairtner
partridge *n.* pairtrick (M, C); paitrick (S, M1)
party *n.* pairty; shine; (for women) henshine
pass *v.* (something to someone) rax; (through or over) owergae; **pass the time away** fite the idle pin
passage *n.* closs; pass; throw-gang; (in a house) trance
passing, in the *phr.* i the bygaein; i the bygaan
past *prep.* by
pat *v.* (fondle) clap
path *n.* roddie; waakie
patron *n.* paatron
patronage *n.* paatronage
patronise *v.* paatroneese
pattern *n.* pattren

pause *n., v.* devall
pavement *n.* planesteens
pay *n., v.* pey
payment *n.* peymen
peace *n.* quaitness
peak *n.* snoot
peaked *adj.* (of a cap) snootit
pearl *n.* pairl
peas *n. pl.* piz
pease meal *n.* piz-meal; pizzers
peat *n.* (individual) cloddie; (pile of) stack; **peat-cutting** mossin; **peat dust** drush
peck *n., v.* (of birds) dorb
peculiar *adj.* unco
peddle wares *v.* cadge
peep *v.* keek; teet; **peep-bo** keek-a-bo; teet-a-bo
peevish *adj.* girnie; nibawa; nyattery; orpiet (A2); **peevish person** wittrel, witterel
pelt *v.* clod; daad, daud
pen *n.* (for cattle) pumphel
penholder *n.* penner
people *n. pl.* fowk; folk
perched (on) *ppl.* cockit (on)
perhaps *adv.* ablins; aiblins; mebbe
periwinkle *n.* buckie; wulk
perplexed *adj.* hobbelt
persevere *v.* hing in
person *n.* bodie; leevin; wicht
persuade *v.* gow (ower); perswaad
pertain *v.* perteen
pert girl *adj., n.* clip; (person) smatchet
perverse *adj.* camsteerie; contermin't; ill-gatit, ill-gettit
pester *v.* (with entreaties) deeve, deave
pet *v.* daat; dawt; *n.* daatie; tae-ee

155

Peter *pr. n. dim.* Patie
Peterhead native *pr. n.* Blue-moggener
petrol *n.* peetrol
petticoat *n.* kwite; quyte; *n. pl.* cotts; (made of wincey) winceys
pew *n.* (square) pumphel
phlegm *n.* haach
physical *adj.* feesickle
physically *adv.* body-bulk
physician *n.* physeeshun
piano *n.* peanny
pick *v.* pyke
Pict *n.* Picht
picture *n.* picter, pictur
piece *n.* (large) daad, daud; fordel (B1); knyte; (very small) nimp; nippock(ie)
pierce *v.* prob (*incl.* piercing of cow's stomach to release gas)
pig *n.* (fisher word to overcome taboo) grunter; Sandy Campbell
pigeon *n.* doo
pigeon-toed *adj.* pirn-taed
pigsty *n.* swine's hoose
pilfer *v.* pilk
pill *n.* peel
pillow *n.* pilla
pimple *n.* plook
pimply *adj.* plooky
pin *n.* preen; (or knob) knag; *v.* preen
pinafore *n.* peenie; (loose) slip
pincers *n. pl.* turkis
pinched *adj.* wainished-like
pine *v.* dwine
pine torch *n.* fir
pin-headed *adj.* preen-heidit
pinnacle *n.* toopachin, toopican
pipe *n.* (short tobacco pipe) cutty; (chain of tin pipe-lid) rackle
pitch-dark *n.* pick-mirk
pitcher *n.* craggin; pig; (wooden) stoop(ie)
pith *n.* fushen, fushon
pitiful *adj.* peetifu
Pitsligo *pr. n.* (nickname) Kyack
pity *n.* peety; *v.* meen; peety
place *v.* plank
plague *n.* pleege
plaice *n.* plashie; plash fluke
plaid *n.* faik; fayich; fyaaak
plain *adj.* (blunt) aff-han; (simple) hamal(t)
plank *n.* (of wood) plunk
plantation *n.* plantin
plaster *n.* plaister
playground *n.* playgrun; playgreen
plaything *n.* plaik
plead *v.* prig
pleasant *adj.* couthie; leesome; lichtsome; pleesint; plizzant
pleased *adj.* pleased, pleast; plaised (S, C1); **pleased with** teen wi
pleasure *n.* pleesur(e)
plentiful *adj.* raffy
plenty (of) *n.* rowth, routh (o)
pliable *adj.* weffle
plight *n.* plicht; pilget (B1); plisky (B1)
plod *v.* stowff
plough *n.* pleuch (A, M1); ploo; (projecting wing on sock) ploo-feathers; (handles) ploo-stilts; *v.* ear (A2); pleugh; ploo; (shallow furrows) ebb-ploo; brak-fur; (fallow land) fauch
ploughed land *n.* red-lan
ploughing *n.* earin (A2); plooin
ploughing marker *n.* prop

ploughman *n.* plooman
ploughshare *n.* sock
plover *n.* plivver
plump *adj.* sonsy
plum pudding *n.* dumplin; (boiled in a cloth) clootie dumplin
plunder *n.* herry; *v.* reive; (bird's nest) harry; herry
plunge churn *n.* plump churn
pocket *n.* pooch; pock (J); (inside) oxter-pooch; *v.* pooch
poet *n.* makar
point *v.* pynt
point of, on the *prep. phr.* aweers o; on the weers o
poison *n.* pooshan, pooshin; pyshon
poisonous *adj.* pooshinous
poke *v.* dab; pirl; powk
pole *n.* stang
polecat *n.* foumart
police *n.* pleece; pollis (J)
policeman *n.* bobby
polish *n.* (black polish) blake
politician *n.* politeeshun
politics *n.* poleetics
pond *n.* (for watering cattle) coble; stank
pony *n.* shalt(ie); shelt(ie); shult; (suffering from stringhalt) cleekit shalt
pool *n.* peel
poor *adj.* peer, puir
pope *n.* pape
porridge *n.* porritch; pottich; parritch (J) (plural in Doric)
Portessie *pr. n.* the Sloch
portion *n.* pairt; trail; (small) tait
position *n.* poseetion; (posture) powster
possess *v.* acht, aucht

possession *n.* acht, aucht
postman *n.* postie
pot *n.* pat; **went to pot** gaed worth
potato *n.* tattie; pitaatie (B1); **potato-masher** tattie-chapper; (pit for storage) tattie-clamp; **potato digger** tattie-howker; (implement) deevil; **potato harvest** tattie-howkin, -liftin (J); **potato foliage** tattie-shaw
potter *v.* plowter; plyter; scutter
poultice *n.* pultice; steepit loaf
pound *n.* (sterling) poond; pown; pund; (in weight) pun; pund
pounded oats *n.* bruised corn
pour *v.* poor
poverty *n.* poortith
powder *n.* pooder
power *n.* pooer
practical joke *adj., n.* hyze; rig
practise *v.* practeese
praise *n.* (high) reeze; *v.* reeze
pram *n.* coach
pranks, mad *n.* madden-dreem
prate *v.* gab
prattle *n.* gab
prattler *n.* a gab
prayers *n. pl.* gweed-words
precise *adj.* perjink; preceese; *adv.* preceesely
predicament *n.* frap; hobble
prefer *v.* prefar
preference *n.* prefairrance
pregnant *adj.* muckle-bookit, -boukit; in the faimly wye (A2); **make pregnant** *v.* bairn; nick
prejudice *n.* prejudeece
present *adv.* aside; *n.* praisent; (bought at a fair) fairin(g)
presentable *adj.* gatefarrin

presently *adv.* belyve
preside *v.* (at a Presbyterian Church court) moderate
press *v.* birse, birze
press on *v.* kneip on
press-stud *n.* dome
pressure *n.* (*esp.* from a crowd) birse
pretence *n.* mak-on
pretend *v.* mak on
pretentious *adj.* upsettin
pretty *adj.* bonnie, bonny; protty; **a pretty penny** a protty penny
pretty well *adv.* geylies
prick *v.* brob; job; **pricked** *ppl.* brobbit
prickly *adj.* jobby
prim *adj.* mim; mim-like; mim-moo't, -mou't; perjink; primpit
prime *n.* potestatur; pottiestattur
prince *n.* prence
principle *n.* prenciple
print *n., v.* prent
privilege *n.* preevilege
probably *adv.* belike
proclaim *v.* scrie, scry
procrastinating *ppl., adj.* aff-pittin
prod *v.* prob
prodigious *adj.* prodeegious
profit *n.* (high) rug
progress *n.* fordal, fordle
project *n.* projeck
promoter *n.* deester
proof *n.* preef, pruif

properly *adv.* the richt gate
prophesy *v.* prophesee
protect *v.* proteck
protest *v.* oot-cry
proud *adj.* poochle; prood; pridefu (J)
prove *v.* pruv
provisions *n. pl.* proveesions
provoking *adj.* angersome
prudent *adj.* canny
prune *v.* sned
prying *adj.* lang-nebbit, -nibbit
puff *n.* (of wind) waff; **puffed up** *ppl., adj.* (of a person) ful, full
pull *v.* poo, pu; tit; (forcibly) rive, *ppl.* rivven
pullet *n.* yearock
pulpit *n.* poopit
punch *n.* plowt
punctual *adj.* punctwal
puny *adj.* nochtie
pupil *n.* scholar
puppy *n.* fulpie
purple *adj.* purpie
purr *n.* (of a cat) three-threids-an-a-thrum; *v.* spin his/her thrums
push *v.* shiv; shive; putt; (push to) birse tee
puss *n.* bau(l)drins; bawdrons
put *v.* pit, *pt.* pat; **put away** pit past; **put by, put aside** *ppl.* pat tee; **put out** *ppl.* pitten, putten oot; **put together** *v.* ranter
puzzle *v.* bleck

— Q —

quaff *v.* skowf. *cf.* **scoof**
quake *v.* shak; trimmle

quandary *n.* swither
quantity *n.* a curn; sowd; wheen;

(large) gweed curn; feck; hantle;
(small) bittock; pick; starn(ie);
tait; tooshtie (very small) skirlie;
(small, of liquor) skite; tootie;
(tiny) stime, styme

quarrel *n.* cast-oot; faa oot;
scashle; sharrie; split; strush(ie);
throw-the-muir; tulzie; *v.* scashle;
strive, *pt.* streeve, *ppl.* striven;
threep

quarrelsome *adj.* camsteerie; din-
raisin

quarter *n.* (of oatcake round)
corter, korter; (of a year) raith

quart measure *n.* (with knobbed
lid) tappit hen

queer *adj.* unco

quench *v.* (thirst) slack; slock,
sloke; slocken, sloken

querulous *adj.* girny; orpiet (A2)

question *n.* quisson; *v.* back-speir

quibbles *n. pl.* fittie-fies

quick *adj.* faist; slippy

quick-tempered *adj.* short-i-the-
trot

quiet *adj.* quait; **be quiet** hud yer
tongue; hud yer wheesht

quietness *n.* quaitness

quit *v.* quat

quite *adv.* (completely) fair; *excl.*
fairly

quiver *v.* chiver; trimmle

quiz *v.* backspeir

quoth *v.* quo

— R —

rabbit *n.* rubbit; ribbit (S); (used on
board ship to avoid taboo word)
mappie; (Russian) Roosian

rack *n.* (for fodder) haik

radish *n.* (wild) runch

rafter *n.* couple, cupple

rag *n.* (thin cloth) flinrikin;
(worthless) peltin-pyock; *chf. in
pl.* duds; **rags and tatters**
tatterwallops

rage *n., v.* rampage, rampauge

ragged *adj.* duddie; raggit; **ragged
person** tatterwallop

raging *ppl., adj.* ragie

ragweed *n.* weepies (J)

ragwort *n.* tansy

rain *n.* reyn; (light, good for crops)
growin shoorie; (a heavy fall)
onding; spleeter o weet; (fine)

smirr; smoocherin; *v.* (slightly)
spirk; spit

rainbow *n.* (broken) a teeth in the
sky

rainy *adj.* drappie; weety

rake *n.* (small) smiler; *v.* raik

range *v.* (roam) reenge

ransack *v.* raffle; rype

rascal *n.* a bit o a lad; limmer;
scypal, skypal

rash *adj.* ramsh

raspberry *n.* risp; sivven

rat *n.* rottan

rather *adv.* gey; geylies; raither;
redder; some; **rather cold** some
caal

ravenous *adj.* yamph

ravine *n.* cleuch; glack

ray *n.* (of sun) blink

reach *v.* (a place) win
ready *adj.* redd
real *adj.* rale
really *adj.* ralely
reap *v.* cut; shear
reaper *n.* raeper, raiper
reason *n.* rizzon
reasonable *adj.* rizzonable
rebound *v.* skite
recently *adv.* newlins
recipe *n.* recaipt
reck *v.* (care) raik
reckon *v.* rackon
recline *v.* (lit.) lig
recognisable *adj.* (easily)
   kenspeckle
reconsider *v.* fell-think
recover *v.* weer tee; (one's health
   or spirits) cantle; (from) cower
recuperate *v.* recreet
red *adj.* reed, reid
red-cheeked *adj.* reid-chikkit
red-combed *adj.* reid-kaimed
redcurrant *n.* rizzar
red-headed *adj.* reid-heidit
red-hot *adj.* reid-het
reed *n.* sprot
reel *n.* (on which yarn or thread is
   wound) pirn
refer *v.* refar
refusal *n.* na-say
refuse *n.* orrals; *v.* refeese; na-say
regard *n., v.* regaird
register *v.* (for proclamation of
   banns of marriage) beuk
regret about, express *v.* remorse
regular *adj.* reglar
rein *n.* rine, ryne
related *adj.* sib
relationship *n.* sibness

relax *v.* rist; hud doon the deece; lat
   the theats slack
reliable *adj.* siccar
relief *n.* easedom
religion *n.* releegion
religious *adj.* releegious
remain *v.* bide
remains *n. pl.* hinner-en
remainder *n.* the lave
remark *n.* (quick-witted) upcome
remarkable *adj.* unco
remedy *n.* remeid
remember *v.* mynd; myn
remind *v.* mynd; myn
removal *n.* (from a tenancy)
   ootgang
renegade *n.* ranegill
renewal *n.* (replacement) retour
rennet *n.* yirnin
rent *n.* rint
repent *v.* remorse
replacement *n.* retour
replete *adj.* (after food) ful; ful up;
   stappit; weel-sairt;
reprimand *n.* owergaan, -gaun
reproof *n.* (severe) owergaan,
   -gaun
reprove *v.* repree
require *v.* requar, requair
reserved *adj.* poochle; puchal
resin *n.* rosit
resinous *adj.* firry; rositie
respect *n., v.* respeck
respectable *adj.* douce; wice-like;
   (of appearance) gatefarrin
respectful *adj.* mensefu
responsible *in phr.* **to be**
   responsible for it tae be the deed
   o't
rest *n.* rist; flap; (the remainder)

lave; *v.* rist; hud doon the deece;
lat the theats slack

resting-place *n.* ludgement

restive *adj.* reistin

restless *adj.* (of a horse) tittersome

retailer *n.* merchan

retch *v.* cowk, kowk

retort *v.* rebat

reveal *v.* kythe

revel *n.* splore

reverse *n.* revarse; (of a horse etc.)
into reverse intae the britchin

rhododendron *n.* rhoddie

ribbon-ends *n. pl.* fattrels

rib-grass *n.* carl-doddie

riches *n. pl.* graith

rick *n.* ruck; (large, or hay or corn)
moo; (small, of corn or hay)
hooick; scroo

rick-yard *n.* stack-yaird

ricochet *v.* skite

rid *adj.* redd; *v.* redd; **get rid of**
wun redd o

riddance *n.* reddance; **good
riddance** gweed reddance; **off
you go and good riddance**
mirra-hine; merry-hyne

ridge *n.* rig; riggin; (on which
plough is turned) fleed; (side)
side-rig

ridiculous *adj.* rideeclous

riff-raff *n.* raff; scruff; warriedrags,
towrags an swypins o the pier (B)

rifle *v.* rype

right *adj., n., v.* richt

righteous *adj.* richteous

right thing, do the *v.* dee the richt
gate

right turn *phr.* (command to
plough-horse in Buchan) wish

rigid *adj.* strait

rigmarole *n.* la(m)gamachie;
linglairy (B1)

ring *v.* (of a tolling bell) jow

rinse *v.* sweel

ripple *v. intr.* bicker; pirl

risky *adj.* oonchancie

rivet *v.* clink

road *n.* (narrow) roddie

roam *v.* raik, rake; reenge

roar *v.* (of cattle) rowst, roust; rowt
(G1)

roast *v.* birsel, birstle; roast; *ppl.*
roasin, roassin; **roasting hot**
roassin

Robert *pr. n.* (familiar form)
Rob(bie)

rod *n.* (for stirring porridge)
spurkle; spurtle; theevil; (in
chimney for hanging pots over
the fire) swey; (fishing) waan

rode *v. pt.* rade

roe *n.* raan

rogue *n.* widdiefu; (term of
endearment for a child) rogie

roguery *n.* joukerie pawkerie

roll *n.* (morning) buttery-rowie;
buttery; rowie; (floury) bap; *v.*
rowe; wammle

roof *n.* reef; riggin

room *n.* (best) the room

roost *n., v.* reest

root *n.* reet

rope *n.* raip, rape; tow; (round
eaves of a stack) eave raip; (ball
of straw-rope) edderin; *v.* (twist
ropes round a stack) edder; (used
to lash a load on to a cart) girdin;
(for hanging nappies) hippen-
towie; (double ropes for skipping)

lundies
rope-twister *n.* thrawcruik;
tweezlock; twiner
rose *v. pt.* rase
rough *adj.* roch; reuch (J); grofe;
(unmannerly) menseless; (~ in
manners) roch an richt; **rough
character** ranegill
rough-and-ready *adj.* hull-run
rough-cast *v.* (a wall with mortar)
(sneck)-harl; **rough-casting** *n.*
harlin
round *adj., adv., prep.* roon
round-shouldered *adj.* roon-
shoodert
rouse *v.* (to anger) roose
route *n.* gate
row *n.* gyang; raa, raw
row *n.* (rumpus) reerie; sta(r)shie;
stushie; **make a row** kick up a
reerie
rowan tree *n.* rantree; rodden tree
rub *v.* faach, fauch (B1)

rubbish *n.* pelt; perlyaag
ruddy *ppl., adj.* kindlin (J)
ruin *n.* gowf(f); (cause of) herrial
rule *n., v.* rowle
ruler *n.* rowler
rumble *v.* rummle; (of the stomach)
womle
rummage *v.* reemish
rumour *n.* raiverie; reverie
rumpus *n.* ran-dan; rammie; reerie
run *v.* rin; skelp; (off quickly)
skice, skyce; skite; uptail; (in
excited or aimless fashion) fudder
runny jam *adj., n.* elbuck jam
rush *n.* (plant) rash; sprot; *v.*
(forward impetuously) breenge;
(of the wind) sough
Russian *adj.* Rooshian
rustle *n., v.* reesle, reeshle; (of grain
indicating ripeness) buzzle
rust *n., v.* roost, roust; *ppl. adj.*
roostin
rusty *adj.* roosty

— S —

saa *v. pt.* saw, *neg.* saana, sawna
Sabbath *n.* Saabath, Sawbath
sabre *n.* saabre
sack *n.* saick, seck; **sackcloth and
ashes** harn bags an shunners
sad *adj.* doolsome; dowie; wae;
waesome
saddle *n.* saiddle, seddle
safe *adj.* saff; (~ to deal with)
chancy
sag *v.* seg
sagging *adj.* seggit
sago pudding *n.* (nicknamed)

birdies eenies; puddock's eggs
saint *n.* sant
saintly *adj.* santly
salary *n.* sailary
sallow *adj.* hyaave
salmon *n.* reidfish (to avoid taboo
word at sea)
salt *n.* saat, saut; **worth his salt**
wirth saat till his kail; *v.* (fish)
roose; **salty** *adj.* saatie, sautie
salt-box *n.* saat-backet, saut-backet
salt-brick *n.* (for cattle) saat-lick,
saut-lick

salter *n.* saater, sauter
salve *n.* saa, saw
same *adj.* **all the same** aa ae claith
sample *n.* swatch
sanctify *v.* santifee
sand *n.* saan
sand-eel *n.* sile; sunnel
sane *adj.* aa come; aa there
sapless *adj.* foggy
saps *n. pl.* flannen broth
Satan *pr. n.* Saatan, Sawtan
sate *v.* sair
satiate *v.* sair; stech; *ppl.* sick sairt
satisfy *v.* saitisfee; (*esp.* with food or drink) sair
Saturday *n.* Saiterday, Setterday
saucy *adj.* sanshach
saunter *v.* pammer, paumer
savour *n.* saar
saw *v. pt.* saa
sawdust *n.* saadist
saxifrage *n.* fou
scabbed *adj.* scabbit; scabby
scabby *adj.* scabbit
scald *v.* scaad, scaud; plot; (slightly) scam, scaum
scamp, *n.* fang; widdiefu
scan, *v.* scance
scandal *n.* ill-win
scandal-monger *n.* sclave
scarcely *adv.* jimp
scare *n.* gliff (B1); *v.* fley
scarecrow *n.* bockie, bokie; scare-craa, scarecraw; tattie-boodie (A); tattie-bootie (C); tattie-doodle (S); tattie-dulie (J)
scarf *n.* graavit, grauvit
scavenge *v.* scran
scheme *n., v.* skaim, skem
school *n.* skweel, squeel; skale (S);

schule (J); (attendance officer) wheeper-in
schoolmaster *n.* dominie
school pupil *n.* scholar
scientific *adj.* scienteefic
scissors *n. pl.* sheers
scivvy *n.* sciffie (S)
scoff *v.* scowff
scold *v.* ban; banter; coonjer; flyte, *pt.* flate; get on tae; gie intae trouble; (severely) bully-rag; rally on; scaal, scaul; seeg (G); tongue. *cf.* **flyte**
scolding *n.* bark-an-bowff; scaal, scaul; sedarin; sortin; (severe) dixie; kail-throwe-the-reek; owergaan, -gaun; (mild) ragie;
scoop *n.* (metal ~ for use with herring) sheil
scope *v.* scooth; scowth; scouth
scorch *v.* birstle; plot; scam, scaum; scorching, *ppl.* birstlin
scoundrel *n.* scoon(e)ral; *(joc.)* bleck
scour *v.* scoor
scowl *n., v.* glower; scool
scraggy person *adj., n.* sharger
scrape *v.* screeve
scratch *n.* scart; scrat; (large) screeve; *v.* claa; faach, fauch (B1); scart; scrat; screeve
scratching-post *n.* claain-post
scream *v.* skirl; skwaal
screech *v.* scraach, scrauch; skraich
scrimmage *n.* bicker; shangie
scrounge *v.* cadge; mooch; (of people and dogs) skweenge
scrounger *n.* moocher
scrubbing-board *n.* scoorin-buird
scurry *v.* skyce, skice

scythe *n.* robsorbie (from make of scythe); **scythe handle** sned

sea anemone *n.* pap

seagull *n.* (Buckie) gow; (M1) maa, maw; (Fraserburgh) myaave; (Gardenstown) pule, pyool; (Peterhead) scurry; (M1) scurry-waster; (A1, R) sea-goo; (M1) seamaa

search *v.* rake

season *n., v.* sizzon; *v.* (food) hire

seasoning *n.* kitchie

seat *n.* sate, **take a seat** sit doon; lean yersel doon; loot ye doon

seaweed *n.* (heavy with thick stalks, broad fronds) carlers; (coloured) dallies clysies; (dulse) dilse; (a species) tangles

second day's broth *phr.* yavil-broth

second thoughts, to have *v., n.* fell-think

second-year crop *n.* yavil

secret *n.* saicret; **divulging a ~** *phr.* lattin oot the pooder

secretly *adv.* stown-wyes

secure *adj.* siccar

sedge *n.* seg(g)s

see through a dodge *phr.* twig

seed *n.* sid

seek *v.* sik, seek

seemly *adj.* wice-like

seep *v.* sype

see to *v.* sort

see-saw *n.* coup-the-ladle

seething *adj.* hotchin

segment *n.* lith

seize *v.* cleek; mitten; nab

seizure *n.* jamaica, *in phr.* jist aboot hid a jamaica

select *v.* seleck, wale; wyle

selection *n.* wale; wylin

self *n.* sel

self-important *adj.* puchal, puchil (A2)

selfishness *n.* selfitness

self-righteous *adj.* unco-gweed

send *v.* sen

senna *n.* sinna

senseless *adj.* glaikit

sensitive *adj.* (of an issue) kittle, kittlesome; (of a person) thin-skinnt

sent *ppl.* putten

separate *v.* sinder; sinner; (used in curling) split

sergeant *n.* sairgint

serious *adj.* sairious

serve *v.* sair; ser; (~ a cow) bul(l)

serving *n.* sairin

set *in phr.* all set, riggit oot; set off, get roadit

setback *n.* backset; snipe, snype

settle *n.* deece, deese; *v.* sattle

settlement *n.* (usually at marriage) doon-sittin

seven *adj.* saiven; seiven; seyven; siven

seventeen *adj.* saiventeen; seiventeen; seyventeen

seventy *adj.* saiventy; seiventy; seyventy

several *adj.* (a) twa-three; a wheen

sew *v.* shoo, shew

sewing *n.* shooin, shewin

sewing-machine *n.* shewin-machine

shabby *adj.* orra; scabbit; (mean) wheetie

shadow *n.* shadda

shaft *n.* (of barrow, cart) tram

shake *n., v.* shak; shog; shoggle; shoogle; (roughly) cadge; (wave) wag; **no great shakes** nae great dell

shaker *n.* (in a mill) shakker

shaky *adj.* shakky; shoggly; shoogly; (from weakness) waffle

shall *v.* sall; **shall not** sanna

shamble *v.* baachle, bauchle

shanks' pony *n.* shanks' meer; waaker's bus

shape *v.* fack (B1)

shaped *ppl.* shapit

shard *n.* (of earthenware) lame

share out *n.* pairtin; pairt-oot (S); *v.* pairt; **badly shared out** ill-pairtit

shark *n.* (basking) muldoan, muldoon

sharp *adj.* (of mind) gleg; glegsome; (of tongue) ill-hung; (of the wind) snell

sharpen *v.* sharp

shatter *v.* chatter

shaved *v. pt., ppl.* shaven

sheaf *n.* shafe, shaif; shave; (last sheaf on top of a stack) heid(in)-shafe

shed *n.* lean-tee

sheep *n.* (female) yowe; (young, before first shearing) hog(g); (having died a natural death) braxy; (disease) braxy; (fluke worm on lung) the hooze; (hurdle for penning) flake

sheep-fold *n.* bucht; fank, faul(d)

shelf *n.* skelf; skelve (B1)

shell *n.* shall; *v.* sheel; **shell sand** shall san

shelly *adj.* shally

shelter *n.* biel; bield; leethe; lythe; scoog, scoug

sheltered *adj.* bieldy; lown; lythe

sheriff *n.* shirra

sherry *n.* shirry

shiftiness *n.* hunker-slidin

shiftless *adj.* fen(d)less

shilling *n.* shullin

shine *n., v.* shine; (gaudily) skyre

shingle *n.* chingle

shirt *n.* sark; sarkit

shiver *v.* chitter

shock *n.* an astonishment (A1); begeck; gliff; gluff; stammy-gaster; *v.* stammygaster

shock *n.* stook; **put into shocks** *v.* stook

shoe *n.* shee; *pl.* sheen, shune; shoon; **old shoe** baachle, bauchle

shoe-lace *n.* baachle-, bauchle-ban; lacer; pynt, pint

shoemaker *n.* sooter, souter; **shoe-maker's awl** ellieson; eshin; **shoemaker's last** sooter's deevil

shoot *v.* sheet

shop *n.* chop; shop; (small) shoppie

shop-assistant *n.* coonter-lowper

shop-keeper *n.* merchan

shopping *n.* messages; **do the shopping** go the messages

short *adj.* (and stocky) laichy-braid

shortcomings *n. pl.* shortcomes

short-tempered *adj.* capernicious

should *v.* sid; shud; sud; **shouldn't** sudna

shoulder *n., v.* shooder, shouder; shoother, shouther; (one higher than the other) shoother-the-win; (of an animal) spaal, spaul; **shoulder joint** shooderheid

shout (for) *v.* cry (on);
(incoherently) gollar
shove *v.* putt; shiv; shive
shovel *n., v.* sheel
show *n.* (fine) braivity, brevity; *v.*
kythe (B1); shaw
shower *n.* shooer; (sharp) blatter;
(heavy) spleeter o weet; (heavy,
putting a stop to work) lowsin-
shooer; (passing) scuff o rain;
(slight) shoorie
show off *n.* palaiver; *v.* cock
showy *adj.* skiry, skyrie
shrewd *adj.* lang-heidit; fell (J);
pawky
shrewdness *n.* smeddum
shriek *v.* scraich; skry; walloch
shrink *v. intr.* crine; (with age)
creep doon; *v. tr.* nirl, *ppl.* nirlt;
skurken
shrivel *v. intr.* crine; gizzen, *ppl.*
gizzent; *v. tr.* nirl, *ppl.* nirlt;
skurken; wizzen(t)
shroud *n.* shrood
Shrove Tuesday *pr. n.* Faster's
Eve(n), (Een); Fasten's Eve
shudder *v.* grue, groo
shuffle *v.* fuffle; scooshle; scushle;
sclaap, sclaup; shaachle, shauchle
shut *v.* (the mouth) dit; (the door,
your eyes) steek; **shut the door**
caa the door tee
shy *adj.* baach, bauch
sick *adj.* sick; seek (S); (of)
scunnert wi/o
sickly *adj.* gowsty; paewae; peelie-
wally
sickly-looking *adj.* fauchie
side-by-side *adv.* cheekie-for-
chowie

side ridge *n.* siderig
sideways *adv.* sidelins; sidiewyes
sieve *n.* riddel; sey; (with solid
base) blin sieve; wecht
sigh *n., v.* sich; sooch, soogh,
souch, sough
sight *n.* sicht; **a welcome sight** a
sicht for sair een
signature *n.* signaatur
silence *n.* seelence; **silenced** *ppl.*
dusht
silent *adj.* seelent
silver *n.* siller. *cf.* **money**
simmer *v.* hotter
simple *adj.* haimal(t); (of a person)
saft
simpleton *n.* nosy-wax (B1)
since *adv.* seen; sin; syne; *prep.*
seen; sin; *conj.* sin; **since then**
sinseen; sinsyne
sincere *adj.* aefaal(d), aefaul(d)
sing *v.* (of birds) chirm; (in low
tone without words) diddle
sing-song speech *adj., n.* sing-sang
singe *v.* scam, scaum; *sing., ppl.*
sung
sink *n.* jaa-hole, jaw-hole; *v.* (in
bog or mud) lair
sip *n.* sup(pie); bleb; *v.* (a small
amount) blibber; (noisily)
slubber; (take food or liquid *esp.*
with a spoon) sup
sister *n.* (*chf.* child's word) titty
sit *v.* (down) lean doon; (down with
a bump) dyst; **sit down!** *imp.* faal
yer fit; lean yersel doon; reest
site *n.* stance; seet
sitting *n.* (of eggs) laachter,
lauchter
situated *ppl.* sitiwat

situation *n.* (lot) billet; powster; seetivation

six *adj.* sax

sixteen *adj.* Saxteen

sixty *adj.* sixty

sixpence *n.* saxpence

skid *n.* skite

skilful *adj.* kittle; nacky; skeely

skill *n.* skeel

skim *v.* skum

skimmer *n.* (for surface soil and weeds) skreefer

skin *n.* bark; peelin; *v.* bark; flae; **skinned** barkit; **by the skin of his teeth** by the briers o his een

skulk *v.* scook, scouk

skull *n.* riggin

sky *n.* lift; welkin (M1)

skylark *n.* lav(e)rock; livrock

slab *n.* skelp

slake *v.* (thirst) slack; slock; slocken

slander *n.* ill-win; *v.* misca

slant *v.* sklent, sklint

slap *n.* sclaffert; (on the hand with a leather belt) the scud

slate *n.* sklate; sclait

slate pencil *n.* skaalie; skaillie; skeily

slater *n.* sklater

slattern *n.* trail

slaughter *n.* slaachter, slauchter

slaughter-house *n.* slaachter-, slauchter-hoose

slaver *n., v.* sliv(v)er

sledge *n.* sled; (heavy, used on farms) puddick, puddock

sleek *adj.* sleekit

sleight *n.* sleicht

slept *v. pt.* sleepit; **overslept** sleepit in

slice *n.* (of bread) sheave; (thin) skelf; *v.* hash

slid *v. pt.* sleed (S)

slide *n.* (children's) rone; (on ice) skip; *v.* (suddenly) skite

slight *adj., n.* slicht

slime *n.* (from fish, ill-smelling) goor

slip *n.* skite; *v.* skite; (awkwardly) sklyte, sklyter

slipper *n.* saftie

slippery *adj.* skitie; sliddery

slop *n.* slabber

slope *n.* brae; **situated on a slope** braeset; *v.* sklent, sklint

sloven *n.* trail

slovenly *adj.* strushel; struchlach (B1)

slow *adj.* slaa, slaw; latch; **slowly** *imp.* heely! **slow person** creepin-eevie. *cf.* **convolvulus**

slow-coach *n.* warridrag

sluggish *adj.* smeerless

slush *n.* snaa-, snaw-bree; slabber

slut *n.* limmer

sly *adj.* (*chf.* re humour) pawky; slee; sleekit; sneck-drawin (A2)

slyly *adv.* sleely

smack *n.* lick; skelp

small *adj.* sma; wee; *n.* (person) picht

small-holding *n.* huddin

smart *adj.* smert; (grand) fantoosh

smear *v.* clart; clort; sclarry (J); skaik; *ppl.* skaikit; (with tongue, *liter.*) sklaik

smell *n.* guff; (sharp, disagreeable) kneggum; (of fumes) yowder; *v.* smell about (like a dog) snowk

English–Doric

smiling *adj.* mirky
smithereens *n. pl.* crockaneeshun
smock *n.* (for working) vrapper
smoke *n., v.* rik, reek; **belch of
smoke** reek-book, -bouk; (of a
pipe) feuch; lunt
smoky *adj.* reekie; smeeky (G1)
smooth *adj.* smeeth; (and glossy)
sleekit
smother *v.* smore
smoulder *v.* smuchter
smudge *n.* smad; smird
smut *n.* smad; smird
snack *n.* (portable) piece
snap *v.* (with the teeth) gnap;
snappy *adj.* nibawa; snappus
(A2)
snare *n.* girn
snarl *v.* girn
sneak *v.* sneck
sneaky *adj.* sleekit; thiefie
sneer *n., v.* jamph
sniff *n.* snifter; *v.* snifter; (noisily)
snocher
snigger *v.* snicher
snivel *v.* sneevil
snod *adj.* tidy
snood *n.* (of horsehair, made by
fishermen) tippen
snore *v.* snocher
snotty-nosed *adj.* bibbly-nibbit
snout *n.* snoot
snow *n.* snaa, snaw; snaave;
snyaave (slight squally shower)
fluffert; (heavy fall) onding;
(driving) blin-drift, yowden drift;
(melted) snaa-, snaw-bree; *v.* (in
big flakes) flag
snow-flake *n.* (large) flag
snow-white *adj.* snaa-fite

snowy *adj.* snaavie (S)
snuff *n.* sneeshin
snuffle *v.* snotter; (like a dog)
snowk
so *adv.* as; sae; that; **so much** as
much; **it was so cold that** it wis
as caal
soaked *ppl.* sypit
sob *v.* sab; (deeply) swult
sock *n.* ploughshare; (short) fit-
sock; (with legs cut off) fittock
soft *adj.* saft; (spongy, *e.g.* of rotten
vegetables) fossy; fosy, fozie
soft drink *n.* ale; dazzle
softness *n.* saftness
soil *n.* yird; (shallow) ebb land;
(thin, poor) scaap, scaup; *v.* fyle
soirée *n.* siree
sold *v. pt., ppl.* selt; saal, saul
solder *n., v.* sooder, souder
soldier *n.* sodger
some *adj.* a puckle
somebody *See* **someone**
someone *pron.* some-een, some-ane
sometimes *adv.* fyles
somewhat *adj.* gey
son *n.* sin; **son-in-law** *n.* gweed-sin
song *n.* sang; (farmworker's) bothy
ballad; cornkister; (silly) strood;
strowd; stroud
soon *adv.* seen
sooner *adv.* seener; sheener, shuner
(S)
soot *n.* sitt; (on pots) brook
sooty *adj.* (of pots) brookie
sore *adj., n.* sair
sorely *adv.* sair
sorrel *n.* soorocks
sorrow *n.* dool; sorra
sorrowful *adj.* dool; dowie;

sorrafu; wae; waesome

sorry *adj.* vexed; (extremely) ill-peyt; (for) wae for

sought *ppl.* socht. *cf.* **seek**

soul *n.* saal, saul; sowl

sound *n.* soon(d); myowte; *v.* soon(d); soun(d)

soup *n.* (made with offal) womble-brees

sour *adj.* soor; (of disposition) sturken; **sourness** *n.* soorness

south *adj., n.* sooth; **southern** *adj.* southron; suddron; sooth-kwintra

southernwood *n.* sudderinwid

sow *n.* soo

sow *v.* saw (S), *pt.* sew; shaw, *pt.* shew; shaave, shauv, *pt.* shew, *ppl.* shaaven, shauven

sower *n.* sawer

sowing machine *n.* broadcast

spacious *adj.* spaacious, spawcious

spade *n.* spaad, spad, spaud; (two-handed for cutting turfs, peats) flaaghter-spaad, flaughter-spaad

span *n., v.* spang

spanking *n.* buttock-mail

spare *adj.* (of figure) sober

spare room *n., adj.* spence

spark *n.* spirk; (from wood fire) flaesick

sparrow *n.* (house) spurdie; spurgie (O); sparry (J)

spate *n.* speet; speeth

spatter *v.* spairge

spawn *v.* spen

speak *v.* spik; (angrily/fretfully) nyatter, rally on; (ill of) misca; (again) rebat

special(ly) *adj., adv.* speeshal(ly)

speckle *v.* spraikle, *ppl.* spraiklt;

speckled (of cattle and sheep) brookit

spectacle *n.* (a sight) moniment

spectacles *n. pl.* glesses

speech *n.* (of an area) spik

speed *n.* nip; **at high speed** at a gweed lick; at the iverleevin gallop; at howdie haste

spelling-book *n.* spell-beuk, -buik

spend *v.* spen; waar, waur; wair, ware; (of time) hud

spider *n.* ettercap; nettercap; wyver; **spider's web** moosewob

spike *n.* (of a railing etc.) pyke, *ppl.* pykit

spill *v. tr.* jilp; *tr., intr.* skail, skale, skel; splyte; spull

spillings *n. pl.* spleeters; spullins; skaillies

spill over *v.* jibble ower

spindle *n.* spinnle; **spindly legs** spinnle shanks

spinning-bee *n.* rockin

spinning-wheel *n.* wheel

spirit *n.* gurr; speerit

spiritless *adj.* saarless, saurless

spiritual *adj.* speeritool

spite of, in *prep. phr.* mager, mauger

spit out *v.* splew

splash *n.* jilp; skirp; *v.* skite; skirp; spark; sperk, spirk; spurk (J); splyter

splash about *v. intr.* jilp; (in mud or water) plowter

splashings *n. pl.* spleeters

splatter *v.* daad, daud

splay-footed *adj.* skew-fittit; skyow-fittit

spleen *n.* melt; milt

splendid *adj.* (first rate) bencape; (excl.) capital; **splendidly** *adv.* brawly

splendour *n.* braivity

splinter *n.* skelb; skelf

splints, put in *phr.* scob

splutter *v.* splooter, splouter

spoil *v.* blad, blaud; connach; spile, spyle; *ppl.* bladdit, blaudit; (completely) connacht; geen tae potterlow

spoke *v. pt.* spak

sponge *v.* cadge; sorn

sponge-cake *n.* (in paper cup) sairheidie

sponger *n.* cadger

spoon *n., v.* speen

spot *n.* (splash) spirk

spout *n.* spoot; (of teapot etc.) stroop(ie); *v.* (talk volubly) lay-aff

sprawl *v.* sprachle, sprauchle

spring *n.* spang; (elastic force) sprent; *v.* spang

sprout *n.* (Brussels) sproot; *v.* sproot; (of grain) breer

sprouting *n.* (of new grain) braird; breer

spruce *adj.* jinipperous

spue *v.* splew

sputter *v.* hotter

squall *v.* (scream) skwaal

square *adj., n., v.* squaar, squarr

squat *v.* (on the haunches) hunker

squeal *v.* skwyle, squile; squallach

squeamish *adj.* cackie-stammackit; **be squeamish** *v.* womle

squeeze *v.* birse, birze

squelch *v.* plowter; plyter

squint *adj.* gley; *n.* cockle-ee, gley; **eye with a squint** gleyed ee

squire *n.* laird

squirt *v.* skite

stack *n.* ruck; (steaming) het ruck; (thatched for winter) thackit ruck; (badly built and porous) wattert ruck; (foundation) ruck-foon; (support for off-centre stack) ruck-post; (stack ladder) ruck-ledder; (rectangle of hay/straw) soo

stack-yard *n.* corn-yard

staff *n.* (heavy) rung

staff-in-hand *adj.* staffy-nevel

stagger *v.* stacher, staucher; staamer, staumer, styte, stoit; styter, stoiter; stot; stotter

stake-fence *n.* palin

stale *adj.* wachy

stalk *n.* (of kail or cabbage) castock; runt; *v.* stilp

stall *n.* sta(a)

stallion *n.* staig

stalwart *adj.* beerdly, buirdly

stammer *v.* habber, hubber; mant

stamp around *v.* (noisily) haamer; pammer

stampede *v. intr.* (of cattle to avoid insect bites) prick

stand *v.* stan

star *n.* starn(ie)

starch *n.* stairch; stiffen; *v.* stairch

stare *v.* gowp, goup; gype

starling *n.* stirlin

start *n.* aff-go; *n., v.* stairt, stert **starting-time** *n.* (at work) yokin-time

starvation *n.* stairvation

starve *v.* stairve, sterve; knap (B1)

state *n.* (of excitement) feerich; **in a state** in a feerich

stately *adj.* (would be) pensy
statue *n.* staito (A2)
staunch *adj.* stanch; stainch, stench; stinch
stay *n.* stey; *v.* bide, *ppl.* bidden; stey; (at an address) stop
steading *n.* steadin; toon
steal *v.* nab; rype; stale, stail; stow; *ppl.* stowen
stealth, by *adv.* stown-wyes
steam *n.* stame; **steam-driven threshing-maching** stame-mull; stem-mull
steep *adj.* stey
steeple *n.* toopachin; toopican
steer *n. sing., pl.* nowt
steering-rod *n.* stang
step *n.* stap
stick *v.* stick, *pt.* stack, *ppl.* stucken
stick in *v.* persevere
stickleback *n.* (or minnow) bandy
stiff *adj.* satteral
still *adj.* (of weather) lown; *adv.* aye
stilt *n.* stilpert
sting *n.* stang; job; *v.* job; **stinging nettles** jobby nettles
stingy *adj.* grippy
stint *n.* stent
stipend *n.* steepin
stir *n.* steer; stur; *v.* gee; jee; kirn; pirl; steer; stur
stitch *n.* steek; *v.* (coarsely) ranter; steek
stock, take *phr.* tak taik
stocking *n.* hose; (sometimes used as a purse) moggan; (being knitted) shank; **footless stocking** moggan; **shoes and stockings** hose an sheen

stomach *n.* kite, kyte; stamach, stam(m)ack; *v.* stammack; wame; wime, wyme; (of a calf) yirnin
stomach-ache *n.* belly-thraw
stomp *v.* stodge
stone *n., v.* steen, stane; **stone's throw** steen-cast
stone-chat *n.* steen-chackert
stonecrop *n.* fou
Stonehaven *pr. n.* (to outsiders) Steenhive; (locally) Stonie
stony *adj.* steeny, stany
stood *v. pt.* steed
stool *n.* steel, steil; creepie; (square-shaped) buffet steel; (with short legs) cutty steel
stop *v.* stap
store *n., v.* fordal, fordle
stormy *adj.* (of weather) cankert; gurlie, gurly
story *n.* (tall tale) binder; (old and stale) caal kail het; (long, about nothing) lab(b)ach (R); (drawn out) la(m)gamachie; linglairy (B1)
stout *adj.* brosie; stoot, stout
straight *adj., adv.* eyven; stracht, straucht
straight, off the *phr.* agley; agee
straightaway *adv.* strachtwye, strauchtwye
straighten *v.* strachen; straichen; stracht, straucht; **straighten your tie** set yer tie eyven
straightforward *adj.* (honest) fair-furth-the-gate; stracht-oot-the-gate
strain *v.* (milk through a sieve) sey; **strainer** *n.* (of milk) seyer
strange *adj.* keerious; unca, unco

stranger *n.* ootlin; unco man; *n. pl.* the fremt; unco fowk

strangle *v.* worry

strap *n.* (leather – for punishment in school) tawse

straps *n. pl.* (buckled leather, worn below the knee by farm-workers) nicky-tams; waal-tams

straw *n.* strae; (loose, e.g. on field after harvest) strab; (bundle of) win(d)lin; **the last straw** the croonin shafe; *v.* (one's boots) strae (T), stra (R) yer beets

strawberry *n.* straaberry

straw-rope *n.* (ball of) clew, cloo

stray *v.* rake

streak *n.* spraing

stream *n.* burn; (small) strype

street *n.* causey; (narrow) wynd

street-sweeper *n.* scaffy

strength *n.* strenth, strinth

stretch *v.* rax; streek; streetch

strict *adj.* streck, strick

stride *v.* spang; sten(d) (A2)

strife *n.* sturt (C)

strike *v.* cloor, clour; clowt, clout; strick, strik; (sharply) wap

string *n.* twine; tow

strip off *v.* tirr

stripling *n.* callant

strive *v.* strive; *pt.* streeve

strode *v. pt.* strade

stroke *n.* straik, strake; (blow) daad, daud; (on the palm) paamie; sclaff; sclaffert; (sharp) wap (of good luck) raise-o-the-win; *v. pt.* strack

stroll *n.* taik; *v.* danner, dauner; dander, daunder

strong *adj.* baul (B1); beerdly, buirdly; fere; kibble; stoot strang; (of wind) reevin; **strongly** *adv.* starkly

stronghold *n.* haald, hauld

strove *v. pt.* streeve, struve

struck *v. pt.* strack; *ppl.* strucken

struggle *n.* pilget; tyaave, tyauve; (hard) sair fecht; sair tyaave; ae pot an row; *v.* tyaave, tyauve; strive, *pt.* streeve; waachle, wauchle; warsle, warstle

stub *v.* (the toe etc.) stob

stubble *n.* stibble

stubborn *adj.* thraan, thrawn

stubbornness *n.* gee

stucco *n.* stookie

stuck *v. pt.* stack; *ppl.* stucken

stud *n.* tacket; **studded boots** tackitie beets

student *n.* colleeginer (A1); (first year) bajan

stuff *v.* stap

stumble *n., v.* hyter; styter, stoiter; (of a horse) snapper

stump *v.* stowff

stun *v.* daver

stunted *adj.* crynt; (in growth) settril; shargart; **stunted person** sharger

stupid *adj.* bleat; dylt, doilt; dytit, doitit; donnert; feel; gaakit, gawkit; gapus; glaikit; **stupid fellow** stirk. *See* **fool**

stupidity *n.* feelness; gaakitness, gawkitness; gypery

stupify *v.* daver; dozen

sturdy *adj.* buirdly; fere; kibble

stutter *v.* habber, hubber; mant

subject *n., v.* subjeck

substance *n.* graith

such *adj.* sic; siccan; **such and such** sic an sic; **such-like** *adj.* siclike

suck *v.* sook

sucker *n.* (of tree) sooker

suckling calf *n.* sookin caafie

sudden *adj.* suddent (C)

suddenly *adv.* in (on) a suddenty

suddenness *n.* suddenty

suffocate *v.* scomfish; skumfish

sugar *n.* succar

suit *n., v.* shoot; sheet, shuit

sulk *v.* mump; funk (B1); **sulky** *adj.* sturken; **look sulky** *v.* glumph

sullen *adj.* drumly; **sullenness** *n.* gee; soorness

sum *n.* soom; (large) sowd; (small) triffle; trifflie

summer *n.* simmer

summit *n.* toopachin; toopican

sumptuous *adj.* lordlifu

sun *n.* sin; **sunburned** *adj.* sin-brunt; din-skinnt

sunder *v.* sinder; sinner

sundown *n.* sindoon

sundry *adj.* sinry

sunk down *adj.* seggit

sunset *n.* sindoon

sunshine *n.* sunsheen

superannuated *ppl.* sooperanniwat

superior *adj.* skichent

superstition *n.* suppersteeshun; a fret

superstitious beliefs *adj., n. pl.* feart things

supervisor *n.* owersman

supper *n.* sipper

supple *adj.* soople, souple; swack, swak; **make supple** swacken

support *n.* stey

sure *adj.* seer; shair (S)

surely *adv.* seerly; shairly (S); fairly

surface *n.* (of water) screeth

surfeit *n.* forleithy (B1)

surliness *n.* soorness

surly *adj.* strunge

surmise *n.* sleumin

surpass *v.* cow(e)

surprise *n.* astonisher; (excl. of) goshie; govie-dick(s); jings; loshins; loshtie (be here); loshtie-goshtie guide's; meggins alive; megstie me; michty me; serve's

survive *v.* (as a race) store the kin (*chf.* used in *neg.*)

suspect *v.* jaloose, jalouse; suspeck

suspense *n.* tig-tire; **in suspense** in captire

suspicious *adj.* (giving rise to suspicion) ill-thochtit

swagger *v.* cock

swallow *n., v.* swally; (quick(ly)) scoof, scouf

swarm *n.* hobble; smarrach; swarrach

swathe *n.* (cut by scythesman) bout

sway *v.* swey; swye; swig (J); (influence) swye

swear *n.* sweer, sweir; *v.* sweer; ban; (vehemently) sweer blue lowes (B)

sweat *n., v.* swat, *pt.* swat, swattit; swate (A2); swite, swyte; (state of sudden heat) feem

swede *n.* swad; Swaddish neep

sweep *v.* swipe, swype

sweet *n.* (round) sweetie-boolie; *pl.* galshachs, galshochs; smachrie

sweetheart *n.* lad; jo (J)
sweet-seller *n.* (female) sweetie-wife
swell *v. tr., intr.* swall; hive, *ppl.* hoven
swept clean *ppl., adj.* besom-ticht
swerve *v.* jink; jouk
swift(ly) *adj., adv.* swith
swig *n., v.* scoof, scouf; waach, wauch
swill *v.* sweel
swim *v.* sweem; soom (C)
swimmer *n.* sweemer
swindle *v.* swick
swindler *n.* swick

swing *n., v. tr., intr.* showd; sweeng; swey
swing-boats *n. pl.* (at the carnival) showdin-boats
swingle-tree *n.* swingle-, sweengle-tree
swirl *v.* sweel
swish *v.* sweesh
swivel *v.* sweevle
swollen-headed *adj.* swall-heidit; swale-heidit (S)
swoon *n., v.* swarf
sword *n.* soord; swoord; soward
Synod *n.* seenit
syrup *n.* seerup

— **T** —

table *n.* brod; buird
tackle *n.* taikle
tag *n.* (game) tackie, takie; tik an tak
tail-board *n.* (of cart) back-door
tail end *n.* tail-eyn
tailor *n.* tyler; tylie; (itinerant) whip-the-cat
take *v.* tak, *pt.* teuk, *ppl.* teen; taen (S); **take care of** tak aboot; **take it easy** lat the theats slack
talk *n.* blether; jaa, jaw; (idle, silly) clashmaclavers, clish-ma-claver; gypery; (intimate) collogue; (low, muttered) toot-moot; (foolish) yaam; yaum (R); *v.* jaa, jaw; blether; (nonsense) blether; haver; (idly and at length) lyaag; laig; (volubly) lay-aff; (excitedly) (yab-) yabber; *adj.* (given to unwholesome talk) kyaard-

tonguet; **talking about** on aboot
talkative *adj.* crackie
talking-to *n.* dixie; hanlin; sedarin
tall *adj.* (and agile) strappin; **tall person** traleel; (lanky, ill-shaped person) trypal
tangle *n.* snorl; (of objects) wumple
tangled *ppl., adj.* raivelt
tantalise *v.* tantaleese
tap *v.* tig
tapioca *n.* (nicknamed) puddock's eggs
tardy *adj.* latch
tare *n.* teer
tart *adj.* satteral
tassle *n.* tossil; toshil
tasteless *adj.* saarless, saurless; wersh
taught *ppl.* taacht, taucht
tavern *n.* cheenge-hoose; chynge-

hoose

tea *n.* tay; (sly cup) fly-cup; fly; (made in the cup) tinkie's maskin

teach *v.* lairn; leern

teacher *n.* missie (S)

team-picker *n.* (in games) chyser

teapot *n.* taypot; (earthenware) trackie

tear *n., v.* rive; (rip) teer

tear-stained *adj.* begrutten; grutten

tease *n.* tarraneese; *v.* tarraneese; *tr.* banter

tease out *v.* tase oot (S)

teaspoon *n.* tayspeen; **teaspoonful** tayspenfae

teat *v.* tit; pap; **blind teat** blin tit

tedium *n.* langer

teetotum *n.* tottum, totum

tell-tale *n.* clipe, clype

temper *n.* birse; dander; teen; **bad temper** ill teen; **get angry** get yer dander up

temples *n. pl.* (of the head) haffets

tent *n.* tint

term *n.* (at school) raith

tern *n.* (Arctic) tarick

terrified *ppl.* terrifeet

terrify *v.* terrifee

testament *n.* tasment; tastement; tesment

tether-peg *n.* baikie

than *conj., quasi-prep.* nor

thank *v.* thank; thenk (S)

that *adj., pron.* aat; thon; yon; *conj.* at

thatch *v.* thack; theek (J); (by means of stob or stake) stob; (rope-thatch with a cloo) swap; **thatched** thackit; stobbit

thaw *v.* thow

thawing *ppl.* (of weather) fresh

the *def. art.* e; the

themselves *pron.* (*also* **by themselves**) theirsels

then *adv.* syne; than

thereupon *adv.* syne

these *adj., pron.* aat; thase; thon; yon; thae (S, J, C)

thick *adj.* (of water) drumly; **thick with** thrang wi

thief *n.* reiver

thigh *n.* (lower part of human thigh) hoch, hough

thimble *n.* thummle

thin *adj.* (of a person) skinny; wainisht-like; **thin legs** spurtle-shanks; **thin person** skinnymalink

thing *n.* (the very) the verra dunt

thingummybob *n.* thingumboob; thingumenderry

thirst *n.* thrist; **thirsty** *adj.* droothy, drouthy; thristy

thistle *n.* thrissle, thristle

Thomas *pr. n.* Tam

thorn *n.* stob

those *adj.* (*or* **these**) aat; thon; yon; thae (S, J, C)

thought *n., v., pt., ppl.* thocht

thousand *n.* thoosan(d)

thrash *v.* ledder; lick; aam, aum; creesh

thrashing *n.* ledderin; lickin; limerin; peelin

thread *n.* threid; (unbleached) whitet-, whitie-broons; **losing the thread of his thought** aff his stotter

threat *n.* threet

threaten *v.* thraten; threet; threeten

threatening *adj.* threetnin; (of weather) cankert; gurlie, gurly; (supernaturally) uncanny
threshing-mill *n.* thrashin-mull
threw *v. pt.* ceest
thrill *v.* thirl
thrived *v. pt.* thrave
throat *n.* craig; thrapple; witters
throb *n., v.* stoond, stound
throng *n.* thrang
throttle *v.* thrapple
through *adv., prep.* ben; throw
throw *n.* (heavy) doosht; *v.* fung, haive; thraw; (with a bump) dyst; (down with a thud) doosht; (of rope or fishing line only) shyve
throw off *v.* (a coat) cast
thrush *n.* mavis (M)
thud *n.* dird
thumb *n.* thoomb
thumb-rope *n.* thoomb-raip
thump *n., v.* dird; dunt
thunder *n.* thunner
Thursday *n.* Fiersday
thwarted *ppl.* stickit
tickle *v.* kittle
ticklish, tickly *adj.* kittlie, kittly
tidy *adj., v.* trig
tidy up *v.* snod
tie *v.* (tightly) hank
tight *adj.* ticht; **tighten** *v.* tichen; **tight-fisted** *adj.* grippy; near the been; **tight-fitting** *adj.* nippit
tile hat *n.* (black) lum hat
till *conj.* ontill, oontill
timber *n.* timmer; **seasoned timber** wun-timmer
time off *n.* afflat
time-serving *adj.* time-sairin
timid *adj.* bauch

timorous *adj.* arch (**ch** *gutteral*)
tinful *n.* mulfa
tingle *v.* dirl; thirl
tinker *n.* caird; cyaard; gate-ganger; tinkie; tinkler; kyaard
tinware *n.* fite iron
tipple *n.* bleb
tipsy *adj.* foo, fou, fu; far on; weel on
tiredness *n.* tire
tithe *n., v.* teind
title *n.* teetle
tittle-tattle *n.* claik; clash
to *prep.* tae; (*usu.* before a vowel) till; tull
toad *n.* ted
toadstool *n.* puddock-steel
toast *v.* birsel, birstle
tobacco *n.* tobaacca; (unconsumed in pipe) dottle; **tobacco pouch** spleuchan, splochan
today *adv., n.* the day
todo *n.* adee
toe *n.* tae
together *adv.* thegidder; thegither
told *ppl.* bidden; *v. pt., ppl.* taal, taul; telt
tolerance *n.* merciment
tolerate *v.* bide; thole; tolerat
Tomintoul *pr. n.* Tamintowl
tomorrow *adv.* the morn; **tomorrow night** the morn's nicht
tongs *n. pl.* tyangs; (hinged wire-tightener in fencing) taings
tongue-tied *ppl., adj.* tongue-tackit
tontine *n.* tamteen
too *adv.* an aa; tee; tae (S)
took *v. pt.* teuk; tyeuk
tool *n.* teel

toothache *n.* teethache
tootle *v.* (on a wind instrument) tweetle
top *n.* tap; (spinning) peerie; (card with pin passing through, resembling a teetotum) tipperteen; *v.* tap; **top man or woman** tapster; **over the top** (in behaviour) throw the bows
topsy-turvy *adv.* tapsalteerie
torch *n.* (paraffin torch used at sea) bubbly
tore *v. pt.* rave. *cf.* **rive**
torment *v.* tarraneese
torture *v.* (as a martyr) martyreese
totter *v.* styter; (from age) tite, tyte
touch *v.* lightly tap; (lightly in passing) scuff
touched *ppl., adj.* affeckit
touchy *adj.* kittle
tough *adj.* teuch, tyeuch
tousle *v.* tossle; toosle; **tousled** *adj.* toosy, tousy
towel *n.* tool
tower *n., v.* toor, tour
towering *ppl., adj.* toorin
town *n.* toon
town-dweller *n.* toonser
toy *n.* plyaak
trace *n.* theat; **kick over the traces** kick ower the theats; (the slightest) sinacle (B1)
tractor *n.* (Field Marshall diesel) pom-pom
train *v.* (animals to go in traces) track
tramp *n.* gangrel; trump; (with quarters on farm in exchange for work) quarterer
transaction *n.* transack

trash *n.* pelt; trag; trock, troke
travel *n., v.* traivel
travelling people *n. pl.* tinkies
treacle *n.* traikle, trykle
treacle toffee *n.* claggum; claggieleerum
tread *v.* treid (J)
treat *n.* cheery-pyke; gallshach, galshoch; trait; *v.* (harshly) ool; **harshly treated** oolt
treble *v.* threeple
tremble *v.* chitter
trench *n.* sheugh
trencher *n.* truncher
trestle *n.* mason's mear
trick *n.* aivis; begeck; gaa, gaw; (of the weather) widder-gaa; ginkum; ginkmen (B1); rig; jink; (mischievous) plisky; *v.* begeck; begowk; **to play a trick on** tae hae a hyze wi; tae play a rig; tak the rise o
trickery *n.* joukerie pawkery
trickle *v.* treetle
tricky *adj.* (of a task) fykie; kittle, kittlesome; quirky
trifle *n.* triffle; trifflie; (worthless) quinkins
trifling *adj.* nochtie, noughtie
trim *adj.* jinipperous
trip *v.* hyter
triple *adj.* threeple
triplet *n.* threeplet
trollope *n.* limmer
trot *v.* tite, tyte; treetle
troth *excl.* trogs
trouble *n.* fash, dispeace; trebble; tribble; **troublesome thing** tribbler; *v.* fash; **don't trouble yourself** dinna fash yer thoomb,

yer heid; **make trouble** raise din
trouble-maker *n.* din-raiser
trouble-making *adj.* din-raisin
troublesome *adj.* fykie
trough *n.* troch
trousers *n. pl.* breeks, briks; (of
thick cotton) moleskins; troosers;
trouser braces galluses; **trouser
fly** spaver
trout *n.* troot
trowel *n.* trool
truant *n.* fugie (rhymes with
budgie); true (the skweel); **truant
officer** catcher (S)
truce *n.* (in games) parley, after the
cry 'parleys-on'
trudge *n., v.* traik; trail
trust *v.* lippen tae; troo
truth *n., int.* trowth; **truthful** *adj.*
trowthfu
trysting-tree *n.* covin-tree
tuck up *v.* (skirts, sleeves etc.) kilt
Tuesday *n.* Tyesday
tug *n., v.* rug; tit; yark
tumble *n., v.* tummle
tumbledown *adj.* tummle-doon
tumbler *n.* (glass) tummler
tumult *n.* shirrameer; shirramineer
tune *n.* teen; (lively, on the
bagpipes) port; (lively) rant;
spring
turf, a *n.* a divot; truff
turkey-cock *n.* bubbly(jock)

turn *n.* (to play etc.) shottie; *v.*
(over) wummle; whummle; (of a
river) wumple; (inside out) flype;
(sudden) jink; twine; **turn and
twist** weemple an wample
turncoat *n.* turnkwite
turnip *n.* neep; **turnip-slicer** neep-
hasher; **turnip-lantern** neepie-
lantrin; **turnip-hoeing** neep-
rinnin; **turnip and potato soup**
lefts an richts; **turnip watch**
neep waatch
turret *n.* toopachin; toopican
Turriff *pr. n.* Turra
twelve *adj.* twal
twelve-month period *n.*
towmon(d); twalmont(h)
twenty *adj.* twinty
twice *adv.* twise
twig *v.* (of shrub or bush) cowe
twilight *n.* gloam; gloamin;
gloomin
twine *n.* (strong) tow
twirl *n., v.* birl
twist *n.* crook; thraw; *v.* kinsh;
thraw, *ppl.* thrawn; twine
twitch *v.* tit
two *adj.* twa; **two-faced** *adj.*
dooble; **two-handed** *adj.* twa-
han
type *n.* teep
tyrant *n.* tirran

— **U** —

udder *n.* aidder; ether
ugly *adj.* ill-, ull-faart
umbrage *n.* umrage

umbrella *n.* umberella
un- *prefix* on-; oon-
unaware *adj.* onwuttin

unbaptised *ppl., adj.* oonbapteest
uncanny *adj.* eldritch; oonchancie
uncaring *adj.* ooncarin
unceasing *adj.* oondevallin
uncivil *adj.* oonceevil
uncommon *adj.* ooncommon
uncontrolled *adj.* oon o han
uncouth *adj.* hull-run
uncover *v.* tirr
undamaged *adj.* clear
undecided *adj.* i the deid-thraw; **to be undecided** *v.* swither
under *prep.* oonder; ooner
under-cattleman *n.* little bailie
underground *adj., adv.* oondergrun
undermost *adj.* naithmaist
underpants *n. pl.* (long) draars; draavers
undershirt *n.* semmit; linder; linner; sarket, sarkit
understand *v.* oonerstan, *pt., ppl.* unnersteed
undertake *v.* tak in han
undertaking *n.* oonertakkin
undigested *adj.* ondisjeestit
undoubtedly *adv.* oondootitly
undress *v.* tirr
undulate *v.* wammle
unearthly *adj.* eldritch; uncanny
uneducated *adj.* unedicat
unending *adj.* oonendin
uneven *adj.* shammelt
unexpected *adj.* oonexpeckit
unfair *adj.* (used by children) skicie
unfeeling *adj.* onfeelin
unfortunate *adj.* misfortnat
unfrequented *adj.* lown
ungenerous *adj.* ill-willie; (used by children) skycie
ungrateful *adj.* peyed-thankless;

pickthank; pykethank
unhappy *adj.* oonhappy
unheeding *adj.* onheedin
unintelligent *adj.* preen-heidit
unkempt *adj.* hudd(e)ry
unkind *adj.* ill; ull; **unkindly done** ull-deen
unknown *adj.* oonkent; unco
unlawful *adj.* oonlawfu
unless *conj.* onless, oonless
unload *v.* unlade; (a catch of fish) liver
unmannerly *adj.* menseless
unmethodical *adj.* ramshackle
unmindful (of) *adj.* onmynit (o)
unnatural *adj.* oonnaitral
unpleasant *adj.* (in behaviour) ull-farrant
unprincipled *adj.* oonprenciplt
unquenched *adj.* oonslockent
unreasonable *adj.* oot o theat
unrighteous *adj.* oonrichteous
unroof *v.* tirr
unruly *adj.* (of children) royd, royt
unsettled *adj.* (of weather) tittersome
unsociable *adj.* saachen, sauchen
unsought *ppl., adj.* unsocht
unsporting *adj.* skycie
unstable *adj.* oonstable
unsteady *adj.* (of a table, etc) shoogly
untidy *adj.* strushal, strushel; ill-shooken up; struchlach (B1); throw-idder; throwder; **untidy person** eeshich (B1); ticket; track; wallydraigle
until *conj.* or; ontil, oontill
untiring *adj.* ontirin
untroubled *adj.* oonfasht

unwashed *ppl., adj.* oonwaashen
unwell *adj.* oonweel; paewae; **to be unwell** *v.* ail
unwilling *adj.* oonwullin; sweer, sweir
unworked *adj.* (of land) unvrocht
unyoke *v.* lowse
up *adv.* up; hup
upbringing *n.* upfessin, -feshin
uphold *v.* uphud
upon *prep.* upo
upper hand *n.* wheep han
uppermost *adj.* eemaist; **upper part** (of field) eemaist wynin
uproar *n.* collieshangie; dirdum; gilgal (hard **g**) (B1); rammy; reerie; remishin; rippit; shirrameer; shirramineer; sta(r)shie; stramash; stushie
uprooted *ppl., adj.* (by the wind) win-casten
upset *v. tr.* kittle; vex; (overturn)

cowp; (a plan) cowp the creels
upwards *adv.* upwuth
urine *n.* strang; (stale, used as detergent) maister; **urine jar** maister-pig
urinate *v.* pish
urination *n.* rin-oot
us *pron.* hiz; huz
usage *n.* eesage
use *n.* eese (*pro.* eece); **full use of** *phr.* weelins; *v.* eese (*pro.* eeze); **used to it** eest wi't; **useful** *adj.* eesefu; essfu
useless *adj.* eeseless; feckless; **useless person** footer
usual *adj., adv.* eeswal(ly)
utmost *adj.* itmaist
utter *v.* moo-ban
uvular 'r' *n.* (sounded in throat) burr; hurl in the throat; *v.* to use the uvular 'r' burr

— V —

vacant *adj.* vaacant, vawcant
vagrant *n.* gangrel; gyangrel
vain *adj.* full; vantie, vauntie
valentine *n.* valinteen
valley *n.* strath; (narrow) glen; howe
valuable *adj.* vailyable
value *n.* vailye; (something of little value) wanwurth; (something of no value) tinkler's curse
vanish *v.* vainish
vapour *n.* vaapour, vawpour
variable *adj.* immis (B1)
vegetation *n.* growthe

vehicle *n.* viackle; (old and rickety) shan-dre-dan
venomous *adj.* veeperate
very *adj., adv.* fair; foo; gey; verra; unco
vessel *n.* veshel; (drinking) pint-stowp,-stoup
vestige *n.* sinacle
vetch *n.* (tufted) fidgick; **wild peas** fidgick piz
veterinary surgeon *n.* ferrier
vibrate *v.* dirl; tirl
vibration *n.* dirl, tirl
vicious *adj.* veeperate; veeshus

view *n.* (range of vision) vizzie;
(mental attitude) opingan
vigour *n.* fushen, fushon; vigour;
lacking vigour fushenless
vilify *v.* (vilipend) wilipen
village *n.* clachan; toon; (with
parish church) kirkton; **village
green** loaning(s)
violence *n.* (to person or property)
bangstrie
violent *adv.* veelent
violin *n.* fiddle
virago *n.* randy

vision *n.* veesion
visit *n.* veesit; *v.* (briefly) ca in by;
cry in by
visitor *n.* veesitor; (the first to meet
a marriage party or call on New
Year's Day) first-fit
voice *n.* vice, vyce
voluble *n.* lairge
vomit *n.* splewin; *v.* byock (B1);
kowk (A); spue; splew
vouch *v.* vooch
vow *v.* voo
vulgar *adj.* grofe

— **W** —

waddle *v.* shochle; waachle,
wauchle
wade *v.* wide, wyde
wager *n., v.* waager, wauger
wages *n. pl.* waages, wauges;
(farmhand's) fee; (in advance)
sub
wagon *n.* (two-wheeled, open)
bogie
wail *v.* walloch
waistcoat *n.* waskit; weskit;
(sleeved) shafter, shaftit weskit;
(under-jacket) fecket
wait *v.* bide; wyte; *imp.* heely
wakeful *adj.* waakrife, waukrife
waken *v.* waaken, wauken
walk *n.* waak(ie), wauk; traivel (S);
(stroll) taik; (long, wearisome)
trail; *v.* waak, wauk; leg, shank it;
traivel; (noisily) clamp;
(awkwardly) fuffle; (unsteadily)
hyter; (hand-in-hand, arm-in-arm)
link; (clumsily) haamer;

(aimlessly) pammer; (in mud or
water) plyper; (slowly) stodge;
(with a spring) stot; (with heavy,
swinging gait); slewie (B1); (in a
stumping way) stumpart, stumper;
(in flat-footed way) sclap, sclaup
walker *n.* waaker, wauker
walkway *n.* waakie
wall *n.* wa; (of stone) dyke; (dry-
stone) dry steen dyke; (built of
sods) feal dyke
wall clock *n.* (with pendulum) wag-
at-the-wa
wall-cupboard *n.* press
wall-eyes *n. pl.* ringel-een
wallow *v.* (in mud) slocher
wand *n.* gad, gaad; waan
wander *v.* rake; stravaig; wanner;
(in speech) raivel
want *v.* wint; wunt; sik
wares *n. pl.* gibbles; waares
warm *adj.* waarm; *v.* (before the
fire) beek; bek; byke; (warm, dry

weather, good for growth) forcie
warped *ppl.* gizzent
warrant *v.* warn
was *v. pt.* wis, *neg.* wisna
wash *n.* waash; (quick) cat's dicht;
  v. waash, *pt.* weesh(t); *ppl.*
  waashen
washing-line *n.* claes tow
waste *n.* waistry; wastry
waste away *v.* dwine
water *n.* watter
water-closet *n.* wattery
waterfall *n.* linn
water-glass *n.* (for preserving eggs)
  watter-gless
water-hen *n.* beltie (G1)
watering-can *n.* rooser
water tap *n.* stroop
watery *adj.* (of flavour) waable,
  wauble
wave *n.* waav; (at sea) jaa, jaw; *v.*
  wag
way *adv.* wye; wa; wan; **come
  away in** come yer was ben; **in
  the direction of Kintore** Kintore
  wye/wan; *n.* gate; wye
weak *adj.* feckless; saft; waffle;
  waik; wyke; **weak-minded
  person** *n.* saftie
weakly *adj.* sober
weakness *n.* waikness; wykeness
wealth *n.* gear; **accumulate wealth**
  fog
wealthy *adj.* walthy
wean *v.* speen; spen
wear *n., v.* weer; **wear yourself out**
  ca yersel deen
wearied *ppl.* dylt; wabbit; weariet
wearisome *adj.* dreich; langsome
weary *v.* jaap, jaup

weasel *n.* futrat, futtrat; **weasely
  person** futtrat
weather *n.* widder; wither; (warm,
  dry, good for crops) forcie;
  (conducive to growth) growthie
weather-beaten *adj.* din-skinnt. *cf.*
  sunburned
weave *v.* wyve
weaver *n.* wabster
weaving *n.* wyvin
web *n.* (spider's) (moose)wob; (of
  small spiders) slammach; (woven
  fabric) wab
wed *v.* wad, *pt.* waddit; mairry
wedding *n.* mairritch, mairrage;
  waddin
weed *n.* wide, wyde
week *n.* wik; ook, ouk; **a week
  today** this day ook
week-end *n.* wik-en
weigh *v.* wye, *pt.* wyt
weighed down *ppl.* wechen doon
weighing machine *n.* (steelyard
  type) steilert
weight *n.* wacht, waucht; wecht;
  (for fastening horse in stall)
  sinker
weighty *adj.* wachty, wauchty;
  wechty
weird *adj.* uncanny
weld *v.* (by hammering) clink
we'll *pron.* with *v.* we's
well *adj.* weel; *adv.* brawlies;
  brawly; brulies; weel; *int.* aweel;
  weel; wale (S); *n.* waal
well-bred *adj.* mensefu
well-built *adj.* kibble
well-favoured *adj.* weel-faart,
  -faurt
well-fed *adj.* brosy; sair-maitit

well-known *adj.* weel-kent
well-loved *adj.* leal-loved
well-mannered *adj.* weel-mennert
well-off *adj.* foggit; weel-geddert
well-to-do *adj.* bien; geddert
went *v. pt.* gaed, gid
wept *v. pt.* grat, *ppl.* grutten; (noisily) roared an grat
we're *pron. with v.* we's
were *v. pt.* war; wur, *pt. neg.* warna
west *adj., adv.* wast; **western** *adj.* waster; **westward** *adv.* wastlins; wastward
wet *adj.* wat; weet; plytery; (of weather) drabbly; *v.* drabble
wether *n.* (castrated ram) wedder
wetting *n.* steeping
whack *n.* skelp
whale *n.* whaal, whaul
what *adj., pron.* fat, faat; fit; fut; **what a lot of** fat a; **what sort of** fatna; **what-do-you-call-it** fat-ye-ca't
whatever *adv., conj.* farivver
wheedling *ppl., adj.* fraiky
wheel *v.* (a barrow) rowe
wheeze *v.* clocher; whazzle; wheezle
whelk *n.* wulk
whelp *n.* fulp
when *adv., conj., pron.* fan, faan; fin
where *adv.* faar, faur; whaar (G1), whaur
whereas *conj.* forbyes
where else *interrog. adv.* faar idder
wherever *adv., conj.* farivver
whether *conj.* fidder; fudder; futher; gin
whey *n.* fy

which *pron.* whilk; *rel. pron.* whilk; fit (S)
whiff *n.* waff
while *conj., n., v.* fyle; (little) fylie; wee; whilie; whylock; **stay a while** bide-a-wee
whim *n.* gee; maggot; **full of whims** maggotive
whimper *n., v.* girn
whin *n.* fun, funn; **whin mill** fun mull
whine *v.* peenge; yammer
whinny *n.* nicher
whip *n., v.* fup; wheep; whup
whip-hand *n.* fup-han
whipper-in *n.* dog-dirder
whirl *v.* furl; **whirly** *adj.* furly
whirr *n.* birr
whisk away *v.* wheech
whiskers *n. pl.* fuskers; **whiskered** *ppl.* fuskert
whisky *n.* fusky; whusky; the cratur; **small whisky bottle** cutter
whispering *n.* fusperin; toot-moot (B1)
whistle *n.* fustle; (of the wind) sough; (whistling sound) wheeber; *v.* fustle; sough; wheeble; wheeple; (in a low tone) sowff
whit, not a *phr.* dag the bit
white *adj.* fite
whitlow *n.* futlie (beelin)
Whitsunday *n.* Wutsunday
whittle *v.* fite; futtle
whizz *v.* wheech; wheek
who *pron.* fa, faa; wha (G1)
whole *adj. n.* hail(l), hale
wholesome *adj.* halesome

whom *pron.* wham
whooping cough *n.* kinkhoast
whore *n.* hooer, hure
whorl *n.* (flywheel on spindle) forl
whose *pron.* whase (G1), whause
why *adv.* foo; fit wye; hoo
wicked *adj.* ill; ull; wicket
widow *n.* weeda; widda; widdie (J)
wife *n.* goodwife (A2); gweedwife;
  kimmer; wife
wight *n.* wicht
wild *adj., adv.* wil; wudden; wull;
  (unfrequented) bosky; (of
  children) royd, royt
wild-like *adj.* wull-like
wild mustard *n.* skellach
will *n.* (testament) tasment;
  tastement; tesment; wull; *v.* wull,
  neg. winna; wunna
William *pr. n.* Weelum; Wull(ie)
willing *adj.* redd; wullin
willow *n.* saach, sauch; (abounding
  in willows) sauchy; **willow wand**
  saach-waan, widdie-waan
wind *n.* win; (gust) flan; (sudden
  gust) howder; (off the sea) oot-
  win; (high) reevin win; **break
  wind** *v.* pump; let off
wind *v.* (a rope) kinsh; (of a river)
  wimple
windbag *n.* gab
windfall *n.* capshun
wind instrument *n.* tooteroo
window *n.* windae; windy (J);
  winnock (A1)
window-catch *n.* windae-sneck
window pane *n.* lozen
windy *adj.* winny
wing *n.* weeng
wink *v.* blink

winnow *v.* winny; (for the first
  time) cuff
winnowing machine *n.* fan; fanner
wipe *v.* dicht; *n.* dicht; dirrum-dicht
wire *n.* weer; **wire-tightening lever**
  peer-man
wise *adj.* wice, wyce
wish *n., v.* wiss; wuss
wishbone *n.* thocht-been
wisp *n.* wusp
wit *n.* wut; **wits** *n. pl.* wuts
witch *n.* carlin(e)
with *prep.* wi
wither *v.* widder
withered *adj.* (of flowers) wallant
without *prep., conj.* athoot; wi-oot;
  withoot; on (used with *pt. ppl.*);
  without being on-been; **without
  having** on-hed; **without doing**
  on-deen etc.
witness *n.* wutness
wizened *adj.* foggie
wobble *v.* waable, wauble
wobbly *adj.* waable, wauble
woe *n.* wae
woe-begone *adj.* hingin-luggit
woeful *adj.* waefu
woe-is-me *phr.* wae's me
woman *n.* umman; wife; wifie; *pl.*
  weemen; (married) kimmer; (old)
  carlin(e); *(derog.)* besom; (of
  doubtful character) kiltimmer; (of
  ill repute) runk; (loose-tongued)
  randy; (dirty, untidy) trail; (loose)
  vyaig; (worthless) baggerel
womb *n.* wyme
won *v. pt.* wan
wonder *n.* ferlie; winner; *v.* winner;
  wonner, *ppl.* winrin
wonderful *adj.* winnerfu

wood *n.* (substance) timmer; (trees) wid; wud; (small) widdie; shaw (J)
wooden *adj.* timmer; widden
wood pigeon *n.* cushie-doo
wood-shaving *n.* flaesick, flezick; spell
wood-turner *n.* (maker of caaps) caaper, cauper
wool *n.* oo; woo; (knitting) worsit*;*
wool-bag *n.* worsit-bag
word *n.* wird; **words** *n. pl.* langidge
work *n.* wark; (day's work) darg; (messy or difficult) scutter; *v.* darg; wark, *pt. reg.*, also vrocht, wrocht; (in a flurried way) foorich; (in a slovenly way) kirn; (clumsily) haamer; (at high pressure) hash; (vigorously) link at; (messily) plowter; plyter; (at domestic chores) scudge, skudge; (awkwardly, messily) scutter; (vigorously) timmer on/up; (ineffectually) tooter; (strenuously) tyaaave, tyauve; (hard) yark; **start work** yoke, yoke intae; **set to work** wire intae; **stop work** lowse; **at work** *prep. phr.* ayoke
worker *n.* warker; wirker
work-house *n.* peer(s)-hoose
working period *n.* yokin
world *n.* wardle; warl(d); wordle
worldly *adv.* wardly
wordly-wise *adj.* warly-wise
worm *n.* wirm
wormwood *n.* wormit
worn *adj.* tasht
worn out *ppl., adj.* forfochen; forjeskit; foonert; (with hard work) fochen-deen; puggled; sair awa wi't; sair come at
worried *adj.* pit/pitten oot; vext
worse *adj.* waar, waur; **the worse for wear** waar o *(or* i) the weer
worst *adj., n.* warst
worsted *adj., n.* wirsit, worsit; (fine, from spun wool) fingerin
worth *n.* wirth
worthless *adj.* orra; weirdless; (anything worthless) *n.* wa-cast
worthy *n.* woorthy; *adj.* wordy
would *v.* wad, wid, wud; **would not** wadna, widna, wudna
wound *n.* hagger; sair; *v. pt.* wun
woven *ppl.* wivven
wraith *n.* wreith
wrangle *n.* dibber-dabber
wrap *n.* hap-waarm; *v.* wip; wup
wrath *n.* wraith
wreath *n.* (of snow) vreath
wreck *n.* wrack
wren *n.* vran
wrestle *v.* vrastle; warsle, warstle
wretch *n.* vratch
wright *n.* vricht; jyner
wring *v.* vring
wrinkled *ppl.* runklt, wrunkelt
wrist-bone *n.* shackleebeen, -bane
write *v.* screeve, screive; scrive; vreet
writer *n.* vreeter
writhe *v.* wammle
writing *n.* (long piece of) screed
writing-desk *n.* vreetin-dask
writing-paper *n.* vreetin-paper
written *ppl.* vrutten
wrong *adj., n.* vrang; wrang
wrote *v. pt.* vrat; vrote
wrought *v. pt.* vrocht

— **Y** —

yard *n.* (unit of measurement) yaird, yerd

yardstick *n.* ell-wan

yarn *n.* (woollen) worsit; (ends of) thrums

yawl *n.* yole; (used for catching cod by hand-line) ripper-yole

yawn *v.* gant

year *n.* year; **last year** fernyear; was-a-year; **year before last** fernyear was-a-year

yearn (for) *v.* mang for; green (efter) (B1)

yeast *n.* barm

yell *v.* skraich; skirl; yall

yellow *adj.* yalla

yellow-hammer *n.* yaldie; yeldrin; yirlin

yellow iris *n.* seg

yellow turnip *n.* yalla

yelp *v.* yalp

yeoman farmer *n.* bonnet laird

yes *adv.* ay; ty; yea

yesterday *n., adv.* (*esp.* evening) the streen, yestreen

yet *conj.* still an on; yit

Y-junction *n.* split-the-win

yonder *adv.* yonner; yont

you *pron.* ye; *pl.* (in *vocative* case) you eens

you'll *pron. with v.* ye'll; ye's

your *pron.* yer

yourself *pron.* yersel; **by yourself** yersel

youth *n.* (abstract term) youthheid; (young man) halflin

Yule *n.* Eel; Yeel; (the old Christmas season continuing until after New Year) hale Eel

Publisher's note:

Whilst the publishers are confident that this dictionary contains most of the Doric words in current usage within the north-east of Scotland, as well as some much older ones, they are also aware that there are bound to be omissions or alternative entries that could have been included.

So that our database can be updated, the publishers would be pleased to hear from anyone who would like to provide further information. Should there be a second edition of this dictionary, all such informants will be duly acknowledged in it.

Please send us any words or phrases, enclosing this form, or write out your words on a separate sheet of paper, but please remember to include the area you were brought up. You do not need to provide your address if you do not want to. However, for your information to be duly acknowledged in a future edition we will need to have your name.

✄--

A DORIC DICTIONARY
Amendments and omissions from the First Edition
(please write/type as clearly as possible)

Supplied by (name): _____

address: _____

Born in (town/county): _____   Year of birth: _____

Word(s)/Phrases	Meaning

(use a separate sheet if necessary)

When completed, please send to:

Doric Dictionary Editor
Scottish Cultural Press, Unit 14, Leith Walk Business Centre,
130 Leith Walk, Edinburgh EH6 5DT